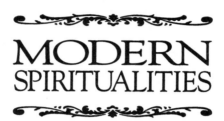

MODERN
SPIRITUALITIES

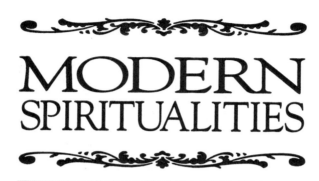

MODERN
SPIRITUALITIES

AN INQUIRY

EDITED BY
LAURENCE BROWN
BERNARD C. FARR
R. JOSEPH HOFFMANN

 WESTMINSTER COLLEGE-OXFORD: CRITICAL STUDIES IN RELIGION

Prometheus Books
Amherst, New York
Oxford, England

Published 1997 by Prometheus Books

01 00 99 98 97   5 4 3 2 1

Library of Congress Cataloging-in-Publication Data

Modern spiritualities : an inquiry / edited by Laurence Brown, Bernard C. Farr, R.
    Joseph Hoffmann.
        p.   cm.
    Includes bibliographical references.
    ISBN 1–57392–112–2 (cloth : alk. paper)
        1. Spirituality—Congresses. I. Brown, Laurence Binet, 1927–
II. Farr, Bernard C. III. Hoffmann, R. Joseph.
BL624.M633   1996
291.4—dc20   96–41522
                                                                              CIP

Printed in the United States of America on acid-free paper

Contents

PART FIVE: SPIRITUALITY AND SCIENCE

Preface

Modern Spiritualities joins a long list of titles on a subject that has begun to intrigue the unchurched as much as the churched, and opponents of state-sponsored religious education as much as those who stress, in a Christian context, the need for a more "traditional" form of moral and *spiritual* development. Once the exclusive property of Western monastics and Eastern mystics, the term *spirituality* has now become one of the disturbing metaphors that lingers, like the rising sun and the four corners of the earth, to remind us of more ancient cosmologies and anthropologies.

No doubt the term is troublesome. Cheslyn Jones, one of the editors of the distinguished book *The Study of Spirituality* (Oxford, 1985) confesses as much when he notes that it is difficult to trace its contemporary meaning much before a 1967 conference at Durham, whose discussions were published under the title *Spirituality for Today.* Jones, former master of Pusey House Oxford, noted with some impatience that "the term *spirituality* bounces round these pages [without any] systematic attempt to define it except through off-the-cuff phrases, not all coherent." The contributors define the concept variously as "the form and structures of the life of prayer," "the spir-

9

itual life," "some kind of wholeness," "a search for meaning and significance by contemplation and reflection on the totality of human experiences in relation to the whole world which is experience." In short, spirituality means what one wants it to mean.

At the conference from which *Modern Spiritualities* emerged, Antony Flew with his characteristic impatience for fuzzy logic professed not to "know what the term means": When school governors implement religious education syllabi calling for spiritual development as a superadditum to intellectual and physical development, what precisely are they after? There is a lingering suspicion that what is really being solicited is, if not obedience to a certain formulation of a particular set of religious doctrines, then perhaps a form of conduct roughly equivalent to such obedience. Flew is not the first to notice that the image of spiritual development as something distinct from the intellectual and physical perpetuates the tripartite division of the soul into vegetative, sensitive, and rational powers (Plato, *Republic* 4.350–53), a slicing up of human personhood into interactive but often disagreeable parts.

For Flew and others like him, the term is—if I may be a little extreme—dangerous because unlike the rising sun, four-cornered earth, and three-personed God, it has "policy implications." School principals and boards of education in America and Britain wring their hands over a lack of "spiritual" development (by which they often mean appropriate conduct or better English-language skills). Church leaders deplore the loss of spirituality in their congregations, by which they mean the attraction of shopping malls over churches. Baptists, Unitarians, and (even) secular humanists "bounce" the word as though there were nothing left to guesswork in its meaning. In the United State particularly it vies with school prayer as a politically safe alternative to what the courts have seen as enforced religious observance, safe because, unlike prayer, no one quite knows what spirituality is. Pressed for the mysterious something "missing" in everyday life, spirituality is cited as the ingredient that seems to have disappeared from modern society and left it, and us, struggling for a meaning that transcends the ordinary—the humdrum.

And yet, "We live not by things but by the meaning of things," as one of the displays at the Crewkerne Flower Festival proclaims. The floral scene for this verse is a marble bust of a child reading (originally in the Unitarian chapel at Hminster). There is a faint trace of pleasure, not quite a smile, on her lips, but the expression is softened by the intensity of the reading experience—Victorian satisfaction tempered by serious-mindedness. At this level the experience is neither wholly "physical" (not merely an excitation of cerebral neurons by the optic nerve) nor "intellectual" (a perception and acquisition of content). There seems to be no term in the positivist's lexicon to give the moment, here frozen in stone, the meaning its intensity deserves. To make it more complicated, what name do we give to the process through which the living model of the "reading experience" has been expressed spatially and precisely, but in a way clearly different from the meaning of the sentence: Here is a girl reading a book?

In a 1996 lecture to the Oxford Centre for Critical Studies at Westminster College, Irving Singer did not shy away from using the terms *spirit* and *spiritual* to get at the "meaning of things." Having traced the concept from the pre-Socratics to the postmodernists, he is well aware of the linguistic and metaphysical objections that can be leveled against a concept like *spirituality*. Singer, however, does not believe in a divisible soul, a personal God, nor a "realm" of spirit in which mortals participate through an outpouring of immaterial essences. (Does anyone today recognize this as the classical Christian doctrine of redemption by the spirit of the living God?) Instead, he regards spirit as the definingly human aspect of nature: to be human means to be capable of art and expression, ranging from the construction of simple sentences to the crafting of the *Odyssey,* and from the building of sandcastles to the creation of the pyramids. The human spirit, as Singer argues his case, is "exemplified" if not proved by art; and insofar as human nature is defined in the phrase *man the maker* (*homo faber*), it is also the nature of man to be spiritual (*homo spiritualis*). Before the *Odyssey* and the pyramids are held to be typical exhibits of "the human spirit," Singer concedes that there are pornography, offensive architectural styles, rap music, and Quentin Tarantino

films to account for: in short, that human nature and spirit are not necessarily defined by "masterpieces" and canons of taste.

As the debate goes on, the definition of spirituality threatens to sta-
bilize. Prayer and meditation are no longer seen as the trademarks of
"spirituality" except in the pages of manuals of ascetic (or spiritual)
theology. Nor is it clear that in speaking about "spirituality" one is dab-
bling in theosophy or lapsing into the obscurity that characterizes
Paul's digression on "spiritual bodies" in 1 Corinthians 15:42–49.
What then is spirituality, asked Jacques Madaule in a *Le Monde* review
(October 28, 1980) of the tenth edition of the prestigious *Dictionnaire
de la spiritualité*: "It is by no means to be confused with theology,
which is chiefly an elaboration of concepts. . . . Although the notion of
spirituality is definitely a Christian notion, it by no means limits its
attention to the Catholic world nor even the Christian world. To exhibit
the spirituality of human reality is to embrace this reality to its full
extent, and such a quest does not interest just a few specialists."

In this volume, more than a few specialists show the wisdom of
Madaule's comment. The essays contained here range over a wide
variety of themes: early Christian humor; the influence of heresy on
Christian ideas of the spiritual "man"; the lessons to be learned from
becoming a connoisseur in spiritual development, and analogies
between the habit of marijuana smoking and leading a spiritual life;
the "quantum metaphysics" of the religious physicists and of Teilhard
and Tipler; Buddhist and modern African varieties of spiritual enlightenment. Here you will find the definability of the concept criticized
(Antony Flew); the easy availability of Eastern spiritualities challenged as a "smorgasbord syndrome" (Margaret Chatterjee); the
syzygy between some forms of spirituality and the experience of the
paranormal defended (Paul Kurtz); the possibility of an enlightened
spirituality in the Islamic context argued (Clinton Bennett).

The conference on Modern Spiritualities was a mixed if evocative
experience for those who participated in it. Many observers left feeling they had been treated to an overabundant meal that—as one
attendee put it—would take weeks to digest. Others, who had come
for a clarification of ideas or hoped to leave with a definition in their

pocket, went away feeling that the term is too stubborn to define. Readers of this volume now have in front of them the transcripts of this experience and will be able to judge for themselves.

There is one sad omission in this collection. No essay appears on the theme of millennial or apocalyptic spirituality despite a growing interest in the religious studies and theological communities in the phenomenon of millennialism and its influence on religious ideas as we near the landmark year 2000. It is undeniable that such occasions express themselves in religious terms and that Christianity, whose anniversary the millennium is, is especially susceptible to both ecstatic and domesticated forms of millennial spirituality. For this the editors apologize, while at the same time noting that the diversity of the "spiritualities" and critiques of the phenomenon included here—perhaps the collection itself—points to the enormous energy of modern spiritualities seeking to define themselves in human communities that sense the end of the old religious order.

R. Joseph Hoffmann
Westminster College
Oxford

Part One

Definitions

1

The Smorgasbord Syndrome: Availability Reexamined

Margaret Chatterjee

INTRODUCTION

I wish to begin by setting up front some initial difficulties. I doubt one can properly proceed to a typology unless the phenomenon of which species are alleged to be identifiable is itself identified. Even family resemblance does not serve us too well, for it is a fuzzy concept. Overlapping categories, moreover, still trail the concept of resemblance, scandalous though this may be, and so we do not get very far from the odor of essentialism. Moreover, what deserves including in the smorgasbord seems to require an exclusion principle, and the resources of family resemblance do not serve us here either. So let us go back a bit.

When a letter writer in the early part of the fifth century urged his correspondent, *"Age ut in spiritualitate proficias"* (So act as to advance in spirituality), his meaning would have been understood. For centuries Greek resonances were heard in the contrast between *spiri-*

Reprinted from the *Journal for the Critical Study of Religion, Ethics, and Society* 1, no. 1 (Winter/Spring 1996). By permission of the publisher.

tualitas and *materialitas*. The specifically Christian way of spelling out the latter concept in terms of corporeality was certainly not derived from Jewish sources. There does not seem to have been anything outside Christendom quite like the world/flesh/devil package singled out for eschewal by Christian aspirants to the realm of spirit. Other religious traditions (perhaps Jainism excepted) were on balance more able to recognize the worldly as our proper place and to be without hang-ups about fleshly existence. The extent to which a fall from *spiritualitas* would be reckoned to bring about descent into the nether regions cannot be underplayed, for the fear of hellfire must have been a dominant feature of the human psyche during the centuries when the chariots of war were dragged across Europe. Mutter Courage and all she represents knew well enough that hellfire was right here and nowhere else. It is ironic indeed that the world, the flesh, and the devil are very much the "in" thing in certain contemporary new-look lifestyles. If these are deemed to be "spiritualities," one can note not a sea change but a whole planetary shift in the use of the term. But in between there was much that transpired.

The "worldliness" of pioneering sects in the new world can be taken as embodying the insight that the spirit must manifest itself in community. *Schwärmerei* and *Gemeinschaft* did not necessarily pull in different directions; indeed, more often than not they were in tandem. Once manifestation in community was taken as a natural outcome of the fervor of the like-minded, the way was open for participation in the body politic, that is to say, for following through the implication of acting as the "leaven" in society. A way was now available for providing an energizing factor in society that could later function beyond the confines of dissent. Many contemporary new-style religiosities, on the other hand, seem marked by a mood of retreat. Some no doubt, by giving a *topos* to certain sorts of utopianism, provide implicit comment on current society. Those that resurrect archaic practices strike me as identifiable within twentieth-century fin de siècle romanticism. No doubt cults, sects, and movements need to be distinguished. But where do spiritualities fit in? Presumably they are not forms of social organization. Are they then reckoned to be a kind of epiphenomenal steam issuing from the same? How would they be identified? The criterion of "by their fruits" might prove embarrassing.

Perhaps the factors that have weakened traditional allegiances in our own time might offer a clue as to how the notion of multiple modern spiritualities should have risen at all and whether such phenomena are evidence of the retreating sea of faith or whether they indicate a tidal flow capable of flooding the dry sands of the late twentieth century. I take it that the following factors have in various measures played a role in transforming traditional beliefs: the scientific outlook, secularism, religious pluralism, distress leading to a credibility crisis (e.g., where was God during the Holocaust?), democratic revolt against hierarchies, and pulverization of communities consequent upon industrialization. This is by no means an exhaustive list. It does not, for example, include the factor of sheer indifference, nor does it include surrogates of the kind listed by John Smith of Yale under "quasi-religions." And yet none of these brings us any nearer to answering the question why the term *spiritualities* should be in vogue to the extent that it is.

An invitation to write for an encyclopedia of world spirituality included the caution that spirituality "as such should be distinguished from the history of religions, theology, and the philosophy of religion, although it will draw from these disciplines." A request for further clarification elicited the reply that the editors had not been able to agree on any initial statement as to what spirituality was and therefore I could treat it as I pleased. In other words, what we had was a putative reification and a confession of *je ne sais quoi.* Having said this, the various meanings left behind through Greek and Latin terminology culminate in a nucleus that seems to be characteristically Christian. If this sounds tendentious, let me put it this way: Coining the phrases *Hindu spirituality* or *Buddhist spirituality* needs to be compared with coining such phrases as Judaic *sadhana,* Christian *dharma,* or Islamic *satori* to see how odd such expressions are. But it is even more complicated than this. To say that the word *spirituality* trails largely Christian associations is to set loose a bag of contrary winds, for does the expression "Christian associations" have uniform conno-

tations? I rather suspect it does not. What I shall try and do is to keep
on a diagnostic track in what follows.

MAINLY DIAGNOSTIC

I believe the current interest in spiritualities to be a fin de siècle phenomenon that speaks of the ontological insecurity experienced by
many today, and, more psychologically, that speaks of the fragmentation of the self, a condition for which remedies are being sought. This
quest currently involves a ransacking of both centuries and continents.
This strikes me as a cultural phenomenon noticeable largely in the
Western Hemisphere and even more specifically in the English-speaking world. Let us then retain the word *spiritualities* in the plural for
the sake of argument, bearing in mind that the term may not eventually be found to carry more cognitive weight than locutions such as
religious styles of life or *religiosities.* Since linguistic usage seems to
be currently installed on the altar, we can pass politely by without
pious genuflection.

Now comes one of my hard sayings. I believe that the apparent
availability of "other spiritualities" (perhaps a more attractively packaged expression than the older usage "other religions") is in no small
part a function of the end of the colonial context which *seems* to make
other people's styles of life "available" without occasioning the
frightful stigma of "going native." The wry effect this can have in the
countries of origin of some of the acquired ideas can be illustrated by
the following anecdote. I was present at a function in Visva Bharati,
the university founded by the poet Rabindranath Tagore, where the
comparative study of religion was being discussed. The interplay
between ethnic and religious identity came in for special mention and
a young Westerner, perilously attired in a dhoti (I say perilously
because only the initiated can manipulate it with proper decorum),
rose to his feet to say that he regarded himself to be a Hindu. Where-
upon an elderly gentleman to the manor born retorted, "Ah, but *we*
don't regard you as such." How "available," in fact, was the way of

life that belonged to a different people, a way of life where there were no creeds to provide firm coordinates and to define group membership? Issues about "otherness" thereupon raise their heads, and I think such issues are relevant in view of the key word *spiritualities.* Does one spirituality exclude another? The rise of sects no doubt evidences a process of demarcation at work, but this is compatible with considerable retention of the style of religiosity (if this question-begging phrase can be pardoned) of the parent institution from which a breakaway is effected (Methodism would be a case in point). Borrowings from elsewhere may also be incorporated. Investigators into such developments, delving into history, would find themselves looking into that often ill-matched pair, modes of experiencing and behavior.

It looks as if spiritualities are often constructed from dismembered earlier forms, a strategy that bears some analogy to the building of mosques, temples, and churches from the debris of earlier structures. A different analogy takes us to geology. This might be even more illuminating: layers of sedimentation becoming visible through fault lines, and an occasional upthrust revealing a primal layer well-nigh buried. The archaic and, for that matter, the atavistic can show themselves when least expected.

It should not be forgotten that the processes that generate what our contemporaries like to call spiritualities can contain strategies of protest. This includes protest against authoritarian structures such as an established church or, in more general terms, protest against a homogenized culture. I deliberately use a word associated with a kind of milk that many in the United States avoid on account of its indigestibility.

The availability of dissent per se has a wide scatter. In societies where the proliferation of Protestant sects goes along with the democratic ethos, varieties of religiosity fostered by successive waves of immigration occasion no surprise. American life shows this most clearly. The occasion of dissent in Latin America is a much more problematic affair, the reason for which lies both in the nature of the clerical establishment in that part of the world and in the economic institutions which generate immiseration. New styles of religiosity in such conditions can develop nonetheless through an impinging of secular ideology on some of the clergy and/or a discovery of revolutionary potential either in scripture or in papal pronouncement.

In countries where such religiosities are to be found we would not expect to find available the kinds inspired by, say, Eastern religions. But there are other examples. The upthrust of religiosity at the folk level has been cleverly incorporated by the establishment in Mexico and the Philippines. How is this to be interpreted? In such societies the ontological insecurity (a rather pretentious expression for what in many areas of the world amounts to the sheerest deprivation) calls forth indigenous sources of meaning beneath an apparatus of belief and practice left behind by, for example, the culture of the conquistadores.

So far it would look as if the referent of the word *spiritualities* can be unpacked into clusters of behavior, experience, and belief, all intricately interwoven and loosely regarded as "religious." They require investigation in a historical manner on the analogy of understanding individual life histories. So what we are looking for is not modes of validation, but ways of understanding. This is why facets of the postcolonial situation, resistances, patterns of migration, economic inelasticities, and the privileging of certain sorts of experience by those purporting to have them—in fact, a ragbag of diverse factors—are so relevant to our inquiry. The trends, needless to say, point in contrary directions. Among these we come across rear-guard actions on the part of diehard traditionalists, new-look accommodations by others, primordial attachments reinforced by ethnicity, transplants retaining a tenuous link with their place of origin (symbolized, for example, by Ganges water carefully transported and liberally diluted in order to go round), revivals of the archaic (in Britain, this can bear a trace of an imagined and perhaps imaginary Anglo-Saxonry)—and this is only a small sample.

SOME QUESTIONS POSED

The questions that can be asked include the following:

(1) If religious discourse and practice can be taken as both partly constitutive of changing social identities and symptomatic of it, can we inquire if the discourse and practice of spirituality does likewise? The problem is that putative spiritualities show themselves mainly in behavior rather than in discourse. The discourse proliferating currently seems to provide more in the nature of a typology of religiosity rather than anything else. My question was posed in terms of social identity, but it can be posed as easily in terms of individual identity and, of course, the relation between the two.

(2) This brings me to my second question. How are we to interpret the reconstruction of the divided self shored up by cultural scaffolding selectively appropriated in the course of a post-colonial free-for-all? I speak of those for whom, particularly in Britain, the parish church or local chapel is no longer the focus of religious life.

(3) And now my third consideration. There are those who do not resort to such scaffolding but who cling to the nucleating factor provided by a revelatory experience or, more exactly, one regarded as such. The narratives generated are perhaps too slender to serve as an Ariadne's thread in the maze of contemporary existence. More serious, their privacy amounts to a believed privileging which, in fact, increases personal isolation, producing a cocoon that in no way compensates for the loss of social identity for which the alleged "epiphany" is supposed to compensate. Are such narratives of the "When I was in Poona" variety or should they be given a religious weight?

(4) What are we to make of turning-point experiences which do not fall into the conversion category? I take the latter to involve, classically, a *metabasis eis allo genos* (change into another kind), a total turning which is evidenced in a change in way of life, presumably accompanied by qualitative changes in feeling-tone. At first sight a purported experience which has no identifiable manifestation may seem to lack validation. And yet, if civilized behavior (?) goes along with patterns of inhibition, should we always *expect* a manifestation of experience in behavior? The one who sees men as trees walking might be well advised to keep this peculiarity to himself. The fact remains that we do expect there to be some manifestation of religious experience in behavior.

(5) I next ask whether patterns of experiencing are equally available to all. At first sight the reply seems to be a definitive no. The soil clings to our roots. Yet one of the things maintained by those who claim to have had revelatory religious experiences is that no one else can possibly fathom how "epiphanic" they were and, even so, they wish to talk about it. The claim made in this respect runs counter to the usual way of establishing something in a scientific manner, on the lines of "Any observer under conditions A, B, C, with standard sense endowments is likely to experience X, other things being equal." So when the validating criteria of consequent behavior and/or being, available to others placed in similar circumstances, are absent, the phenomenon remains a piece of personal history, of absorbing interest to the experient, of clinical interest to the analyst probably, but not of any great importance otherwise. However, it might be objected that the condition of availability to others in similar circumstances can never apply in the nature of things in that circumstances can never be similar given that the *people* concerned are different. And this brings me to my sixth question.

(6) Do spiritualities have any cognitive import? There is an obvious sense in which the narratives that people come up with provide information about *them*. But this is presumably not what we are looking for. Claims are advanced as to the existence of a noumenal order (perhaps numinous as well). To deal with this would mean recapping several decades of philosophical debate and so I pass this over.

(7) I now turn to a teasing question concerning the concept *modern*. It may not be wide of the mark to say that the discourse of modernity opposes the religious to the secular. If spirituality is located on the side of religion, could it be that we miss one of the intriguing features which the phrase *modern spirituality* may denote, for the very phrase suggests an intermediate territory between religion and the secular? New-style religiosities, including transplanted ones, which have lost a good deal of their native flavor in their countries of origin, generate their own organizational forms and rituals, setting off new sets of expectation. The institutions created strive to satisfy a clientele not wanting to be provided with the same mixture as before. Modern spir-

itualities, in the sense I speak of them here, presuppose traditional ones and need them just as any rebound phenomenon, whether in personal or social life, presupposes what is rebounded from. That there is a strong secular element in some of the so-called modern spiritualities can be illustrated in the rituals proposed, none too successfully, by Auguste Comte in his cult of humanity, and in the form of "service" favored by some British ethical societies early in the twentieth century.

Started originally in connection with spelling out what content could be given to nonreligious moral instruction in schools, the British ethical societies had links with the New York Society of Ethical Culture through Felix Adler, and through his father with Reform Judaism, and on a more conservative wicket, with transcendentalism of an Emersonian brand. No less a person than Ramsay Macdonald characterized the proponents of ethical culture as those who believed that conduct is "the only medium through which religious conviction can be expressed, and that the body is more than raiment." The London-based Union of Ethical Societies affirmed that "moral ideas and the moral life are independent of beliefs as to the ultimate nature of things, and as to a life after death." The 1909 statement of aims goes further. The moral ideal must be set up as "the object of religious devotion." The phrase *moral fellowship* echoes evangelical language where one would least expect it. The provenance of the ethical societies was intriguing. Steering clear of Unitarianism, which was on a sympathetic wavelength but, so they thought, not rationalist enough, the ethicists constructed a kind of Universalism which found a ready outlet in social criticism. All this was almost a century after Raja Rammohun Roy in India found in Unitarianism a useful ally in combating obscurantism and the Trinitarianism of his missionary critics. That he was closely connected with freemasonry provides another aspect of the story. What is worth noting is how consonant the agenda of the ethical societies was with rationalism and humanism of various kinds. The outcome was what could be called a mode of spirituality free of ecstasy and oriented in the direction of "fruit" rather than "experience." It is not surprising to learn that Mahatma Gandhi was attracted to these societies and wrote a Gujerati version of *Ethical*

Religion, which William M. Salter, founder of the Ethical Society in Chicago, had first published in 1889. Gandhi's paraphrases, however, reveal his own bent. For example, the eighth and final paraphrase published in *Indian Opinion* contains this line: "One's way of life is not to be judged by one's visible outward actions, but by one's inner leanings." How inner leanings are to be gauged other than by overt actions is not indicated.

My purpose in including the concept of ethical religion is to illustrate my suggestion that there might be an intermediate territory between the religious and the secular and that some of the "spiritualities" proffered may be identifiable in this area. To this extent, spiritualities are ambiguous vis-à-vis rationality. Some are antirational in being centered on a mystique and yet rational in an Enlightenment manner in voicing the right to freedom of expression in civil society. Some new spiritualities certainly seem to operate between faith and ideology. However this may be, they retain their character as fin de siècle phenomena puncturing the overarching canopy of global civilization in diverse ways. Applying the criterion of soteriological efficacy to some of these may be an irrelevancy. Having said this, I turn next to some facets of current interest in so-called Eastern spirituality, confining myself for the sake of convenience to phenomena from India.

EASTERN SPIRITUALITY

I indicated earlier that I think the contemporary interest in various spiritualities applies a yardstick drawn from a particular tradition, the Christian one, and to that extent remains locked into a Ptolemaic perspective. In this respect the identification of putative spiritualities as likewise different sorts of "believers" (as if religious affiliation were always centered on belief) reflects assumptions that can be seriously questioned. There is no word for *spirituality* in Indian languages. Most pertinent of all there is an immense difference between *atman* and "spirit." To begin with, *atman* is not an individuating principle, and furthermore, there is no way in which, by using the word *atman,* we could distinguish between the human individual non-ontic self and an absolute principle since the texts make no such distinction. I refer to the Upanishads here since it is in these texts that *atman* talk is found in its root form. A term like *adhyatmika* connotes "pertaining to the Self" in contrast with what pertains to material elements or to deities. What Nachiketas attains at the close of the Katha Upanishad is knowledge of the Supreme Self, not the self in any common or garden sense but a sphere beyond the accounting of merit and demerit and therefore beyond good and evil.

The construction of the concept of Hindu spirituality in the modern era was a follow-up on the work of German Indologists anxious to find something analogous to the realm of *das Geistige* and was effected mainly by Swami Vivekananda and Radhakrishnan. But they used the medium of English, which had over centuries selectively assimilated a Greco-Latin heritage whose family of concepts differed fundamentally from the coinage of Hindu or Buddhist metaphysical thought. Vivekananda and those successors of his who were like-minded made capital out of an alleged dichotomy, that between the spiritual East and the materialist West, which they were able to exploit with a motive that was nationalist rather than scholarly. The idea was that if there could be no chance of superiority as far as material wealth was concerned, an as yet subject people could still score as far as spirituality was concerned.

What I have called the smorgasbord syndrome received a considerable fillip in the West as cultural pessimism deepened. Perhaps an Eastern shot in the arm would have a regenerative effect—or at least so some thought. India's main export on the spirituality market by this time was various brands of yoga. This was a clever move as it was able to capture both the market for physical fitness and the market for edification. This time missionary efforts were not following a flag, but what they were providing was very much in the nature of a return compliment.

I suggest that the "spiritual" exports were particularly welcome to the *déraciné,* the uprooted, the frustrated, and those alienated, for whatever reason, from their own traditions. A more philosophical type of Hindu missionary marketed a different product, inspired by the Farquhar thesis in reverse: not Christianity but Vedanta was the unacknowledged essence behind other religions. A third type, able to offer the mini-ecstasies induced by singing and percussive instruments, catered to the need for colorful processions which are a relative rarity in colder climes. They provided a strung-out open-air witnessing that contrasted noticeably with the fervors of the mission tent. Stylistically this category to my mind is clearly classifiable under *Schwärmerei.* The intriguing twist added is the clash of two separate rights, the right of expression and the right of others not to have their passage obstructed on public highways.

All this might well be hailed with delight by a votary of the market economy. The days of monopoly are over, frontiers are down, at last everything is available. Why miss out? The smorgasbord invites nibbling at this and that, leaving the unconsumed on your plate. The committed vegetarian will presumably not take a ham sandwich, but your Laodicean might.

Is this availability not a good thing, it may be asked? It is not for me to say as I seek to understand the phenomenon rather than to judge it. What I wish to stress is that the exported products are prepared for a market and are to be distinguished from the homegrown product. So when we speak of availability I tend to think that the original forms of life are not exportable, shorn of habitat, history, and ambience. Immigrant communities who miss their lost habitat every day of their lives would testify to the vast gulf between life in the old country and in the new. New generations learn to forget inherited memories, and the genuine article experienced on visits to ancestral places often proves an embarrassment. I now consider whether it is proper to think of the spiritual as in any way autonomous.

IS THE SPIRITUAL AUTONOMOUS?

My problem is as follows: To hunt for the distinctiveness of any phenomenon X presumes that it is possible to demarcate it from other phenomena, to pin down its quiddity. But what if this cannot be done? Is there not a sense in which either the spiritual pervades the whole of life or it is otherwise a luxury of interiority, which in Kabir's words "shames the outer world of matter" and leaves out that most important factor, the fruits? For these are, after all, the only accessible evidence of the particular dispositions that we happen to have.

From what has been gathered so far it looks as if current usages of the term *spirituality* reflect a selection of the following: a desire to avoid the reified concept of religion per se, a stress on ambience rather than on belief, and a wish to point up the experiential. The historical and sociological factors that have shaped current perceptions were briefly touched on earlier. To say, at this juncture, that the spiritual is not autonomous is to recall the multiple derivations and contexts of any particular spirituality, a matter of extreme complexity. But cutting across this consideration, another reflection offers itself. The nonautonomous nature of the spiritual refers no less to its deep interfusion with the aesthetic and the moral. One could invoke at this point Newman's reminder about the beauty of holiness, or Kant's analysis of the moral consciousness. It seems to me that the interplay between the aesthetic and the moral in Kant and Kierkegaard serves in a subtle way to adjust the passion for infinity to those anchorages of the spirit which tug the moral impulse.

What I suggest next is that it is the very nonautonomous character of the spiritual that can set limits to its availability. Spirituality, after all, was traditionally hardly *opted* for. It was a manifestation of rootedness in a tradition, the outward and visible sign of inward growth. To insist on availability, the traditionalist may well say, is to ignore the heritages into which new generations enter through birthright and through lifetimes of nurturing. But nothing ventured, nothing gained.

It could be claimed that your innovator, the one who embarks on a new style of life, is not so much *opting* for as *creating*. If that is so, two reminders may be in order. The first is that such creativity need not have any truck with religion at all. When Kandinsky wrote of the spiritual life as a complicated but definite movement forward and upward, he was speaking of the life of the artist, and Stravinsky could have spoken likewise.

What I suggest then is that the spiritual does not have to be identified with the religious any more than the mystical does. The second reminder is that freedom from key-relationship (our root metaphor now coming from music) goes along with the liberation of dissonance, and for this we should be prepared. Such is the kingdom of availability.

And so the table is spread. Not everything is easily identifiable, so choose carefully and then do not mix your drinks. I may well choose what is not set out on the smorgasbord at all, and being contrary, like Alice, use words as I please, not a private language but a different one. So here goes. I see the spiritual as whatever is a solvent of all that makes us invisible to one another, all that eradicates shadows. I speak of a regeneration that can come through art, music, nature, and what Martin Buber called *hagshamah* or community. It dwells especially in those personal relationships that succeed in raising a Jacob's ladder that extends both downward, reclaiming the underworld, and upward into shared dimensions of life. The spiritual so conceived is inevitably temporal, elusive no doubt, and not necessarily religious as commonly understood. It is delicately poised as all that is human must be, and never the object of direct pursuit. In sum, within the C major of life resonances can be heard. However, this gives us no claim to have made a raid on the absolute. It is enough to be capable of undergoing a metamorphosis within the dimension of the empirical, and this is itself a kind of transempiricality. This was what Wordsworth meant by intimation and Tagore by the flute whose notes were not lost in space and the streams whose waters had not been entirely swallowed up by the sands of the desert.

2

What Is 'Spirituality'?

Antony Flew

In the world in which I was raised, the word *spiritual* was pretty well synonymous with the word *religious*; and, since that was long before the mass immigrations into Europe of adherents of non-Christian religions, *religious* was in practice equivalent to *Christian*. For me, therefore, talk about spiritual life was talk about worshipping and praying to the Mosaic God of Judaism and Christianity. Since ceasing in my middle teens to believe in the existence of that God, I have in consequence simply not had, at any rate in that understanding, any spiritual life at all.

The question which I have been set is perhaps approached by way of some preliminary consideration of the meanings of some shorter words with which the word *spirituality* is etymologically associated. In that consideration we shall find occasions to develop certain fundamental distinctions which will need to be drawn in the subsequent discussions. These shorter words are *spirited, spirit, spiritist, spiritual,* and *spiritualist.*

Let us dispose first of *spirited.* Everyone knows what is meant by a high-spirited or a poor-spirited person; the latter being what would today be dismissed as a wimp. The most famous and the last irrelevant

31

employment of the word *spirited*—or rather of its Greek equivalent—is by Plato in *The Republic*. There Plato distinguishes three parts, or slightly better, elements in what is always translated as the soul:[1] the desiring, the spirited, and the rational. The point for us to note about Plato's spirited element is that it is not itself a spirit. It is one element in or one characteristic of or one disposition of the single hypothesized entity which, Plato argues, is an incorporeal, immaterial, spiritual being.

In arguing for these conclusions[2] Plato became the inspiration of one of the two great rival, traditional views of the nature of humankind: the Platonic-Cartesian and the Aristotelian. On the latter view people simply are, what in most of our weekday thinking and talking and doing we all assume them to be, members of a very special species of creatures of flesh and blood. As Aristotle himself put it, in his scandalously sexist and politically incorrect way, man is the rational animal.

Where Aristotelian views of the nature of humankind are unitary, Platonic-Cartesian views are dualist. On such views we are constructs out of two radically disparate elements: the one—the body—corporeal and perishable; the other—the mind or soul—immaterial and perhaps imperishable. According to the Platonic-Cartesian tradition, these invisible and incorporeal minds or souls are the people, the agents, the thinkers, the sufferers. To this the Aristotelian responds that people actually meet and shake hands or dance or fight with one another. Such everyday transactions are truly and immediately interpersonal: they are not vicarious transactions between the containers in which people are packaged, the bodies in which they are imprisoned.

We come next to the word *spirit*. It is of the first importance to recognize that this word is not and never has been employed only and unequivocally to refer to supposedly existent substantial but nevertheless incorporeal entities. Here, of course, the word *substantial* is being employed in its prime philosophical sense; the sense in which substances—let us christen them philosophical substances—are things which can significantly be said to exist separately and, as it were, in their own right.

Perhaps the most effective and certainly the most agreeable way of fixing this concept of philosophical substances in mind is by contemplating two examples provided by one of Oxford's most considerable philosophical logicians. These examples show that not all significant substantives are words for sorts of substances, in this present or indeed in any other sense of the word *substance*. Everyone, even in what Wittgenstein so loved to call "the darkness of these times," will surely recall the subtraction sum which in *Alice in Wonderland* the Red Queen set for Alice: "Take a bone from a dog, what would remain?" The answer that nothing would remain is rejected. For the dog losing its temper would depart while the lost temper would remain. Again, everyone will remember from *Through the Looking Glass* how the grinning Cheshire Cat disappeared with only the grin remaining. The substantives *temper* and *grin* are thus shown not to be words for what we call philosophical substances, for it is absurd to talk of tempers or grins as if these were objects which could conceivably exist separately and, as it were, in their own right.

At this point we have what is always welcome, an occasion to quote one of the greatest of Oxford philosophers. Thomas Hobbes was in his twenties when the King James Bible was first published, and subsequently achieved a remarkably comprehensive knowledge of its contents.[3] Hobbes insisted that in that work the word *spirit* is rarely if ever employed to refer to a member of a supposed kind we would rate (but he could not have characterized) as philosophical substances. Instead, he maintained—for instance, in chapter 34 of his *Leviathan*—that the word *spirit* in the Bible usually refers to a:

> Disposition or *Inclination* of the mind; as when for the disposition to controwl the sayings of other men, we say a *spirit of contradiction*. For a *disposition to uncleannesse, an unclean spirit;* for *perversenesse, a froward spirit;* for *sullennesse, a dumb spirit;* and for *inclination to godlinesse, and Gods service, the Spirit of God;* sometimes for any eminent ability, or extraordinary passion, or disease of the mind, as when *great wisdome* is called the *spirit of wisdome;* and *mad men* are said to be *possessed with a spirit.*

Again a little later, in chapter 36, Hobbes asserted that:

> When therefore a Prophet is said to speak in the Spirit, or by the Spirit of God, we are to understand no more, but that he speaks according to God's will, declared by the supreme Prophet. For the most common acceptation of the word Spirit, is in the significance of a man's intention, mind, or disposition.

But now, what is to be said about the alternative interpretation of talk about spirits, the interpretation which takes it to be referring to members of a sort of immaterial philosophical substances? This interpretation is of course presupposed by the teaching of the Spiritualist church and by the beliefs of the people called *spiritists*. For whatever are to be said to survive the death and dissolution of persons, as conceived by Aristotelians, have to be entities "which can significantly be said to exist separately and, as it were, in their own right." To the suggestion that there could be such immaterial entities, Hobbes makes his first and most emphatic response in chapter 5 of *Leviathan*: "If a man talks to me of 'a round quadrangle'; or 'accidents of bread in cheese';[4] or 'immaterial substances'; I should not say that he was in error, but that his words were without meaning: that is to say, absurd."

Later, in chapter 44, Hobbes goes on to claim that: "The *Soule* in Scripture, signifieth alwaies, either the Life, or the Living Creature; and the Body and Soule jointly, the *Body alive*." After giving several Scriptural examples of such talk he contends that from these "if by *Soule* were meant a *Substance Incorporeall*, with an existence separated from the Body, it might as well be inferred of any other living Creature, as of Man." He concludes the paragraph: "And for the places of the New Testament, where it is said that any man shall be cast Body and Soul into Hell fire, it is no more than Body and Life; that is to say, they shall be cast alive into the perpetual fire of Gehenna."[5]

Talk about immaterial substances Hobbes sees as absurd because he is taking the word *substance* to be synonymous with the word *stuff*, as when we talk of a mysterious or a sticky substance. Interpreting the expression *immaterial substances* in this way, as virtually equivalent to *nonstuff stuffs,* does indeed make it obviously self-contradictory and absurd. But it is not so obviously absurd—indeed, most would claim that it is not absurd at all—to maintain that there could be and are immaterial philosophical substances.

To characterize a supposed something as immaterial or incorporeal is, however, to make an assertion which is at one and the same time both extremely comprehensive and wholly negative. Those proposing to hypothesize such recherché philosophical substances surely owe it both to themselves and others not only to reveal what positive characteristics might significantly be attributed to their elusive hypothesized entities, but also to specify how such entities could be identified in the first place and thereafter be reidentified as through the effluxion of time still the same individuals. At the very least we surely ought to be told how theoretically and in principle this conceivably might be done, even if for some reason it is and will remain forever impossible in practice.[6]

Next we come to the adjective *spiritual.* A survey through the relevant item in the big *Oxford English Dictionary* reveals that those who do give employment to this word employ it in what are in fact two very different and by no means necessarily connected sorts of senses. In senses of the first sort this word is used to distinguish what are perceived as higher and hence less material and more spiritual human characteristics from the lower, more earthily material remainder. In the other, the second sort of sense, the spiritual appears to be virtually synonymous with the religious, as when spiritual courts and powers used to be distinguished from earthly powers and interests.

Among the definitions offered are "of or pertaining to the higher moral qualities, especially as regarded in a religious aspect" and "of or pertaining to higher faculties." Since the first of these two definitions was offered to elucidate one of the earliest of the usages recorded, the word *moral* should probably be interpreted as it was in the now obsolete contrasts between moral and physical sciences and moral and physical causes,[7] rather than as opposed to amoral or immoral.

The association between the idea of religion and the idea of higher and distinctively human characteristics is so ancient and remains so persistent that secularists who would enthusiastically support musical and artistic education become at best uneasy and at worst positively hostile when these laudable cultural activities seem to be confounded with or described as spiritual education and/or the encouragement of growth in spirituality.[8] It appears that confusions of this kind, together with the consequent tensions, presently afflict the (state) maintained school system in the United Kingdom.

The 1944 Education Act, which established a framework that continued into the early nineties, contained a clause requiring all pupils have some instruction in a nondenominational and, at that time, fairly noncontroversial form of Christianity. Since that time there has, in this country, been both a big fall in the number of active Christians and a very substantial increase in the number of adherents of non-Christian religions. One result of this was that a large but equally unknown number of maintained schools more or less completely ignored that clause in the 1944 act.

The bill which eventually passed as the 1988 Education Reform Act significantly did not contain any substitute clause. It was, perhaps unsurprisingly, not the bishops but a group of strongly committed Christian laypersons who introduced in the House of Lords the amending substitute clause now contained in that 1988 act.

The school of which my wife is a governor was recently inspected. The report of Her Majesty's Inspectors was on the whole strongly favorable. But it did manage to find one thing to complain about: "Spiritual . . . education is underemphasized. Insufficient attention is given to the growth of spirituality through areas of the curriculum. . . ."

I wish I was able to tell what it was that the HMIs had in mind and what they would suggest that teachers should do to enable "pupils to develop personal values, beliefs, and attitudes through the spiritual . . . dimensions of the school's life." But unfortunately, my wife failed in her attempt to persuade her colleagues to make so bold as to ask them.

Some assumptions about the cognitive value of spiritual experience are bound to be made and, hopefully, challenged. If discussion of these issues is to be fruitful, then it has to take into account what is in fact a very frequently neglected fundamental distinction.[9]

This is the distinction between two senses of the word *experience* and of other logically related terms. On the one hand there is the everyday, commonsense sense, let us call it the objective sense: the sense in which a claim to have had experience is a claim to have had dealings with objects existing independently of the existence of the experience. On the other hand there is the sense especially favored by philosophers although it is by no means peculiar to such peculiar people. In this sense—let us call it the subjective sense—a claim to have or to have had experience is a claim about nothing more than what was felt or dreamed or imagined by whoever is supposed to have enjoyed or suffered the experience in question.

Berkeley's ideas, Hume's ideas and impressions, and the sense-data and bodily sensations of twentieth-century philosophy are all kinds of experiences in this second, subjective sense. Notoriously it is impossible validly to infer conclusions about what philosophers since Descartes have called the External World from premises recording the occurrence only of experiences of this sort. A farmer seeking staff with experience of cows would have good reason to be infuriated by an applicant who had dreamed and formed mental images of cows but had never actually milked any.

To bring out the crucial relevance of the fundamental distinction, consider the case of Bernadette Soubirois. If the question is a question about her experience in the second sense of the word *experience,* then her own account of how it seemed to her can be challenged only by doubting either her honesty or her powers of accurate description. But if it is a question, as for the authorities of the Roman Catholic church it clearly was, of whether Bernadette's experience was directly caused by the active presence of Mary the Mother of God, then it becomes a question about experience in the first sense. An affirmative answer could be sustained, if at all, only by evidence of some kind very different from the honest testimony of an unsophisticated peasant girl.[10]

NOTES

1. It would be just as correct, or just as incorrect, to render the Greek word not as *soul* but as *mind*. But since that Greek word is the word from which our *psychology, psychiatry, psychosomatic,* and so on are derived, it would be better still to render it as *psyche*.

2. For a critique of Plato's arguments, see Antony Flew, *The Logic of Mortality* (Oxford: Blackwell, 1987), ch. 2–4.

3. To admirers maintaining that he knew it backwards his many critics would respond—in my view mistakenly—that backwards was precisely how he did know it.

4. The phrase constitutes a characteristically mischievous and derisory reference to the peculiarly Roman Catholic doctrine of transubstantiation. The most devastating and to opponents the most delightful objection which Hobbes deploys against this doctrine is found in chapter 44:

> The Egyptian Conjurers, that are said to have turned their Rods to Serpents, and the Water into Bloud are thought but to have deluded the senses of the Spectators by a false shew of things, yet are esteemed Enchanters: But what should wee have thought of them, if there had appeared in their Rods nothing like a Serpent, and in the Water enchanted, nothing like Bloud, nor like anything else but Water, but that they had faced down the King, that they were Serpents that looked like Rods, and that it was Bloud that seemed Water?

5. Having previously argued that it is perverse to interpret *Everlasting Death* as *Everlasting Life in Torments*, Hobbes in the same chapter finally concluded that:

> the texts that mentioned *Eternall Fire, Eternall Torments, or the Worm that never dieth,* contradict not the Doctrine of a Second and Everlasting Death, in the proper and natural sense of the word *Death.* The Fire, or Torments prepared for the wicked in *Gehenna, Tophet,* or in what place soever, may continue for ever; and there may never want wicked men to be tormented in them; though not every, nor any one Eternally.

6. For a much more extensive treatment of these ultimately perhaps insoluble problems, see Flew, *The Logic of Mortality,* ch. 6–10.

7. For an explanation see, for instance, Antony Flew, *Thinking About Social Thinking* (London: HarperCollins, 1991), pp. 151–55 and ch. 6, passim.

8. One discovery was that the noun *spirituality,* which is now mainly used to refer to the characteristic of being in some sense spiritual, had at one time a more substantial usage. The expression *A Spirituality* was employed as a word for self-conscious collective of religious enthusiasts.

9. For a much fuller treatment see, for instance, Antony Flew, *God: A Critical Enquiry* (La Salle, Ill.: Open Court, 1984), ch. 6. This book was originally published as *God and Philosophy.*

10. It would be churlish not to share the characteristic contribution made by Hobbes in chapter 32 of *Leviathan:*

> For if a man pretend to me that God hath spoken to him . . . immediately, and I make doubt of it, I cannot see what argument he can produce to oblige me to believe it. . . . To say he hath spoken to him in a dream, is no more than to say that he dreamed God spoke to him. . . .

Part Two
Historical Perspectives

3

Plato's Bicycle: Christian Spirituality as a Remythicizing of the Person

R. Joseph Hoffmann

INTRODUCTION

The somewhat mystical title of this essay is meant to suggest what I hold to be two common features of spirituality as a constituent of religious communities: First, its exclusivity when used as a term defining a religious elite within a group of men and women professing common beliefs or adhering to roughly similar doctrines. Second, I want to suggest that this exclusivity functions in the Christian tradition through the conveyance of an eccentric form of the Platonic myth of the human person as a divisible entity of upper and lower parts.[1] Thus my use of the term *Plato's bicycle.*

A bicycle is a conveyance, a vehicle to transport a thing rather than the thing itself. Likewise, what is conveyed in the Christian tradition is not Platonic didache but a Christianized, or more exactly, partially de-Gnosticized myth of the person, propagated chiefly through the heresiological writing of the first three centuries of the Common Era to promote and support specific religious ideas; including the concepts of holiness (saintliness), salvation or savedness, and redemption.

What I should like to attempt is a brief tour of specific "moments"

in the history of Christian forms of spirituality as these define religious elites, recognizing that for every moment I recount there are a
dozen analogous moments and a number of exceptions to the pattern
I hope to establish. I should also want to caution that each moment
deserves—and some have received—full-length studies of the
socioreligious context and linguistic orbits within which variegated
Christian spiritualities emerge. Such concentrated study is especially
crucial if is to be maintained, as some would wish to argue, that
"innocuous" spiritualities exist alongside enthusiastic and charismatic
varieties throughout the church's history. It is my argument here, however, (a) that spirituality as it came to be understood and to express
itself in both forms is rooted in early Christian experience and specifically in what may be termed "Corinthianism" and (b) that this experience, while not foreign to apocalyptic Judaism in first-century Pales-
tine, acquires its characteristic view of human personhood in the
Church's encounter with Gnostic religion and through the social consequences of the *contemptus mundi* propagated by the Gnostic sects.

EXCLUSIVITY AS A FEATURE OF
CHRISTIAN SPIRITUALITY

Half a century ago, Ronald Knox attempted to write a history of the
idea of religious enthusiasm,[2] a word which now suggests gusto, commitment to the company, eagerness to please or to perform a task
well—as in job advertisements that ask for "enthusiastic self-starters."
In John Wesley's day the term meant something very different.[3] It suggested a lack of reasonableness and moderation, as indicated by all
manner of outward appearances: laughing too loud; walking too fast;
talking too much; reading the wrong kind of books, praising Jesus by
moonlight on Christ Church meadow; in short, any sort of behavior
that did not correspond to the conduct expected by *citizens* —a term
then coming into fashion, having been dredged up by republican clas-
sicists—of the self-consciously clockwork world of the eighteenth
century.[4] Above all, enthusiasm was thought to be characteristic of

certain kinds of Christians in the eighteenth century. Moravians, Shakers, Quakers, and born-again Schwenckfelders and Melchiorites and followers of Wesley were called enthusiasts by the high-minded proponents of serious—or to use its other name—rational religion.[5]

But to speak of enthusiasm as a feature of religious groupings of the Enlightenment is to enter the story very late. The prepositional noun ἔνθεος is a derivative of the Greek term for being *en-godded* (literally, full of the god) or possessed by the spirit of God, and this meaning can be traced to the first century of the Church's life, having entered the Christian vocabulary of salvation from two directions: through the mystery or sacramental cults of the Hellenistic world, and through theosophical sects such as those collectively, if misleadingly, named "Gnostic."[6] It is this understanding which attached itself to early Christologies centering on the spiritual presence of the risen Christ within local congregations (cf. John 15:26; 16:12–15), originally perhaps as a response to the apocalyptic preaching of charismatic apostles (Acts 2:1–17) and then in sedentary congregations established by "sign-showing" apostles who spoke of revelations of the absent Lord (2 Cor. 12:1–7).

THE CORINTHIAN PARADIGM

The church in Corinth serves as a model in the development of elitist spiritual enthusiasm. In his letters to the church at Corinth Paul wages a losing battle against two kinds of elite: a merchant or aristocratic elite who tend to shame the poorer members of the congregation with their feasts and drinking contests in the Hellenistic mode; and a spiritual or charismatic elite (whose social origins are harder to pinpoint with certainty) who establish their privileged status in the community through displays of prophecy, and its corollary, speaking in tongues of ecstasy. It may be the case that charismatic elitism in the church at Corinth is a response by poorer members of the congregation to the visible displays of wealth implied in 1 Corinthians 11:22, though in fact the exhibition of spiritual gifts may be linked to drunken abuses of eucharistic practice (including, arguably, "false prophecy" and tongues of ecstasy) condemned by Paul in 11:21f.[7] Paul is dealing therefore with a community where a crisis of spiritual hierarchy has already taken shape, and where contempt for the body has led some members to question the nature of the resurrection of Jesus (1 Cor. 15:15) and the apposite question, the resurrection of the animal body. While a number of studies have mooted the possibility that Paul is up against a sort of proto-Gnosticism at Corinth,[8] the pattern of his argument would seem to suggest that his opposition is a homegrown theosophy that comes into the Church in an informal way through religious dilettantes with attachments to the soteriology of the mystery sects.

Paul's attack on spiritual exclusivism in the community is two-pronged. He claims on the one hand (1 Cor. 14:18) to be as spiritual as anybody; on the other (14:19), to conduct himself differently from the Corinthians, despite possessing abundant gifts of the spirit. In a shocking but probably necessary disclaimer, he offers that he has baptized no one (save Crispus and Gaius), admitting thereby that he regards the sacrament as being misused as an equivalent (1 Cor. 1:16) to a Mithraic lustration. He then attempts to deflate the pretensions of the elite by suggesting criteria for testing claimants of spiritual gifts, making intelligibility and instruction more important than random displays of spirit possession. Paul's God at this point is closer to that of the philosophers than to the gods of the Greek mysteries—a God of order and peace, not of confusion (14:55). He is a bricks-and-mortar kind of God, known by edifying, comprehensible words that build churches: "I would rather speak five intelligible words for the benefit of others as well as myself than thousands of words in the language of ecstasy"(1 Cor. 14:19).

As a test case in the history of Christian spirituality, the Corinthian situation is interesting for two reasons. First of all, it is sometimes missed that the Corinthian church itself is an exclusivist community. Paul's later or further dealings with the church show that he has been rejected for failing to display the kind of spirituality required by the elite (2 Cor. 10:1–18). As a strategy, he may thank God, as he does in 1 Corinthians 14:18–19, that he possesses more charisma than any of the spirituals; but the community seems to reject this claim. His authority may have fallen prey to the influence of a group (so Theissen)[9] of wandering charismatics, but whether or not this is so, it is the triumph of the Corinthians over Paul's sobriety rather than Paul's cautions that define the earliest test case in Christian spiritual enthusiasm. Corinth thus becomes a model in Christian history of the triumph of minority spirituality over an authority based on what Paul terms, at the end of chapter fourteen, decency and order. At this level, it is a contest between a man with church expansion, growth, and structure on his mind (despite a certain apocalyptic inhibition about how long such structures will last) and a community which shows all the earmarks of a charismatic cult: closure, suspicion, and exclusion, and special criteria for its own legitimation and the legitimation of apostolic leaders.[10]

Secondly, the Corinthian case supplies a model for types of spiritual experience: Paul's "Plato" is not the Plato of the dialogues but the dilute, popularized theosophy of street philosophers in Asia Minor. Paul begins with the notion (1 Cor. 13:8) that love—the sort of love that is expressed in the *Symposium* (ἡ ἀγάπη οὐδέποτε πίπτει)—will solve problems and heal divisions, but he does not seem to know that for Plato, human love was more often a source of strife and jealousy than harmony.[11] If he is playing with a term already in use among the Corinthian charismatics, then he does not seem to know how the term functions in a cultic context as a term of exclusion, as it does, for example, in the cultic environment of Johannine Christianity.[12] He knows something about images, archetypes, and ideas: we see shadows of reality through a glass darkly, not things as they are. And he can say in language reminiscent of the philosopher that knowledge is partial—but he then fails to denote the significance of that recognition.

Paul is evidently arguing for a kind of disciplined spirituality in contrast to the undisciplined, elitist-ecstatic spirituality of the Corinthian faction. But effectively he becomes through force of argument a victim of the opposition view that a rational spirituality is less perfect (τέλειος) than an ecstatic spirituality. Moreover, almost any interpreter looking for edification in Paul's digressions in Romans 7 and 8—where he says in close succession that he is unspiritual, the "purchased slave of sin," or that the law is spiritual, but that all Christians are spiritual if only God's spirit dwells in them—will come away greatly confused or theologically taxed.

Clearly Paul works within a religious environment where being "full of the god" was a significant idea and one which could be harnessed to the implicit christology of the absent lord, spiritually present in the body of believers. To be full of Christ was to be perfect (τέλειος), as Paul acknowledges in 1 Corinthians 2:10–13. But the claim of spiritual perfection seems already to belong to the opposition party, and the most Paul can hope for is to bring it under control through moral suasion. He is not able to control, no matter how much his natural pharisaic conservatism would have inclined him to do so, the direction in which spirituality would develop in the hellenized section of the mission field where possession by the spirit of the god transcended the "manifestation of the spirit for the common good" that Paul refers to in 1 Corinthians 12:7. This would suggest, at least, that Paul's stratagem is to democratize a process already threatened by those characterized as the "uncommended" in 11:17.

DEFINING MOMENTS IN POST-CORINTHIAN SPIRITUALITY

The later history of the Church has not only Corinth but the tension between forms of spirituality as a reference point—more specifically, the clash between *ecstatic* (often elitist-collective or "cultic") spirituality wherein the spiritually perfect feel able to defy structures and disciplines of the larger community, and *democratized* (often individualized) spirituality, wherein discipline becomes the way to spiritual perfection.

Montanism

The Montanists of the second and third century almost succeeded in persuading the Roman bishops that a new spirit of prophecy was moving through the Church, until a wavering bishop Zephyrinus recognized that episcopal authority might be jeopardized by acknowledging the claims of the so-called Kataphrygians.[13] As at Corinth, women were singled out as the primary offenders (Paul's advice for women to be quiet in 1 Corinthians 14 comes in his rebuke of the ecstatics, it should be noted); but the main division made by Montanists was between the spiritual and soulish—the pneumatics and the psychics. Tertullian boasts that (ca. 200) he felt compelled to separate from the "natural men because of his acknowledgement of the paraclete."[14] Dead serious in his spirituality, he wanted disciplinary questions settled by a board of prophets; offered the vision of a prophetess as a solution to a metaphysical question; attacked the growing practice of bishops granting forgiveness to those accused of sexual license and adultery; and began the long North African tradition[15] of regarding martyrdom as the ultimate proof of possession of the Spirit. Montanism was the taming of prophecy for spiritual purposes but also an attempt to put authority and organization to the spiritual test.

With Montanism, spirituality enters a new phase in the Church. The Corinthian problem had been the uncontrolled claim of a minority to possess "high spiritual gifts." The Montanist problem was the claim of a church minority to be holier and more contemptuous of life and sex than members of the Church at large—the Catholic church. This claim was based both on prophetic witness, miraculous signs—including speaking in tongues—and especially the rigor of their lifestyle. No doubt the Montanists were rebelling against a perceptibly worldly church which had little room left for prophecy, and thus against a type of protosecularization. But Montanist Christians were also in opposition to a contrastive form of spirituality characterized, especially in some heretical groups like the Marcosians and Phibionites,[16] by a contempt for discipline and restraint, and in the case of the former sect, the practice of ritual prostitution. In short, they were doubly exclusive, setting their faces against both the world, as the puritanical Marcionites and most Christian Gnostic sects had done, and against the worldly church which had begun to outlive the social, structural, and theological limitations of its original apocalyptic witness.

I would suggest that this pattern of double or mutual exclusion holds throughout and beyond the Reformation as part of what Adrian Hastings calls, in another context, the "natural process of fissiparation" within the Christian community. Thus, whether we are talking about the spirituality of the Donatists of the fourth century with their specific claim that the spirit had deserted the church at Rome,[17] or the spirituality of the Desert Fathers, or later on the Benedictines, we are describing the rejection of a majority of Christians by a convinced and enthusiastic minority. Augustine raised the point signally in his first treatise against the Donatists: is the Church a fortress or enclosed garden (hortus conclusus) set against the world—an image which could have described any monastic community of a later day—or a light set on a hill beckoning the faithful and the lapsed, the saint and the sinner?[18]

Early Monasticism

It is simple enough to see the early monastic forms of spirituality as innocuous instances of this pattern of exclusion: men and women living together or apart from the world in order to practice a rule of sexual abstinence, prayer, fasting, and a regimen designed to make the contemplation of God possible. The greatest names of the early movement, however, are those of men who forcefully pursued a life of individual holiness: Gregory of Nyssa was married to a woman named—appropriately—Theosebeia, whom he describes as "illustrious, beautiful, a true priestess, yokefellow, and equal of a priest." He regarded his sexual avoidance of her as triumph over the allures of the flesh.[19] Gregory Nazianzus is described in a recent article by Thomas Hopko as cranky, thin-skinned, self-defensive, easily insulted, often offended.[20] Yet it was among these Cappadocians that Plato's philosophy achieved its closest approach to biblical Christianity, and through their writings that the Philosopher was given a permanent lease on Christian thought.

Syrian spirituality, at a further extreme, took a position which Roberta Bondi has described as being not antiworldly but anticivilization. Its main features, as depicted by Theodoret in the fifth century, included an aversion to food and a high regard for anchorites covered with filth—a visible sign of their rejection of the dung of the body. Jacob of Nisibis, for example, refused to eat any food that he had to work for, and only ate raw what fell to him by chance.[21] Ephraem Syrus complains about the exclusivity of anchorites and the fragmentation caused by the infighting between the styles of spiritual life: the wandering stranger or anchorite was the rule in Ephraem's day rather than the communal monk-in-community, and even the anchorites warred among themselves for the most personalized and interiorized form of the Christian faith. A certain Stephen bar Sudaili (fifth century) claimed that Christ himself is only a stage the mystic must pass through in his interior spiritualized journey, regarding not only communal monastics but other anchorite monastics as heretics of the spirit.

Reformation Spirituality

The pattern of mutual exclusivity continues in the Reformation. The Cathari and Waldensians of the twelfth century—despite orthodox claims to the contrary—were less theologically incorrect than spiritually suspect: they were moral rigorists who threatened to undermine the authority of the sacraments and hierarchy with claims of the purity of their movement.[22] But alongside the spiritual rigorists were radical spiritualists who are less well known: the pantheists, like Amalric of Bena; or the extreme Paulinist David of Dinant who taught that the believer in whom God dwells cannot sin and is superior to moral and civil law. Similar beliefs were held by a variety of mystical sects in the fourteenth and fifteenth centuries, especially among the so-called Brothers and Sisters of the Free Spirit.[23] Luther's roots in the late antique world of the spiritual Franciscans and Brethren of the Common Life is well known, as is the "worldliness" and alleged unspirituality of the Renaissance church he rejected.[24]

It is ironic perhaps that Luther's moral vision of the church provided for marriage as a solution to the spiritual abuses of the very monastic life that had come about as a response to the spiritual lassitude of the Catholic church of the fifth century. Be that as it may, the movement described by George Williams as the magisterial reform—Luther, Calvin, and the reform Christianity of Zwingli—soon enough became a congeries of national churches reflecting the religious ideals of northern Europe as much to pattern as the Roman church reflected, broadly, the religious ideals of southern Europe. Indeed, one way to think of Protestant spirituality is as an antinational countertrend, just as early Catholic spirituality had been an anti-institutional countertrend with a strongly ascetic emphasis. From Müntzer to Wesley, to the Millerites and Adventists, to the Exclusive Brethren formed as a response to the insufficient spirituality of the related Brethren movements, the radical reformers and their successors, or at least the spiritual Anabaptists and the groups that followed them, continued the pattern of an exclusivism based, commonly, on a perceived deficiency in the spirituality of the lumpen mass.[25]

Müntzer defines this pattern in his surprising condemnation of Christendom and his dream of a New Jerusalem of sociospiritual equals led by an inspired prophet: Christendom, he wrote to Duke John in 1520, is senseless. The church, its priests, and its sacraments belong to the devil. The time has come for a cleansing slaughter, *ein Blütvorgeissen,* to identify the true spirituals. Müntzer died trying to prove his point in battle at Frankenhausen on May 27, 1525.

Revivalist Movements

No doubt one ought to distinguish the mysticism of Eckhart from the belligerent spirituality of Müntzer, the discipline of John of the Cross to the sterner discipline of the Albigensian dualists with their rejection of marriage and doctrine of perfection. One of the difficulties in discussing so broad a subject as "Christian spiritualities" is in knowing what color Plato's bicycle is painted at any stop along the way: Monks, anchorites, and mystics tended to be, ideally if not in practice always, ascetics who intended to pursue a life of interior piety apart from the worldly distractions of a church extended throughout the nations; Protestant spirituals tended to reject monks and asceticism as aberrations of the plainer spiritual life that could be constructed from biblical teaching: The six spiritual virtues extolled in a poem by a Nuremberg layman, Hans Sachs, includes the following verse:

> Faith makes us entirely God's / we show our neighbor love, we live each day in hope / we are righteous through the spirit / discretion keeps us vigilant / moderation tames our flesh and blood / endurance helps us through our suffering until life is done and we inherit together the eternal fatherland.

This simple prescription for a spiritual life could be followed by any family, or any collective of communal farmers separated from the distractions of a changing world order, symbolized by the transition from an agrarian Europe still culturally in touch with the biblical world to a preindustrial society which would change the face of commerce, technology, and human interaction.

If Montanism was a nostalgic form of enthusiasm, early monasticism a revolt against the eroded holiness of the Church, and Reformation spirituality a rejection of deciduous monasticism, the evangelical spiritualist and pietist movements from David Joris and Henry Niclaes (founder of the Familist movement) onward regarded the state and society as belonging to the fallen order of creation. Luther, in fact, had argued as much in his 1522 treatise, *Vom ehelichen Leben.* As many of the reformers saw marriage as constituting the basis for the unredeemed social order, they argued its status, equivocally, as a God-given but manmade "ordinance" symbolizing the relationship between Christ and the church (Eph. 5:31ff.).[26] The covenantal idea led to any number of antisacramentarian views of the marriage bond, ranging from monogamy to communalism, and to coupling and polygamy in the case of the Batenburgers, the Thüringian Dreamers, and assorted other "Bible-believing" spiritual sects.[27] On a more docile level, as in the case of the followers of Menno Simons (Wismar Resolutions, 1554), the family was, like the church, essentially "antisocial," a locus for the preservation of the simplicity of Christ's teaching in a complicated and unredeemed world.

Revivalism and Pentecostalism

By the nineteenth century the feeling that spiritual simplicity was, so to speak, too simple was widespread in Protestant circles. Revivalism of various descriptions—from the Great Awakening in New England to the tent revivalism of the American South to the founding of the Elim Foursquare Gospel Alliance—emphasized the importance of religious experience, personal conversion and witness, spirit baptism, and spiritual gifts. The phenomenon was not precisely a back-to-Corinth movement, and certainly not a back-to-Plato movement, but an attempt to revive biblical Christianity in a direct and experiential way. In revival congregations, as indeed at Corinth, the role of the minister, of sacraments, and of doctrine is reduced and the experience of born-again believers greatly expanded. The theme of being saved, or in apocalyptic groupings, the rapture of the saints, becomes the primary focus of believers.

With ideological roots in the radical reformation and its separatist tendencies, evangelical revivalism and pentecostalism were essentially forms of christolatrous spirituality.[28] In the famous Los Angeles Meetings of April 1906, in the preaching of George Jeffreys and others, the movement acquired a reputation for divine healing. While never missing from earlier forms of spiritual exclusivism, the element of divine or "faith" healing has figured more prominently in the pentecostal revival than in previous revival movements as a mark of divine favor. Together with "speaking in tongues," healing is one of the trademarks and hence one of the criteria for legitimation within the movement. While no attempt can be made here to account for the prominence of faith healing as a principle of exclusion, one may point to (a) the virtually magical view of baptism as a source of healing commonly held by spiritual sects (cf. 1 Cor. 1:16f.), a trend which is perpetuated by the Anabaptist spirituals, by Paracelsus, and even by Servetus; and (b) the antiscientific worldview of many exclusive sects, which tends to see petitionary prayer as being of a higher order than medical and technological achievement. While it would be facile to explain this feature of pentecostal spirituality as simply reflecting its general suspicion of book learning and technology, the element of rejection and the desire for "holiness" helps to account for its exclusivist character as much as for its place in the lineage of post-Corinthian spiritualities.

CONCLUSIONS: CHRISTIAN SPIRITUALITY AS NEO-GNOSTICISM

What seems to be a constant in this brief tour, from Paul to the Montanists and from the Desert Fathers to the revivals, is the paramount importance of religious experience in defining what constitutes authentic Christian existence. This perception of the Church can only take shape against the background of other forms of church life, which from the standpoint of the "true" spiritual or born-again believer will seem experientially less rich and probative. This, I suggest, is a common criticism of the *ecclesiola spiritualis in ecclesiam* from Corinth onward.

In this short history debates about celibacy, or purity and virginity and their opposites—antinomianism, sexual license, and ecstatic experience—loom large when one looks at any particular moment. It is a feature of Christian spirituality going back at least to the Donatists that spiritual elites are always at war with themselves and that a movement that begins as pacifist, such as that associated with the spiritual Anabaptists, can turn militant in their prosecution of a holy agenda; or that groups that begin as world-denying and ascetic, such as we think the ptolemaic Gnostics to have been, can produce orgiastic forms of the religion on the premise that the true spiritual owes no debt to his physical nature and can overcome it through sexual excess. The cultural frames of reference, of course, change dramatically: Gnosticized Christians like Clement of Alexandria, a Neoplatonist and intellectual, regarded marriage as an evil and an impediment to pneumatic perfection; Jerome, often a spiritual recluse, thought the bond of marriage tolerable only for the purpose of breeding virgins; the Zwickau prophets and some of the familist sects considered sexual intercourse the "sacramental" and thus the spiritual aspect of marriage; and in certain prophetic movements such as the Cult Davidian, sexual relations with the god-filled prophet acquired a sacramental character and promised spiritual fulfillment.

However variable the cultural determinants and hence the expressions of Christian spirituality, there does seem to be a constant in its development. This is to be found in the view of human personhood formed by the Church in its early encounter with Hellenistic thought. The exclusion of unsaved majorities by spiritual elites has tended to depend, as it did at Corinth, on a myth of the human person derived from first- and second-century Platonic theosophy and especially from Gnosticism. Although New Testament scholars in the Bultmannian tradition have professed to see this myth in the Gospels, and in the Fourth Gospel in particular, the second and third centuries seem to have been the richest time for its development. In relation to Corinth, the anthropology and Christology of the Gospels seem atavistic and perhaps reactionary, the reasons for which cannot be explored here. But there seems little doubt that one of the first effects of the Jewish missionary movement's encounters with Hellenistic culture, as we know that encounter from Paul's letters, was the introduction of certain concepts essentially foreign to the substratum of gospel writing: the defilement of the body; the partitioning of the race into earthy, ensouled, and spiritual beings; the transmutation of animal flesh; the overcoming of cosmic archons who rule the world by an armory of spiritual beings; the death to a cosmocrator's law through an act of lustration (baptism); the emphasis on divine action as a means of God's redemption of divine perfections lost in the process of creation; and so on.[29]

It is best to see these themes not as a Gnosticizing of Paul's (or Paulinist) theology nor as Paul's accommodation to Gnostic trends in Hellenistic congregations but rather as the stock images through which a doctrine of atonement could be conveyed to the uncircumcised. The deductions from it drawn first, so far as we know, at Corinth have remained thematic in the development of Christian spirituality from that time to this. In the transition from the concept of "saved remnant" and "chosen people," concepts with broadly democratic social application within Jewish atonement theology, the Christian encounter with the dilute Platonism of its pagan and then (internal) sectarian opponents served up the image of the spirituality of the *teletoi*, the accomplished, or spiritually complete, whose perfection was not understood as extensible or applicable to the social unit—the church—but limited to the few. In this limited sense, Christian spirituality whether Corinthian, monastic, reformist, pentecostal-revivalist, or New Age shows a consistent tendency for enthusiastic elitism and the exclusivist characteristics that defined the Church's ancient encounter with the programmatically exclusivist Gnostic sects.

It is to the credit of the editors of the University of Chicago's World Spirituality series that in the first volume on Christian spirituality they have included an essay by Robert Grant on Gnostic spirituality, just ahead of the section on the church fathers. This may be an attempt subtly to convey the "prior importance" of Gnostic spirituality to patristic studies, or perhaps an attempt to sequester it. But from the standpoint of the case I have tried to argue the placement of Gnostic ideas as formative ones is significant.

Gnosticism's tortured model of the human person—its anthropology—was never rejected by the Church, despite the broadsides of writers like Irenaeus against its complexity. The Gnostic, says Grant, possessed an essentially negative attitude toward the world, a feeling of hostility and alienation in which the world was somehow an enemy. The Gnostics, like the Corinthian Christians, the Montanists, and the Exclusive Brethren much later, saw spirit as better than soul and opposed to it. Only the pneumatics possessed the inner light, the divine spark, that made salvation possible. According to Irenaeus, one Gnostic described the spiritual man as "gold in the mud."

The Gnostics claimed to possess private revelations through the spirit; they were accused by the orthodox both of denouncing marriage, meat, and wine (habits common among the Syrian spirituals of a later era) and of sexual promiscuity. Chances are, and judging from the evidence of spirituals within the Church and on the fringes of orthodoxy, both characterizations are accurate. According to Clement, a Gnostic once asked a Christian virgin what she made of the text "Give to everyone who asks," and inferring the questioner's purpose she hastened to reply: "On the subject of marriage talk to my mother" (Stromateis, 3.27). Thus, Gnosticism encapsulated within its exclusivist polity both ascetic and antinomian or libertine elements, as later on other spiritual movements would do. They lived apart from the mainstream, though we have little idea how they spent their time or gained support, or what was the precise character of their proselytizing. Like the Montanists later, the community of the Ancrene Wisse, or Mother Ann Lee among the Shaker spirituals, women prophets were prominent in their communities. Yet it is not clear that the prominence of women spirituals among the Gnostics (or at Corinth) is an indication of favor or status. Irenaeus maintained that women spirituals were habitually victimized by the males in Gnostic congregations, "while maintaining that carnal things should be allowed to the carnal nature as spiritual things are to the spiritual."[30] In the same passage, Irenaeus suggests that women spirituals were seduced away from their families by the "perfect," chosen to "bear the elect seed," a charge that can be traced at least to early second-century Corinth, where Clement of Rome complains about the wreckage of families by wandering charismatics.[31] The coincidence of sexual freedom, the simultaneous prominence and subjugation of women among spiritual elites, the wreckage of families, and the exclusivist spirituality extend, given various cultural permutations, from Corinth to Waco.

I would argue in closing that Gnostic Christians are the source of a particular paradigm of humanity in the world which the Church effectively assimilated in the process of opposing. It is this view of the person that Plato's bicycle conveys to successive generations of spiritual elites. No clearer case of this model of personhood and its attendant exclusivity exists than Irenaeus's comments on the teaching of the Valentinian Gnostics of the late second century:

If a person joins with them, he thinks he is no longer in heaven or on earth but has entered into the fulness of God. He struts about with self-esteem and arrogance like a cock. Some of them say that a spiritual man must have good morals, and strike a serious pose; others disdain such scruples and claim to be perfect. They live without shame, despise everyone and everything else and say they already know their place in heaven.[32]

NOTES

1. Cf. Plato, Cratylus 95b-d; Phaedrus 124b-d; Phaedo 251b–254c; Republic iii.358a–559a; Timaeus 453b-c; Laws, v.686d–687c.

2. *Enthusiasm: A Chapter in the History of Religion* (Oxford: Oxford University Press, 1950), especially chs. 5, 6.

3. An indicative title is Wesley's tract, "Predestination Calmly Considered," in Wesley's *Complete Works,* vol. 2 (London: Wesleyan Conference Office, 1972), 233–36.

4. An unofficial vestige of this is the now disregarded Oxford taboo against discussing religion at table during evening meals in hall—a "sconceable offense."

5. Adequate etiology in Kant's *Religion within the Limits of Religion Alone,* trans. T. M. Greene (New York: Harper and Row, 1960), 94–98; and David Hume, "Dialogues Concerning Natural Religion," in *Philosophical Works,* vol. 2 (Boston: Little, Brown, 1854), 432–505.

6. A comprehensive survey of the etymology of *gnosis* is given in H. Marwitz's article, "Gnosis/Gnostiker," in *Der Kleine Pauly Lexikon der Antike,* vol. 2., ed. K. Ziegler (München: Deutscher Taschenbuch Verlag, 1979), 830b–839a.

7. Implicitly the "spirituals" are the ones accused of drinking contests in 1 Corinthians 11:21 and Paul's rejoinder in 1 Corinthians 12:13 to the effect that Jews and Greeks have all been made to drink of the same spirit.

8. Notably, W. Schmithals, "Die Gnosis in Korinth: Eine Untersuchung zu den Korintherbriefen," *Frlant* 48 (1969).

9. "Soziale Schichtung in der korinthischen Gemeinde," *ZNW* 65 (1974): 232–72.

10. Ernst Kaesemann, "Die Legitimatat des Apostels," *ZNW* 41 (1942): 33–71.

11. Symp. 149a–173c; esp. 153b–155c. 1.

12. 1 John 4 exhibits most graphically the cultic cast of the Johannine

church with its stark distinction between those who are "of the world" and those (within the community) "who are of God." The writer goes on to say: "Whoever is of God listens to us and whoever is not of God does not listen to us" (1 John 4:5–6f.).

13. Chief sources among patristic writers are Hippolytus, Stygmata apud. Eusebius, Ecclesiastical History 5.16f.; Epiphanius, Panar. 48. See also J. M. Ford, "Was Montanism a Jewish-Christian Heresy?" in *Journal of Ecclesiastical History* 17 (1966): 145–58.

14. For the study of Tertullian's later involvement with the Montanists, see T. D. Barnes, *Tertullian: A Historical and Literary Study* (Oxford: Oxford University Press, 1971), pp. 130–42.

15. The intellectual history of Christian North Africa is traced by J. P. Brisson in *Gloire et Misère de l'Afrique Chrétienne* (Paris, 1949).

16. Described by Irenaeus, Adv. Haereses 1.7–14.

17. The best treatment of the Donatist schism remains W. H. C. Frend's *The Donatist Church* (Oxford: Oxford University Press, 1952; reprint, 1971), where patristic evidence is exhaustively considered.

18. Augustine, Contra Cresconium 2.34.

19. Cf. De Virginitate, ed. M. Aubineau, *Sources Chrétienne* 99 (1966); and on his attachment to Platonism: H. F. Cherniss, "The Platonism of Gregory of Nyssa," *University of California Studies in Classical Philology* 11 (1930–1934): 1–92.

20. See on Gregory Heinrich Doerrie, *Gregor von Nyssa und die Philosophic* (Leiden: Brill, 1976) and on the Platonism of the Cappadocians, J. Danielou, *Platonisme et Théologie Mystique* (Paris: Aubier, 1944).

21. On Jacob, a leading figure in Syriac church tradition (the "Moses of Mesopotamia"), see A. Voobus, *History of Asceticism in the Syrian Orient*, vol. 1 (CSCO 184, 1958), 141–43, and P. Krüger, "Jakob von Nisibis in syrischer und armenischer Uberlieferung," *Museon* 81 (1968): 161–69.

22. H. Søderberg, *La Religion des Cathares* (Uppsala, 1949); J. Russell, "Interpretations of the Origins of Medieval Heresy," in *Medieval Studies* 25 (1965): 26–53.

23. See in general, C. W. Bynum, "Religious Women in the High Middle Ages," in *Christian Spirituality: High Middle Ages and Reformation* (London: SCM, 1988), 123ff.

24. The factions in the order of St. Francis can be discerned in disagreements between the followers of Elias of Cortona and the Zealots or "Spirituals" who wanted to maintain the original way of life. Under Angelo

Clareno the spirituals tended to become extreme in their positions, and in 1318 John XXII burned four of their number as heretics, having decreed in the bull *Cum inter Nonnullos* that their teaching of absolute poverty of Christ was mistaken and that complete renunciation of possessions did not constitute spiritual perfection. Despite repression, the teaching of the spirituals continued among the Fraticelli and the Beghards of Provence.

25. Discussion and typology provided in G. H. Williams, *The Radical Reformation*, rev. ed. (Philadelphia: Westminster, 1992).

26. Ibid., p. 506.

27. The Traeumer and Blutsfreunde were led by a certain Louis of Tüngeda who renounced baptism as a mark of the covenant in favor of sexual spiritualism that "united the fellowship by a single dream-inspired coition all round"; See Paul Wappler, "Die Steflung Kursachsens und des Landgraften Philipp von Hessen," 13/14 *Reformationsgeschichtliche Studien und Texte* (Münster, 1910).

28. Two older studies can be noted: N. Bloch-Hoell, *The Pentecostal Movement: Its Origins, Development and Distinctive Character* (Oslo, 1964); and J. Hollenweger, *Enthusiastisches Christentum* (Wüppertal, 1969; ET, 1972).

29. That these themes can be discovered in Hellenistic Judaism, in Philo, and in parts of the Jewish wisdom tradition must also be acknowledged. The counter-tendencies in Judaism, however, were much stronger in Judaism than in the Christian churches where for religious as much as for political reasons anti-Hellenistic influences were forsaken at a relatively early period, not least (cf. Acts 6) by Jewish converts to the new religion.

30. Against Heresies, 1.6.3.

31. 1 Clement 6.3.

32. Irenaeus's complete description of Gnostic spirituality, with which he associates carnality, sexual license, and "many other abominations and impieties," is given in Against Heresies, 1.6.2–3.

4

Laughing and Dreaming at the Foot of the Cross: Context and Reception of a Religious Symbol

Justin Meggitt

"Always look on the bright side of life." Monty Python's *Life of Brian* climaxes in some wonderful jokes about the crucifixion of Christ, but perhaps the best is in the final scene. Strung up, waiting to die an unpleasant and uncomfortable death, the assorted bunch of losers and misfits breaks into a banal song with this absurdly optimistic refrain.

However, jokes about the crucifixion are not new. Monty Python certainly did not invent them. We have, for example, a fascinating second-century graffito in which some budding comedian scratched a representation of Jesus on the cross, and a Christian looking up at him, before scrawling below the words, "Alexamenos worships his god": the "god" in question was depicted as having an ass's head. Indeed, even some early Christians found the crucifixion a source of humor. A group among them, the Docetists, believed that Christ himself thought of the whole business as something of a joke. Their savior laughed rather uncharitably at the fate of someone else being crucified in his place: "It was another upon whom they placed the crown of thorns. . . . I was rejoicing in the height . . . laughing at their ignorance" (*Second Treatise of the Great Seth* 56).

Reprinted from the *Journal for the Critical Study of Religion, Ethics, and Society* 1, no. 1 (Winter/Spring 1996). By permission of the publisher.

Perhaps none of this is new or surprising. But what is probably less well known is that jokes about crucifixion actually predate Christianity. And these jokes, it is my contention, are no laughing matter for anyone concerned, as I am in this essay, with examining how the symbol of the cross was received in the popular context of the first century and in determining the contours of the resulting spirituality.

Humor has been for the most part overlooked in the attempt to construct a background against which to interpret earliest Christianity. Firstly, there has always been a reticence to associate humor with Christianity in any way. After all, Christianity is a serious business— Jesus never laughs in the Gospels, he only weeps (John 11:35). Secondly, ancient jokes are often just not funny; studying them can be an unappealing, if not torturous, undertaking. They lose a lot in being made accessible to a twentieth-century audience. As the saying goes, "Nothing gains by translation except a bishop." Thirdly, jokes have always been regarded as rather flippant things, hardly worth remembering, let alone scrutinizing in any depth (with, of course, notable exceptions such as Freud [1960]).

But jokes in general can give us one of our few points of access to the view "from below" in any past society. They can allow us to rescue, in part, the lives of the nonelite from what E. P. Thompson so aptly termed the "enormous condescension of posterity" (1963, 12). They can permit us to reconstruct something of "the mental world" of the "anonymous and undocumented body of people" who fill every age (to borrow the language of Hobsbawm and Rudé 1973, 12). More specifically, jokes from antiquity can let us say something about the popular perceptions of the symbol of the cross *before* the Christian gospel of the crucified messiah was proclaimed. As such they can give an insight into the likely reception of this image, and the spirituality that it engendered among the earliest believers.

A number of types of joke can be distinguished as valuable in our quest. One form, known as the *gallows joke,* which functions to contain, deny, and domesticate the terrifying and unavoidable, is particularly useful. Such jokes can give us a glimpse of the ultimate fears of various groups in society. There are plenty of examples from antiquity involving crucifixion which reveal the dread in which it was held by the nonelite. For example, in Plautus's *Mostellaria* the slave Tranio realizes that his demise looks imminent and remarks, "Anybody here want to make some easy money? Anybody ready to be crucified in my place today? . . . I'm offering a talent to anyone prepared to jump on to a cross . . . after that he can come and claim the money, cash on the nail" (359ff). In Tranio's brave, bitter words we are given a vital clue, albeit a partial and limited one, to the appalling power of the cross in the life of all slaves. This joke is perhaps all the more important given the possibility that Plautus was himself an individual who had experienced life at the bottom of society in the ancient world (Aulus Gellius, *Noctes Atticae* 3.3.14).

Another valuable form of joke, given our concern, is the *ethnic joke.* These tend to hinge upon representatives of certain ethnic groups exhibiting less than flattering qualities, the most common being stupidity. For the most part the humor in such jokes resides in individuals failing to understand obvious or mundane realities. The *Philogelos,* a collection of jokes from the later Empire but containing material from much earlier, includes many such jokes. One interestingly reads as follows: "On seeing a runner who had been crucified, an Abderite remarked, 'By the gods, now he does fly—literally!' " (*Philogelos* 121). Such jokes are significant for our quest, not because of what they tell us about Abderites (they may or may not have been particularly stupid) but what they tell us about the common reality that the Abderite comically fails to comprehend—a man dying upon a cross. The joke gives us a glimpse of the accepted normality of crucifixion in the ancient world.

Taunts are another relevant form of humor. Classical literature is particularly rich in material in which members of the nonelite chide each other on the likelihood of their crucifixion (Hengel 1977, 10). Such jokes reveal the extent of both collective and individual preoccupations with the cross in the everyday lives of such people.

I have only touched on a few types of joke but they are sufficient to alert us to the value of such material in trying to understand something of the reality of the cross for the great mass of Graeco-Romans.

In these macabre attempts at humor we see how the symbol of the cross dominated nonelite mentality.

But, of course, jokes are not the only ways into nonelite mentality. There are a number of other types of evidence (papyri, epitaphs, law codes, curse tablets, domestic artifacts, and the like) which give us significant entry points into their worldviews. Space prevents me from doing any of these even cursory justice and so I shall dwell on one other relevant source of information: books of dream interpretations. These collections were, in some sense, repositories of popular wisdom and reflected to a limited degree common concerns. Like jokes, these sources have tended to be overlooked. Not only is there widescale ignorance of their existence, something only now being rectified with the studies of MacMullen (1971) and Pomeroy (1991), but where such works are known to historians, the continued prevalence of the Freudian assumption that dreams cannot tell us anything about the external world of the dreamer has encouraged their shameful neglect.

This dream literature reveals yet again, albeit *paradoxically,* the terror of the cross. In sleep, the symbol of oppression that dominated most people's waking lives was ironically transformed into one of liberation. The specific details of the barbarous fate of the crucified provided the means for the partial subversion of the symbolic tyranny of crucifixion. Artemidorus, for example, remarks: "It is also auspicious for a poor man [to dream of crucifixion]. For a crucified man is raised high and his substance is sufficient to keep many birds" (*Oneirocritica* 2.53). Being elevated on a cross and exposed to all was altered by the interpretation from being a sign of public shame and dishonor to being an indication of social success. Being helpless and a meal for carrion was changed from being the ultimate ignominy into a portent of wealth. Indeed, to dream of crucifixion boded extremely well for a slave, as it was interpreted as a prediction of manumission: "It means freedom for slaves, since the crucified are no longer subject to any man" (*Oneirocritica* 2.53). The cross, the ultimate symbol of degradation for a slave, became through the medium of dream interpretation a symbol of freedom.

Through jokes and dreams we can uncover some of the resonances of the symbol of the cross to the early hearers of the Christian
message, but now let us turn to the second element of our study and
briefly sketch the interpretation of the cross that this new faith
preached.

The cross was central to early Christian proclamation: it was, as
Hooker says, "the heart of the gospel" (1994, 140). The New Testament narratives clearly reach their climax in Jesus' triumph over the
cross, and other early Christian writings give the death of Christ center stage in their theologies. Paul's words to the Corinthian church are
indicative of this: "When I came to you, brethren, I did not come with
eloquence or superior wisdom as I proclaimed to you the testimony
about God. For I resolved to know nothing while I was with you
except Jesus Christ and him crucified" (1 Cor. 2:1–2).

Of course, there were significant differences in the way New Testament writers portrayed and interpreted this symbol, but the cross
was unalterably there, at the core of their spirituality, albeit a cross
which was transformed by the resurrection (Hooker 1994, 139). However, there are two features of the cross in Christian preaching upon
which I particularly wish to focus: firstly, its unashamed political
character, and secondly, its participatory quality.

Firstly, the cross symbol was understood as redolent with sociopo-
litical meaning. Two examples will suffice. In the so-called Christ-
hymn found in Paul's letter to the Philippians (2:5–11), the composi-
tion pivots upon the confession that Christ was obedient unto death,
"even death upon the cross" (2:8). This ignoble form of execution is
the fundamental component of a stinging attack upon the court rituals
and propaganda that were central to the rule of the Empire. Whoever
wrote these verses has the victim of the cross receive the obeisance
(2:10) customarily given to the emperor ("at the name of Jesus every
knee shall bow"); he or she presents Jesus as having a dominion far
greater than that of the emperor. While the emperor was normally
described as ruling the whole earth (Velleius Paterculus, *A History of
Rome* 2.126.2–5), verse ten describes Christ as ruling everything not
only on earth but above and below it as well. By verse eleven Jesus

becomes "Lord" of all creation, with the implication that Caesar was not. In the letter to the Colossians the cross is described as the means by which the ruling authorities are defeated and turned into a public spectacle (2:15). The language used specifically evokes and therefore subverts the drama of an imperial triumph, that theatrical articulation and confirmation of Roman authority which involved parading the vanquished through the streets of the capital city.

Secondly, as a symbol the cross was not something that was merely a focus of detached devotion. The early Christian proclamation stressed the need for believers to participate in the suffering of the crucifixion. In the synoptic Gospels, for example, the Christians are told to carry their crosses and follow Christ to Golgotha (Matt. 10:38, 16:24; Mark 8:34; Luke 9:23), and elsewhere in the New Testament they are encouraged to think of themselves as being crucified with Christ. As Paul declares: "I have been crucified with Christ" (Gal. 2:20).

We now have before us something of the perception of the symbol among the mass of Graeco-Roman society, and something of the character of the cross as preached by the early Christians. So what kind of spirituality was engendered when context and gospel collided? There is much that could be said, but I hope from the above it will be clear that it was a spirituality that transformed the symbol of oppression and suffering into one of liberation. It provided converts with a personal and collective mythic imperative to demythologize the symbol par excellence of imperial, autocratic hegemony. Just as such people had spasmodically freed themselves from the terror of the cross in their jokes and in their dreams, so in their worship they could produce a total spirituality that chased away its clawing shadow from their everyday lives. The cross may have been a stumbling block to some (1 Cor. 1:23) but for others, particularly those who found themselves at the bottom of first-century society (the slaves and the free or freed poor), the spirituality that was forged would no doubt have had a strong and emotive appeal.

What relevance can all this speculation about the past have for us now? I have no intention of being prescriptive. I am more than aware that the symbol of the cross in today's world means a very different thing to the picture I have just painted. A morbid obsession with Christ's suffering on the cross has led Christians through the ages to inflict atrocious wounds on others and this has in turn changed the Christian cross into a symbol of oppression for many, if not most, people alive today. One need only look at the anger over the ominous cross that, until recently, insensitively dominated Auschwitz. The Christian cross is certainly no symbol of liberation in the contemporary context. It is weighed down with so much "cultural baggage" that the Church of England decided to leave it out of their Easter 1995 advertising campaign, replacing it with a simple slogan—"SURPRISE said Jesus to his friends three days after they buried him" (*The Times,* March 10, 1995, p.1)—as though Christ was an irritating divine jack-in-the-box or adolescent practical joker. But an awareness of the contours of past spiritualities is important in some way for today. Surely, given our contemporary egalitarian impulses, it is particularly significant to try to give voice to the past spiritualities of the undocumented dead, rather than colluding in the crime of historical condescension. I feel this especially keenly as a biblical scholar as I see my own discipline becoming obsessed with interpreting the New Testament in terms of past aristocratic culture and no longer bothering to ask questions about the experiences and expectations of the majority, if not all, of Christianity's earliest adherents, people who shared in the brutal and frugal lives that typified life in the *Pax Romana*. Every modern spirituality has a past, whether it likes it or not. Nothing, except perhaps everything, is created *ex nihilo*.

REFERENCES

Baldwin, B. 1983. *The Philogelos or Laughter-Lover.* Amsterdam: J. C. Gieben.

Freud, S. 1960. *Jokes and Their Relation to the Unconscious,* translated by J. Strachey. London: Routledge and Kegan Paul.

Hengel, M. 1977. *Crucifixion.* London: SCM.

Hobsbawm, E., and G. Rudé. 1973. *Captain Swing.* Harmondsworth, U.K.: Penguin.

Hooker, Morna. 1994. *Not Ashamed of the Gospel: New Testament Interpretation of the Death of Christ.* Carlisle, U.K.: Paternoster Press.

MacMullen, R. 1971. "Social History in Astrology." *Ancient Society* 2: 105–16.

Pomeroy, A. J. 1991. "Status and Status-Concern in the Greco-Roman Dream Books." *Ancient Society* 22: 56–105.

Thompson, E. P. 1963. *The Making of the English Working Class.* London: Victor Gollancz.

Robinson, James M., ed. 1990. *The Nag Hammadi Library.* San Francisco: HarperSan Francisco.

Watling, E. F. 1964. *Plautus: The Rope and Other Plays.* Harmondsworth, U.K.: Penguin.

White, R. J. 1975. *Oneirocritica: The Interpretation of Dreams.* Park Ridge, N.J.: Noyes Press.

5

"Who Knows if the Spirit of Man Rises Upward?": The Bible and the Humanist

Stephen Bigger

> Man's fate is like that of the animals; the same fate awaits them
> both: As one dies, so dies the other. All have the same breath; man
> has no advantage over the animal. Everything is meaningless. All go
> to the same place; all come from dust, and to dust all return. Who
> knows if the spirit of man rises upward and if the spirit of the ani-
> mal goes down into the earth? (Eccles. 3:19–21)*

The Preacher (*Qohelet* in Hebrew, *Ecclesiastes* in Greek) took a sober
look at Hebrew teachings and drew radical conclusions about human
priorities. Wise men do not live longer or suffer less. Indeed, "the
more knowledge the more grief" (1:18). We all die irrespective. Who
knows whether humans and animals have different destinies? A rationalist approach to life is not a modern phenomenon only. As to the
meaning of life, "all is meaningless, a chasing after the wind." Questions about what it means to be human are not romanticized but faced
up to squarely (see Clines, in Bigger 1989, 277–80).

   Bible scholars are a mixed crew. The popular stereotype of them
as conservative believers has not been true for most of this century

---

*Bible references throughout are New International Version.

although it is true of a minority. Indeed, antagonism against "modernists" throughout this century by conservative Christians can still be acute; many of more liberal views have comfortably mixed faith with analysis and found the result enriching. Many Bible scholars are humanists, with an intellectual and not a faith interest. These hold no preconceived assumptions that the Bible is "true" and authoritative, any more than any other form of literature. I wrote in 1989 of how the humanist might approach the Hebrew Bible (popularly known by its Christian nomenclature "Old Testament") and find some meaningfulness in the writings (Bigger 1989: 47–50).* The Bible contains the outpourings of ancient literary minds, with pious and theistic assumptions no doubt, but with human emotions, with traumas to face, and with doubts to resolve. The Bible deals with the past but can impact on present attitudes and future choices.

Whose Bible is it? This seems a simple question but is complex. The Hebrew Bible reflects early Israel and Judaism, and has been preserved both by Jews and Christians. Today it is used devotionally and doctrinally by both faiths. This brings a number of sensitivities. Within these faiths (and especially within orthodox Judaism) a feeling of possession can lead to alienation from biblical criticism. Some hold the view that discussion of biblical texts can only be properly conducted by believers, since nonbelievers can have no empathy for the essential message. This begs the question of what the essential message is and whether traditionalist interpretation has a monopoly on it. The Bible has come to be viewed as a public document, available to novelists, film makers, critics, and rationalists although it has some legal protection in blasphemy laws. Islam has, in contrast, sought to shelter the Qur'an from such treatment. Muslims accept the Bible as part of their own prehistory (unfortunately, in their view, corrupted), giving them a special relationship with many biblical figures whom they regard as prophets. Bahais and Rastafarians also draw on biblical material, the latter using a liberation rhetoric.

Biblical criticism has moved far away from dogma. Consensus is

---

*Further discussion and references to literature can be found in this work.

hard to achieve in that conservative, liberal, and radical scholars take very different views on analytical methods and on much of the detail. Some critical theories became dogma in themselves—for example, the monumental documentary hypothesis of Pentateuchal sources: correctives latterly emerged keeping these questions still open (Whybray 1987). Everything in biblical studies is controversial and hotly contested. Scholars are cautious and skeptical and take nothing on trust. The same material is viewed from many different perspectives—historical, textual, literary, theological, mythological, philosophical, sociological, feminist, liberation, and so on. These books, which have been studied so often and so carefully, reveal little that can be viewed as certain. Studies provide a model for painstaking skeptical and radical scholarship: we have argued elsewhere the importance of learning to take nothing for granted but building each case on its merits (Bigger 1989, xiv). This is particularly true where biblical texts are used to support and define attitudes. Language reflects the worldview of the writers, which may not be found acceptable today. Brenner, for example, recently argued that the husband-wife metaphor is based on male pornographic fantasy in that the women involved are powerless and abused. This metaphor illustrates the ancient writers' assumptions, but is to be rejected as a model for contemporary theology (Brenner 1996; also the earlier work from a Jewish perspective of Drorah Setel, in Russell 1985). Recognizing how popular attitudes have drawn on biblical teaching and assumptions, scholars such as these wish through analysis to lay bare any concept which they deem unworthy.

The study of scriptures in religious studies from a phenomenological point of view stresses respect and seeks empathy with believers. Islamic studies in the West, for example, exist in three camps: that taught by the faith for the faith, that taught by non-Muslims in a manner that is acceptable to Muslims, and rationalist research without reference to Muslim views. In biblical studies the same split occurs: some studies by Christians or Jews for fellow believers may be conservative and confessional, academic studies for a wider audience may seek broad acceptance from faith members, and academic stud-

ies may have little concern for the views of faith members. Phenomenology, the middle of these, avoids critical analysis except for that in
which faith members themselves might engage, so that the analysis
stays within the worldview and theological assumptions of the faith.
The third path is that of unencumbered rationalism: the study is conducted for its own sake, trying to understand the theology in which it
is set but with no brief to accept it.

Studying the Bible is a skilled operation. Textual skills are only
accessible to those with knowledge of the text in the original languages,
and manuscript variation is wide. Readers can note variations in translations, which adopt a particular style and to a greater or lesser extent
paraphrase the meaning. Neither the original text nor any translation can
be regarded as accurate. Historical analysis addresses questions of
authorship, date, sources, and historical authenticity. Archaeology has
been used to support historical reconstruction (e.g., the Albright school
of which Bright is the best-known advocate), but more skeptical scholars see few solid links between archaeology and biblical narrative
(Whitlam, in Bigger 1989, 151–68; Coote and Whitlam 1987). There is
great interest currently in literary characteristics. New Testament redac-
tion critics have read texts as theological statements rather than as history for half a century; Old Testament scholars are analyzing literary
conventions, structure, plot, symbolism, and attitudes. Robert Alter's
influential study (1981) explored sacred history as prose fiction, type
scenes, conventions, narration and dialogue, repetition, characterization,
and the deliberate artistry of the biblical writers. For the literary critic,
the question of historicity is irrelevant: a story is a story, whatever the
content, and story conveys complex kinds of meaning. Inspiration has
also been drawn from anthropology, with important contributions from
Mary Douglas (1966, her pioneering work) and others (see Lang 1985).

GOD LANGUAGE

The literature is theocentric. The Bible depicts God as a personal con-
trolling figure, seeing, hearing, talking, and even walking (in the gar-

den of Eden in the cool of the day). Despite theological assumptions that God is incorporeal, biblical language is very anthropomorphic: Moore (1996) compares the language of God's gigantic body with muscle-building, claiming that we assume too quickly that anthropomorphic language is metaphorical. The writers meant literally what they said even when the language is androgynous. The use of an "intertext" is interesting here—unrelated literature (in this case muscle-building magazines) that might shed light on the literary features of the narrative. Religious and rationalist readers respond differently to God-language, the former linking their assumptions with their own belief in God, the latter finding this a stumbling block to appreciating the literature. Each has to become more detached to open up wider possibilities in interpretation. The concept of God can itself be the object of study.

Language depicting God has a range of functions: it serves as a mark of culture and identity and as a framework for believers to express personal meaning; as an expresser of rights and responsibilities culminating in "given" ethical and legal codes; as a personification of social and cultural values, validating their authority. There are nontheistic ways of expressing these points, and if religion becomes dogmatic rather than expressive, these links may become obscured as specific religious belief becomes the accepted norm. That is to say it can become more important to believe the same doctrine, to sing from the same hymn sheet, than to be concerned with what those doctrines actually express. Religion then becomes a tribal emblem, a badge of "us" as opposed to "them." Such attitudes do not encourage personal, moral, and intellectual growth if answers are *given* and *to be accepted* rather than *explored* and *discovered*. Spirituality implies inner exploration of personal meaning and values that might be inhibited and restricted by dogmatic constraints and might be equally viable outside of theocentric models. Analysis of how God-language expresses human concerns may require the suspension of personal belief or disbelief.

INSPIRATION AND REVELATION

In what sense is the Bible viewed as sacred? Jews and Christians have regarded the various "testaments" as the "word of God" and credited them with ultimate authority for belief and ethics. The lists of authoritative books (or canons) varies, with Jews focusing on the books of the Hebrew Bible (and especially the Torah, the first five books) and Christians being divided according to their affiliation as Protestant, Catholic (who add the Apocrypha), or Orthodox (who add both apocryphal and pseudepigraphal books). The concepts of revelation and inspiration themselves vary. We speak generally of an "inspired" book as something charismatic and particularly meaningful; we might view the source of the inspiration, the "muse," as having divine origin. Doctrines of "verbal inspiration" are a feature of fundamentalist Christian teaching: that the words themselves were written by God through the medium of the human writers. In this the doctrine of inspiration comes close to that of revelation, in which words are "revealed" or brought into the open from somewhere hidden. For many Orthodox Jews, the Torah was "revealed" by God to Moses on Mount Sinai and remains the doctrinal base-point. Fundamentalists resist and reject biblical criticism.

For Jews, the Hebrew Bible is self-standing but has led to the development of later writings such as the Mishnah and Talmud; for Christians it prefaces a renewed theology, the "old covenant or testament" leading to the "new." The complementary relationship between the two literatures can be misunderstood, particularly the concepts of *prophecy* and *fulfillment*. The prophets gave a theological commentary on their time and reflected on the consequences of current policies; this included the hope of an ideal messianic age when wrongs would be righted. Such prophecies, in a vivid apocalyptic format, are found in the New Testament, such as in Mark 13 and parallels, and in Revelation. More generally, however, the New Testament is concerned with fulfillment: that Jesus fulfilled messianic prophecies and was therefore the Messiah. This claim is explicit: an intriguing question is how much Jesus deliberately *intended* to fulfill prophecy. It could be argued that he took suffering servant passages as his own inspiration (Isa. 53; cf. Mark 8:31, 9:12), that he was identified with Son of Man sayings by the church (Matthew replaces "son of Man" with "I"), and he rejected claims that the Messiah was "son of David" (Mark 12:35–40). New Testament writers certainly found "prophetic" fulfillments that Jesus clearly never intended.

The Bible is called "Holy." Sacralizing a text has many functions. It provides:

- an absolute basis for purposes of doctrine and law;

- a focus for reflection by creating an expectation of acceptance;

- a social unifier, an emblem.

The concept of absolute in belief and ethics leads to dogmatism. Since personal attitudes may vary from dogmatic to skeptical, dogmatic doctrines can function as repressive strategies to keep people in line. Skepticism might be viewed as a threat to doctrinal integrity. The varying positions and controversies have given rise to theology as a field of study. In terms of law, revelation on Mount Sinai led to various legal codes, generally identified as the Decalogue, Holiness Code, Priestly Code, and Deuteronomic Code. These in combination provided the basis for historic Jewish law. Christianity has tended to exclusivism, regarding itself as the only right doctrine: the need to convince others of this has led to centuries of missionary activity which has been as much political as religious, an arm of colonialism and imperialism. It is arguable how effective this has been. Any "benefits" are outweighed by the overarching philosophy of dependence that the colonial powers and missionaries attempted to foster, having their vision of the "natives" as infants needing guidance and discipline. Such discipline could have fatal consequences, such as the massacre by the British army of Punjabis at Amritsar in 1919.

As a focus for reflection, revelation can provide a reasonably cohesive framework which provides a common language and mythology that allows people to communicate and develop their ideas. Such a focus, if narrow, can lead to tribalistic loyalties if others outside this framework are viewed as heterodox. We are today becoming more used to multiple frameworks, to viewing conceptual frameworks as perspectives useful for analysis without confining thought. In the Bible this is particularly important: not only are there Jewish, Christian, Islamic, and humanistic perspectives (see Bigger 1989, 31–50), but analyses can be feminist or political (such as in some liberation theologies). One person's focus can be another's anathema.

As a social unifier, a religion, including doctrine, worship, and scriptures, can become an emblem that keeps society together with tradition greatly revered and a deep sense of belonging fostered. The social power of this is clear in Orange parades in Northern Ireland. Religion can play a greater social function in groups exiled from their homeland, helping to keep the community focused. It can have a similar effect in circumstances where people feel a sense of threat such as in war.

The question for the nonmember or nonbeliever is whether sacralized texts can be meaningful *to outsiders*. If God-language mythologizes human values, values such as justice, social responsibilities, human rights, and so on might interest a wider audience. The sacralized documents reveal much about their circumstances, authors, and readership, and can help to develop ideas, ethics, and ethos. We can therefore interrogate the texts as historians, literary critics, sociologists, phenomenologists, or philosophers. Findings are unlikely to conform with traditional doctrine and our conclusions may well be critical.

CREATION

The heat of the debate between Christians and science over the past century has focused on the concept of creation. Literalists from all traditions affirm the story of creation as God's initiative, in history (although perhaps no longer in Archbishop Ussher's date of 4004 B.C.E.), leading to the famous conflicts of the nineteenth century.

Many Jews and Christians find no difficulty in accepting both the concepts of evolution and creation at the same time, viewing creation as the overarching purpose of the world and evolution as the mechanism for change. Science investigates the first few seconds of creation as the big bang unfolds. An explanation more than two millennia old cannot be viewed as being "obviously" true in a scientific sense.

Much is made of the different creation stories of Genesis, attributed to the two writers labeled "J" and "P," the "Yahwist" and "Priestly writer." Indeed, the story of Adam and Eve in the garden seems to create a fresh start, humankind having been created in the previous chapter (Gen. 1:26–27). Genesis 1 seems to function as part of an editorial layer to Genesis as composed into its current form. This was the beginning and the following generations are carefully counted. Even if there were originally different sources, the final text intended the creation story to be read as one story and we need to consider the implications of this: one view supported by later Jewish commentators was that the first humans were androgynous (created male and female [Gen. 1.27]; Moore 1996) and later separated.

Historically, the science-religion debate has focused on whether Genesis is "right" (and if so in what sense): scholarship tends to be less interested in this question and to focus on the construction of the narrative, literary qualities, the author-audience interaction, and the theological ideas expressed. In other words, the passage is analyzed as any other myth would be. All concerned with viewing the narrative as a whole look for ways in which the separate sections complement each other. Those with a conservative religious agenda (both Jews and Christians) are least happy with a source hypothesis. Those who wish to view the myth as history may see in Genesis 2 the creation of *homo sapiens sapiens* out of the wider group of hominids. Historical reconstructions are not, however, to the taste of all scholars; many concentrate on the story as literature and explore the ideas it conveys.

Genesis 1 reveals a world set in water, the water above separated from the water beneath by a solid dome called "sky." Dry land was set in the water below and furnished with vegetation and life, culminating in humanity. Sea monsters were created. In the neighboring Babylonian myth, the world was created from Tiamat, a primeval chaos ocean monster: in Genesis, Tiamat is demythologized and rationalized, becoming the "deep" (Hebrew: *tehom*). Our author, perhaps exiled in Babylon, has rationalized the creation, rejecting but transforming the Babylonian myth. This "rational" account is set within the assumptions of the day.

Humanity was made (male and female) in the image and likeness of God, just as children later were in the image and likeness of their parents (Gen. 5:1–3). The metaphor is one of relatedness, stressing God as "father": much has been made as to whether this means that hominids look like God (or perceive God to look like themselves) or whether the relatedness is moral, ethical, or spiritual. All are speculative. Genesis provides the genealogy of the world: God begat Adam and Eve, who begat the rest. In diet, the first human couple were effectively vegans: this theme continues into the second creation story where after the fall animals are killed to provide clothing. Perversely, the offering of vegetables made by Adam's son Cain was not accepted, while his brother Abel's sacrifice of a lamb was. A consequence of sin was that a life had to be offered to atone, the linchpin of the sacrificial system. Sin destroyed ideal relationships; but for sin, sentient life would live together harmoniously, cooperating and not competing for food. Isaiah returned to this ideal: in the messianic paradise, wild beasts would lie down with vulnerable creatures and children (Isa. 11). However, this rule of righteousness would only be achieved by killing the wicked (Isa. 11:4).

The Eden story exhibits a different style. The man (Adam means "man" or "mankind") is created out of clay and will on death return to dust (the hope of immortality having been lost). So that he is not alone, a woman is created from his side to be a help or companion (the word does not particularly have undertones of inferiority). She has a name, Eve, when the man (*ha'adam*) does not. She is thus the central figure in the story. She encounters the serpent who discusses with her the acquisition of wisdom. She eats the fruit forbidden by God and gives it to the man (who saw that it was good to eat). This poses a threat to God ("they have become like one of us") and the human couple are excluded from the tree conferring immortality. To Eve's desire for wisdom is ascribed pain in childbirth, labor for food, sexual desire, pair bonding, and gender roles. The human couple are no longer dependent with everything provided by God, but are self-reliant and responsible for their own welfare and survival. Feminist analysis has rightly seen this to be a key chapter (Trible 1978).

The desire to understand our origins is really a desire to understand our present. Humanity has evolved into reflective creatures with free will and with choices to make. This brings responsibility and hardship, with problems to solve if we are to survive. This was not in the divine plan, which anticipated humans being obedient vegan dependents, as infants in their playground whose every need was met. This coming of age posed threats for God/the gods (Yahweh speaks in the plural, "like one of *us*") who copes with the problem in a number of ways: by expelling humans from paradise, by shortening their lives (particularly when divine beings took human wives [Gen. 6:1–4]), by drowning them, and by confusing their language. This views God's will as *to control* humankind; any disaster may be interpreted as God asserting this control as punishment. Humans should always therefore be anxious, to be in fear of God: "the fear of the Lord is the root of all wisdom." Underneath the mythology lurks a high regard for human potentiality (which even God sees as a threat), together with a frustration that this is inhibited by natural forces, age, and infirmity. People push for autonomy, but freedoms are restricted. If everybody does what is right in their own eyes, chaos ensues and moral order breaks down: religion therefore provides a necessary restraint that prevents human nature from preferring Sodom and Gomorrah to decent God-fearing lives. Religion is a social necessity, constructed to maintain order in society.

THE LAND

The creation story places humankind as guardians with responsibility for looking after the world, taking for food only that which is ordained as resources are clearly demarcated between humankind and animals. This is a radical agenda, at odds with the view of humans having supreme rights to exploit resources for themselves. The human-centered view of the world exists everywhere today—that the purpose of the world is to provide for human survival and comfort. The death of animals, in this view, is of no account so long as humans benefit: indeed, animals exist solely to be exploited by humans. Genesis 1 gives everything its place and its dignity. Even the great sea monsters, demonized as Tiamat the chaos monster, are viewed as humble creatures.

The death of animals to fulfill human needs comes as a result of sin in the "garden": the fall gives the first couple an understanding of human weakness and fallibility, including embarrassment for nakedness. They cover their nakedness with leaves; Yahweh kills an animal to provide skins. Sin brings a change of values and animal slaughter is legitimated. Abel's sacrifice of a lamb validates the sacrificial system whose line of development culminates in Jesus being the once-and-for-all sacrifice, as seen in the epistle to the Hebrews. If animal sacrifice is not legitimated, then neither is this interpretation of Jesus' death.

The land figures strongly in another doctrine that has ramifications in world politics today. Israel was "the promised land" through a promise made to Abraham and to the Israelites escaping from Egypt. The land is divided, parceled out between the tribes, won and lost, but always viewed as a national *possession*. Rivals receive short shrift even where their claim is older; the curse against such as the Amalekites survives still in synagogue worship. This vision of the land, "Judah and Samaria," has complicated policy in Israel to this day as it geographically constitutes the West Bank, annexed after the 1967 war.

The Old Testament books nevertheless develop an interesting universalism. The book of Ruth depicts the archetypal king David as related to the Moabites. For 2 Isaiah, being the chosen people meant a responsibility to be "a light to the nations." Jonah, a carefully crafted novelette of nationalistic bigotry, ends with severe divine (hence legitimate?) reproof for not recognizing repentance in the Ninevites (Bigger 1989, 198–200; Crouch 1994, 112 puts in Jonah's mouth a "readerly" response to God: "Are you, in this circumstance, really that gullible?"). Jesus praised through story the attitude of helping even Samaritans and showed (Mark 7) that his message also applied to a Syrian woman and was not restricted to Jews. Early Christianity fought this battle hard and won, ensuring that Christianity would not remain a Jewish sect. In his famous phrase declaring that all are equal in the sight of God, Paul (Gal. 3:28) lays a foundation for movements advocating and defending equality and liberty, rejecting prejudice on the grounds of race ("Jew and Gentile"), class ("slave or free"), and sex ("male and female").

GOD IN HISTORY

The biblical authors shared the belief that God intervened in history; yet this is not a simple account of divine succor. Sometimes divine initiative is given to human choices (for example, Abraham was sent from Ur of the Chaldees to Canaan). The exodus was a time when all manner of disasters had happened to the Hebrew people: divine intervention was attributed to natural phenomena (plagues, the drying of the Sea of Reeds, and the consequent destruction of the Egyptian army), the pillar of fire/smoke, and the theophany at the (volcanic?) Mount Sinai. Moses therefore is given the attributes of a divinely appointed messenger. Other legends of the early period point to charismatic leaders ("judges") sent by God to sort out difficulties. Later, lack of political success is interpreted as God's withdrawal as a form of punishment (Jeremiah thus refused to countenance false optimism at the events leading up to the exile in Babylon). There are two major types of reference to divine intervention:

- as a story/legend motif for distinct narrative purposes. For example, the prophet Elijah won his competition with the prophets of Baal when God sent fire from heaven to consume his offering.

- as an editorial device interpreting the significance of the events being described. Natural events can thus be defined as deliberate divine acts. The Torah constantly uses the phrase "And the Lord said to Moses"; the Deuteronomic History offers a punishment/reward system even through this does not always fit the evidence (the narrator is rather quiet about the "evil" king Manasseh who had a long and successful reign).

The New Testament offers a different picture. Divine intervention comes through another messenger, Jesus, who claims less for himself than the church theologians claimed for him. He is the "son of David" who said, "How can the Messiah be David's son?" quoting Psalm 110 as proof-text (Mark 12:35–37). His so-called virgin birth was theologically constructed from Septuagintal readings of Isaiah 6–7 ("A young woman shall conceive and bear a son who shall be called Emmanuel, meaning God with us"). The concept does not appear unambiguously in any text apart from Matthew's Gospel. Resurrection stories do not appear in the earliest gospel, Mark, which ends with Jesus' death, leading to early theories of a lost ending and alternative suggestions appearing. These are generally included as an addendum to current New Testament translations. The theological machine went into action producing many stories, biblical and apocryphal, of resurrection appearances and even ascension into heaven. The intervention is not to provide a charismatic military leader who might drive out the Romans, but a figure who through suffering and service sets an example of unselfish behavior and social action. The picture of Jesus is against the trend of Hellenistic superhero/divine king modeled on Alexander the Great who had no high regard for humble service.

The historicity of biblical stories is greatly controversial. There are some who regard every event described as authentically historical, but this is not a scholarly view. Conservative scholars tend to argue that more events are historically based, but do not press the view that every single detail must be. That the sun stood still for Gideon or the shadow of the sundial went backward remains implausible from any point of view. Scholars differ on scale: many might doubt the historical authenticity of the primeval history and in particular the "myths"; fewer see Abraham as fictitious, fewer still Moses, and fewer still David. All of these characters and events are unsubstantiated by parallel historical texts: some of the later kings like Jehu get a mention in monuments from Mesopotamian powers. There are two separate questions: How much of the detail is historically plausible? Are narratives historical accounts or fiction? The emphasis of biblical studies has focused for most of this century on the former. John Bright's *History of Israel* (first edition 1960) is painstaking in its analysis of historical plausibility, regarding the Old Testament as primary historical data for the events described and comparing this with archaeological data. Martin Noth's *History of Israel* (first edition 1958) asked some more radical questions about legend, drawing on a German tradition going back to and beyond Herman Gunkel. There has been much research over the past two decades, particularly on the Hebrew Bible, focusing on questions of literary style, character, and plot, which draws its impetus from the study of fiction. It is not controversial to analyze biblical texts as narratives created by storytellers—in other words, as fictions.

The picture is different in New Testament scholarship, but not dramatically so. It has been a feature of a strong branch of scholarship to regard the Gospels as theological documents first, leading to the view that the concern for theological meaning put historical questions into the background. The famous slogan highlighting this was Martin Dibelius's "in the beginning was the kerygma [viz., early churches message]." The search for authenticity among sayings and narratives has not produced a consensus. Most scholars would not, however, doubt the existence of Jesus or the broad outline of Christian expansion.

An interesting question is, if biblical narratives are not in general historically true, in what sense if at all can they be regarded as true? A myth might seem naive until it creates the response, for example, "But it's true—jealousy kills." If we are seeking truth, we need first to look at what the story is about in human terms, what it is trying to say. Good biblical examples relate to the Hebrew prophets (Bigger 1989,

185–226). Stories of the prophets resemble theological novelettes whose historical basis is uncertain and probably unimportant, yet they reflect on loyalty, trust, social justice, race, gender, poverty, and other such human issues. Elijah, meaning "Yahweh is God," declares this message amid persecution and is rewarded with fire from heaven to consume his sacrifice as an answer to his prayer; he is taken to God without dying (1 Kings 18; 2 Kings 2). The story of good faith, loyalty, and the need to choose one's side uses universal themes that remain powerful and adapt to new ways of thinking and circumstances, even when the details of the story seem far-fetched. He is a role model of faithfulness. Jonah, swallowed by a "big fish," learns his lesson that even foreigners can repent: his racism stands condemned.

Prophets are traditionally pictured as foretellers and details of fulfillments have been keenly sought, whether messianic (which shaped many Gospel narratives) or eschatological (relating to the end of the age). Prophets were certainly insightful and understood things that escaped others. What "seers" saw were the social, political, and psychological possibilities in everyday actions and choices, the likely consequences of choices. They saw clearly the realities of life, veiled to others with traditionalist and doctrinaire assumptions and "blind faith." Samuel saw and reluctantly shaped political realities with the establishment of the monarchy: his theological and ethical analysis (1 Sam. 8) may come from a later age but may have its roots in Samuel's ideals. Jeremiah foresaw desolation coming out of the complacent attitudes of his contemporaries: he saw the possibilities in accepting the political status quo, indeed, that this was the only way forward (Jer. 27–29). Prophets were often political voices in the wilderness, pointing at self-seeking, power blindness, and greed. They also had ideals: Isaiah's vision of global peace, when weapons become ploughshares (Isa. 2:4), is still inspiring; Jeremiah's new covenant written on the heart (Jer. 31:31–34) inspired Jesus and in translation gives us the name "new testament," although Christianity has not always matched the high levels of personal and ethical renewal implied; Ezekiel's vision of the dry bones becoming refleshed, transformed by new life, symbolized the political restoration and revivification of the nation.

Amos's vision, replacing feasts and sacrifices, was to "let justice roll down like a river, righteousness like a never-ending stream" (Amos 5:24). For Jesus, the ideal was one of service to others, bringing to fruition 2 Isaiah's vision of the suffering servant.

Not only have religions seen themselves as a guide for life, giving legal and ethical direction, but we are encouraged to view our legal and values system as based on Judaeo-Christian principles. In part, there is truth in this: the principles of justice, fairness, and uprightness should underpin a legal system and social mores. The same principles can be seen in all ethical religious systems and in humanism also. In part, however, the claim is phony. Modern law is a mishmash of historical campaigns whose major inspiration is not high ideals but compromise between high-status privileged power groups. Laws are imposed and usually are accepted. A legal system and process needs a degree of validation and legitimation: Hammurabi of Babylon used his own chief deity Shamash (Pritchard 1969, 163–65); the Hebrew Bible claims a divine origin for law through the phrase "And Yahweh said to Moses," describing the corpus as being presented to Moses by God himself on the mountain.

The claim for a divine source for law was its ultimate validator. This is not available to most modern legislators, but its equivalent is the claim for law to be based on religious principles and ideals. The claim that the law is based on fundamental biblical (and hence Christian) principles is made without justification or analysis. It is a vital part of lawmakers' rhetoric. Whatever the real purpose and origin of the law, its promulgation will use ethical ideals and religious principles to stress that it is a good law. The opposition will use the same principles to claim it is not. Political pressure is brought to bear in the United Kingdom to ensure that the school curriculum, and in particular religious education, stresses the validity of the state and of nationhood and informs children of how the Christian tradition underpins the state and culture. Both are political rhetoric and neither bears close analysis: they are, however, perceived as important in underpinning the political status quo, seeking to ensure that those in government benefit to some degree from people's national pride and religious fervor.

Law in the Hebrew Bible is a mixture of religious injunction and social constraint. Laws generally are given a religious motive, such as ensuring that the community is pure in God's eyes. In the Ten Commandments (Exod. 20; Deut. 5), four injunctions stipulated proper attitudes and behavior toward God: one underpins family tradition to ensure continuity of values, three constrain personal behavior in favor of communal harmony, one stresses justice in law by outlawing perjury, and one prohibits wanting ("coveting") other people's possessions. Another decalogue (Exod. 34) gives largely religious injunctions, described in the narrative as being the laws that Moses brought down the second time after breaking the tablets after his first visit. These contain little that is ethical.

Other laws cover many aspects of social life and were in later centuries expanded in Judaism to form the very comprehensive Mishnah and Talmud. Marriage, sexual relations, and divorce are covered, influenced by laws ensuring purity in the community. Religious laws cover all aspects of ritual and religious life, defining and constraining offerings, sacrifices, festivals, worship, and priesthood. Incitement to apostasy is a particularly serious offense (Deut. 13). Laws also control the worst effects of slavery (without abolishing it) and protect aliens, but also define arrangements for holy war. In other words, all the assumptions of society are present in the laws. Some are farsighted; others are introspective, seeking to minimize foreign influence. It was not law in itself that gives modern ethics its foundation—laws were self-serving and small-minded, ensuring social proprieties and religious exclusivism—rather, it was the ethical principles of the prophetic tradition, a world of ideals and values rather than of law. This vision is found in the Torah, which need not be interpreted legalistically. Such principles should be carved on the heart, not on tablets of stone. Jesus supported this by demolishing legalism: the old law said, Do not murder; but I say if you are angry with your brother you will incur judgment (Matt. 5:21–22). Principles such as justice, good faith, love, and forgiveness are stronger bases for personal action. However, principles do not control people: legalism has maintained a strong hold over religious and personal life over the centuries.

UNDERSTANDING LIFE AND DEATH

Although the Bible gives a general impression that faithfulness is rewarded, the writers reflect on life and death in interesting ways. Life was perilous both in terms of health and war. Children were regarded as important, a gift of God, barrenness a cause of unhappiness. Wisdom literature gives interesting perspectives on old problems. Ecclesiastes talks of the mystery of birth: "As you do not know how the spirit comes to the bones in the womb of a woman with child, so you do not know the work of God who makes everything" (Eccles. 11:5). The scientific processes of life are mysterious; this both symbolizes the whole mystery of creation and attempts to validate the mystery of God's power with evidence that there are mysteries beyond our understanding. Job responded to a variety of disasters and losses by challenging everyone, including Yahweh himself, to the unfairness of the situation. The reader knows the real reason—Satan is testing him—but Job has to be satisfied with the notion that humans *cannot* understand. The debate between Christianity and science has revolved around this issue, hampered by literalistic views of creation. Where religion accepts that it complements science (albeit avoiding the scientism of taking science too literalistically), it is better able to express elements of this mystery.

Qohelet, "The Preacher," draws some radical conclusions. We live our lives in the certain knowledge that we will die: this is one of the few sure human realities against which our lives are planned and shaped. There is little point leading a life of acquisition—even where it is wisdom being acquired. Far better to focus on *enjoyment*—enjoying every action and moment and relationship for what it is, a potential for quality. People should find enjoyment in their activities and work (Eccles. 2:24). Much in life is absurd, vanity, meaningless, but it is our lot and we should have pleasure in it.

REFERENCES

Alter, R. 1981. *The Art of Biblical Narrative.* London: George Allen and Unwin.

Bigger, S. F., ed. 1989. *Creating the Old Testament: the Emergence of the Hebrew Bible.* Oxford: Basil Blackwell.

Brenner, A. 1996. "Pornoprophetics Revisited: Some Additional Reflections," in *Journal for the Study of the Old Testament* 70: 63–86.

Bright, J. 1960. *The History of Israel.* London: SCM Press.

Coote, R. B., and K. W. Whitlam. 1987. *The Emergence of Early Israel in Historical Perspective.* Sheffield: Almond Press.

Douglas, M. 1966. *Purity and Danger: An Analysis of Concepts of Pollution and Taboo.* London: Routledge and Kegan Paul.

Lang, B., ed. 1985. *Anthropological Approaches to the Old Testament.* London: SPCK; Philadelphia: Fortress Press.

Moore, S. D. 1996. "Gigantic God: Yahweh's Body." *Journal for the Study of the Old Testament* 70: 87–115.

Noth, M. 1958. *The History of Israel.* London: A and C Black.

Pritchard, J. B. 1969. *Ancient Near Eastern Texts Relating to the Old Testament,* 3d ed. Princeton, N.J.: Princeton University Press.

Russell, L. M. 1985. *Feminist Interpretation of the Bible.* Oxford: Basil Blackwell.

Trible, P. 1978. *God and the Rhetoric of Sexuality.* Philadelphia: Fortress Press.

Whybray, R. N. 1987. *The Making of the Pentateuch.* Sheffield: JSOT Press.

Part Three

Perspectives from the New Age and World Religions

6

The CEBs and the New Age

James Penney

This essay addresses the theme of modern spiritualities by analyzing two significant contemporary movements: the New Age movement and the base ecclesial communities (CEBs) of Latin America—those grass-roots communities which have developed in the last three decades in the Roman Catholic church on that continent. I seek to examine the thesis that New Age embodies a challenge and critique of the Christian tradition in ways which are significantly similar to that of the challenge of the base ecclesial communities in Latin America. I argue that key aspects of the base communities and the theology that underpins these can be discerned in the reflection and practice of New Age communities.

The first section of the essay outlines the genesis and development of base communities in Latin America. These communities have been at the center of the development of liberation theology and the reevaluation of Christian thought and practice in Latin America. In particular, I highlight the social, political, and cultural location of these communities, of the theology which inspires them, and of the spirituality

Reprinted from the *Journal for the Critical Study of Religion, Ethics, and Society* 1, no. 1 (Winter/Spring 1996). By permission of the publisher.

which is at the heart of their reflection and practice. Consideration is given to the language and concepts used by members of base communities to reflect on their faith in a context of poverty, oppression, and marginalization.

The second section analyzes the spirituality of the New Age movement. The growth of New Age in Western Europe and North America has been well documented; its significance for contemporary society assessed in many (often contradictory) forms. My concern is to look more closely at the spirituality of the New Age movement, in particular examining the social, political, and cultural expression of this spirituality, and of its critique of the Christian tradition.

In the final part, I propose that there are important commonalities between New Age spirituality and the spirituality of the base communities. Furthermore, attempts to "indigenize" liberation theology in Western Europe and North America are misdirected, since New Age thought and practice—its spirituality in particular—is an indigenous "theology" which, despite differences not least of which is context, might be described as a liberating theology for late twentieth-century Britain and North America.

A SPIRITUALITY OF THE
BASE ECCLESIAL COMMUNITIES

How might one define a "spirituality of the base communities" in the first place?

In his visit to Peru in 1985, Pope John Paul II visited a shantytown on the outskirts of Lima called Villa El Salvador for an open-air mass with over a million participants. He was greeted by two representatives of the Christian communities,* Victor and Irene Chero. In their speech to the pope (John Paul II 1985, 86f) they said:

---

*In Brazil and other Latin and Central American countries, such communities are often described as base ecclesial communities (CEBs). In Peru, although the characteristics of the communities are virtually identical, they are known as "Christian communities."

Holy Father: we are hungry, we suffer misery, we have no work, we are sick. Their hearts broken by the pain suffered by our wives as they give birth wasted by TB, our babies die, our children grow up weak and with no future. But in spite of all this, we believe in the God of Life, a life of grace and nature.

The pope, in reply, departed from his prepared text, dialoguing with the people. He took up the words of the Chero family (1985, 92):

I have listened with great attention, and I see that here there is a hunger for God. This hunger is true riches, riches of the poor that must not be lost. . . . So to you who are hungry, I wish you a deepening of this hunger for God.

I see also that here there is a hunger for bread. Our Lord taught us to pray every day "give us today our daily bread." So we must do everything in our power to give this daily bread to those hungry for bread; that is, it is a necessity for the good of Peruvian society. THE SHANTYTOWNS CANNOT GO WITHOUT THEIR DAILY BREAD.

So, for you who live in Villa El Salvador, for all the shantytowns of Peru, I wish that the hunger for God remains; and that the hunger for bread be sated. I hope that you may remain hungry for God, but not for your daily bread.

This identification of "two hungers" has become a symbol of the life lived by those in the shantytowns of Latin America, a life characterized by faith and oppression, belief in God, and dire poverty. On his return to Italy, the pope elaborated further on these two hungers, adding a further dimension, the hunger for justice. I would argue that these two hungers—the hunger for God and the hunger for bread—provide us with a useful point of departure for considering the "spirituality of the base communities."

The Hunger for Bread

Within the context of the base communities, the battle for their daily bread is at the heart of their existence. The theological questions which are posed most urgently in this context of immiseration, squalor, and poverty are:

- how to talk of the God of life in a world of death;
- how to tell people who are systematically deprived of their dignity that they are children of God; and
- how to tell people who are treated as no-persons that God loves you.

In terms of their spirituality, this hunger for bread becomes the language of prophecy, the language of denunciation of the unjust structures of society, of all that impoverishes and dehumanizes. It is a shared hunger of those existing on the margins of life, subject to "premature and unjust death," the "crucified peoples" of the urban periphery and rural poverty.

Yet, as indicated above, this hunger is experienced through the eyes of faith. Statistics are always open to misuse and abuse, but it is generally claimed that approximately 80 percent of the Latin American people would consider themselves to be "Christian." Most of these will be Roman Catholics, although the growth of the Protestant churches has rightly been highlighted as a significant dimension of Latin American church life. Nevertheless, in the earliest writings of the theology of liberation, Gustavo Gutiérrez spoke of the people of Latin America as "both Christian and oppressed": their experience of oppression is interpreted through the perspective of faith, but, equally important, the perspective of faith is marked by their experience of oppression.

In this way, the language of the base communities becomes a theological language (I prefer to avoid the word "spiritual" here for obvious reasons), which judges their situation in the light of the God of life in whom they believe.

Although many in the base communities have "multiple membership" through activity in popular movements, in political parties, or in trade unions, the coming together in the context of the base community is an ecclesial gathering. The articulation of their hunger for bread is expressed in relation to the God of the poor, the God who is on the side of the insignificant, the vulnerable, the marginalized. The prophetic call for an end to this "hunger for bread" is one of the key signs of the Latin American church, a call endorsed by the pope in his speech in Villa El Salvador.

The "spirituality of the base ecclesial communities" is thus informed by this prophetic perspective. It is a spirituality of action as well as a spirituality of contemplation and reflection.

The Hunger for God

Central to the experience of the base communities, then, is a hunger for God as a complementary dimension to the hunger for bread. Gustavo Gutiérrez and others have attempted to present this movement between the two dimensions of the lives of the communities in terms of *contemplativos en acción,* as the Jesuits would have it. This is explored further by Gutiérrez in his commentary on Job, in which he identifies two ways of speaking about God: the language of prophecy and the language of contemplation.

It is this language of contemplation that one can see most clearly in the ways in which the people of the base communities express their hunger for God. Again, though it is important to remember that this hunger is also experienced through the material hunger for bread, the two are in relationship to each other, not separated.

The base community gatherings are therefore not simply social protest or political hustings. They are profoundly ecclesial meetings, in which the Bible is the central focus of attention. It is, however, the book of the Bible seen in the context of the book of life: their own lived faith experience. In these meetings, the people try to understand their *realidad* in the light of the witness of the people of God of ancient times: the people of Israel and the people of the early Christian communities. They experience a deep sense of continuity as being the same people of God—the people of the same God who liberated the Hebrews from Egypt, the same God who became incarnate in a stable and was crucified.

And the Church?

These two hungers—for bread and for God—pose particularly hard challenges to a church which has for many centuries been allied to the powerful rather than the powerless, to the oppressors rather than the oppressed, to the significant rather than the insignificant, to the rich rather than the poor.

The base ecclesial communities have thus received a considerable amount of attention from the official sources of the institutional church. The institutional church has at times been fearful that the base communities represent a "parallel church," challenging the authority of the institution. Yet such fears are misplaced. The people of the base communities have no wish to leave the church: the communities are profoundly concerned with their "ecclesiality." The problem they face is that the reality of being church in, say, rural Brazil or in the shantytowns of São Paulo is that the traditional structures of the church are unable to cope with the demands of the people.

Moreover, as the people of the shantytowns and the poor of the countryside have engaged in the process of forging a new democracy and in the struggle to gain a life of dignity, they have become aware of their role as agents of their own history. The models of decision making and distribution of power that emerge from the base communities, the popular movements, and some trade unions present a challenge to the traditional decision-making processes both in the church and in society at large. It is no accident, for example, that the majority of "leaders" of the base communities—and increasingly of the popular movements—are women.

In a number of ways, therefore, the CEBs are, in a real sense, a challenge to the traditional way of being church. Leonardo Boff has stated that the process is one of "ecclesiogenesis"—the poor are reinventing the church. As Marcello de Azevedo writes in his essay "Basic Ecclesial Communities" (1993, 637):

> the basic ecclesial communities are a new way to *live* the church, to *be* church, and to *act* as church. This is not a new way, insofar as the

basic ecclesial communities draw together and revitalize elements of the most authentic tradition of the church since its beginning. But it is a new way of being church if one compares it to the previously existing model of church, which has prevailed for the nearly five centuries of ecclesial presence in Latin America.

A SPIRITUALITY OF THE NEW AGE

Attempts at Definitions

The first section of this essay outlined some of the significant characteristics of the spirituality of the base communities of Latin America. In identifying these characteristics, the task is helped by a general consensus among commentators as to what constitutes the base communities, at least in broad terms. That consensus does not exist in the case of the New Age movement. In fact, one of the greater challenges of investigating the New Age is to attempt a definition of precisely what one means by this term.

For this reason, it is important to set out at least the range of material with which I am concerned. I have chosen to highlight those aspects of the New Age movement which can most appropriately be considered to have implications for Christianity. I know that there are many other aspects of New Age thought and practice which present exciting opportunities for the researcher, but the concerns of this essay are more limited.

Moreover, there are a number of commentators whose analysis of New Age is set firmly within the context of a Christian understanding of this phenomenon. In his unpublished paper "New Age Spiritualities: How Are We to Talk of God?" the Dominican Richard Woods highlights the extent to which he believes it possible to trace the Christian antecedents of New Age (undated, 3):

For [New Age] is, I am convinced, a thoroughly Christian phenomenon. As such it has its origins in late Jewish apocalyptic and certain early Christian expectations. And just as it is the product of a Christian view of the world, its history, and its destiny in relation to God, how *we* speak about God in the light of today's New Age spiritualities, as well as how we look on the New Age "movement" itself will reflect our own Christian vision and attitudes.

It may well be that this is the view of an insider, one within the Christian tradition who seeks to explore the extent to which this tradition is both challenged by, and can learn from what is broadly defined as the New Age movement. Woods is not alone, however, in his thesis that New Age has its origins in a Christian context. Michael Northcott also regards New Age as to some extent a *problem* for institutional Christianity. In his monograph *The New Age and Pastoral Theology: Towards the Resurgence of the Sacred,* Northcott asks a number of critical questions about the development of New Age: whether it should be regarded as a "countercultural" phenomenon within Christianity, or whether it is more appropriately defined as a new religious movement. These two quite different perspectives on New Age clearly have implications for the kind of analysis which would follow. Northcott (1992, 2) challenges the reader to reflect on these perspectives:

> But what social phenomenon or movement is referred to by the phrase "New Age"? Are "New Agers" another part of that burgeoning social phenomenon which sociologists know collectively as New Religious Movements? Or is New Age the reemergence of traditional magic which has always been part of the proto-history of the world from the worship of Isis and Gnosticism, to Rosicrucianism and theosophy? Is New Age a new postmodern, but rather temporary, form of religion or quasi-religion, or does it represent a significant cultural shift in advanced industrial societies, a new phase after the secular rationalist bureaucratic period of Western post-Christian societies?

This identification of alternative representations of New Age has a number of commonalities with the various representations of the base communities in Latin America. There, too, researchers have explored the significance of the CEBs as social phenomena, as an expression of "popular religion" (Northcott's "reemergence of traditional magic which has always been part of the proto-history of the world"), as a post-modern reaction to the peculiarly Latin American form of Roman Catholicism, and as an expression (in the case of the CEBs) of a social, political, religious, and cultural shift in society and in particular against Western society.

Significant Characteristics of New Age

If there is disagreement about defining "New Age," there are, never-theless, a number of characteristics which most commentators would consider significant. Among these, the extent to which New Age con-stitutes a cultural shift in society is particularly important. Whether one focuses on those practices of New Agers that are regarded as "main-stream" (whatever that might mean), or whether one concentrates on practices such as channeling, crystals, and the occult, the New Age movement has given expression—and publicity—to a range of ideas and practices which challenge contemporary hegemonic structures. It is in this challenge that some commentators have sought to identify New Age with postmodernism. So argues Michael York in a recent paper "New Age in Britain: An Overview" in which he also underlines the connection between New Age and the transformation in the under-standing in Western industrialized societies of the relationship between human activity and the environment. He insists (1994, 14):

> The one common theme behind all New Age identity is the metaphor of an imminent quantum shift in collective conscious-ness—whether this shift is a product of divine providence or the development of humanity's full potential.

The two alternatives offered by York—divine providence or the development of humanity's full potential—are reminiscent of the point made above about the different perspectives through which one can evaluate New Age. Moreover, in what follows, York emphasizes that the development of humanity is linked, within New Age thought, as much to rethinking what has happened in the past as to contemplating what should be done in the future.

> The impending change is as much the consequence of what is perceived in ecological terms to be an impending environmental and global catastrophe—the result of overproduction, exhaustion of resources, population explosion, and, especially, industrial pollution.

In this impending catastrophe, a further key characteristic of New Age thought can be identified: the emphasis on "millennial" ideas. Within the writings of New Age, this millenarianism can be represented in a number of sometimes contradictory ways. For some, in a marked pessimism, the impending catastrophe will mark the devastation of the human race. For others, in contrast, the realization of the impending disaster offers the opportunity for humanity to save itself from itself. This more optimistic vision of the future coexists uneasily with its pessimistic counterpart. Together they represent perhaps different strands within the New Age movement as a whole, but they do symbolize the level of concern within the movement for social change —change on a global scale.

The concern for global change, for reimagining the relationship between humans and our environment, is strongly connected with a further dynamic within the New Age movement which pushes for a reconceptualization of interpersonal relationships. Such a reconceptualization has been most clearly articulated in the context of male-female relationships and has been influential in the ways in which Christians have sought to engage with New Age ideas and critiques of "orthodox" Christianity. Through its emphasis on the equality of women as well as through the prominence of women in leadership roles in New Age thinking, the New Age movement has combined ecological concern with feminist concerns. As Northcott argues (1992, 4):

> A major focus in New Age literature and movements is related to gender and feminism. Many women involved in New Age have explic-

itly rejected orthodox religion, particularly Christianity, because of its patriarchal nature. Their experience of gender oppression or suppression within mainstream Christianity generates a desire for alternative religious paths, and also for a new integration of religion and sexuality in contradistinction to the sexual repression of orthodox Christianity.

Indeed, the New Age call to renew our understanding of the nature of human relations, our understanding of our place in the world, and to bring the sacred into the whole of life has contributed a great deal to the ways in which Christian denominations have reviewed their ideas and practice.

However, despite their concern for environmental transformation and for equality for women, the tendency within New Age thought and practice is individualistic rather than social. New Age emphasizes the need for personal renewal, for finding oneself, and for inner cleansing. In this context, social concerns take second place. As a movement, New Age has acquired considerable social significance— one has only to look at the explosion of publications available in high-street bookshops—yet at the same time, it has a strongly introspective foundation. In the words of Northcott (1992, 7):

in New Age thought justice takes second place to the rediscovery of the sacred, for without an awareness of the sacred core at the heart of life and of the cosmos, action for transformative change will ultimately be ineffective.

EVALUATION—A NEW AGE OF LIBERATION?

The previous two sections have summarized some of the principal characteristics of New Age spirituality and of the spirituality of the base communities of Latin America. In the light of these analyses, is it possible to draw any conclusions about commonalities or differences between these two forms of contemporary spirituality?

I believe that some proposals can be made. In the first place, both the New Age and the base communities are concerned to bring a sense of the sacred into the whole of life. This emphasis sits uneasily with the priorities of late-twentieth-century capitalism. The base communities and the New Age movement share a sense of the importance of spirituality; for them, spirituality is not an afterthought or a prelude, but is the way people live their lives. In practical terms, the common emphasis on spirituality is instantiated in a critique of Western lifestyles, of the dominant Western economic priorities, and of "orthodox" Western Christianity. So, both the New Age movement and the base communities appear, in varying degrees, marginalized in relation to the established church and to established society.

At the same time, this marginalization complicates attempts to identify the location of these movements in relation to the contemporary debate about modernity and postmodernity. In both cases, commentators have argued strongly for seeing such ideas and practices as key indicators of postmodern society, while others have defended with equal insistence the view that both movements are the last gasp of modernity (see York 1994, 11). The ambiguity of these movements is reinforced by the transitory character of their membership. It is difficult to find precise numbers of those involved in the New Age and statistics about the number of base communities are notoriously unreliable. In each case, however, one can state with some confidence that members of the respective communities have "multiple memberships"—for example, members of the base communities are often members also of trade unions, popular movements, or political parties. In each case, also, membership can be short-term—a few weeks or months—as well as longer term.

These similarities notwithstanding, there are significant differences between New Age ideas, practices, and community compared to those of the base communities. The most significant of these is their different account of social change. For the base communities, change occurs through a commitment to social justice. The personal dimension is important, but takes second place to the emphasis on *community*. In contrast, those committed to the New Age tend to reverse these priorities. New Age, too, has a strong "otherwordly" apocalyptic dimension, focused particularly on environmental catastrophe. For those who participate in the base communities, finding their daily bread is the most essential issue. They reinforce the need to work for a more just society and community in this world—a commitment which is the responsibility of all people.

In conclusion, I think that there are useful insights to be gained from a study of the New Age alongside that of the base communities. In particular, a number of common features can be discerned, albeit set within very different contexts and different priorities. Perhaps the best way to highlight these points, and thus the argument of this essay, is to end by providing practical examples of the spirituality of the base communities and of the New Age.

The following two popular hymns of the base communities of Brazil help to suggest the character of their spirituality:

Our Father of the Martyrs

Our Father, of the poor, of the marginalized
Our Father, of the martyrs, of the tortured
Your name is sanctified in those who die defending life
Your name is glorified when justice is our measure
Your kingdom is freedom, is fraternity, peace and communion
Cursed be all violence that destroys life through repression
We want to do your will, you are the true Liberating God
We will not follow the doctrines corrupted by the oppressor
We ask of you the bread of life, the bread of security, the bread of
the multitude
The bread that brings humanity, that builds people instead of
canons
Forgive us when through fear we remain silent in the face of death
Forgive and destroy those kingdoms in which corruption is the
strongest law
Protect us from cruelty, from the death squads, from the powerful
Our Father, revolutionary, protector of the poor, God of the
oppressed

Utopia

When the new day of peace dawns again
When the rays of hope shine anew,
Then I will sing
When the people stream into the streets,
When the tables are piled high with food,
Then I will sing
When the doors of the cells are flung wide
And the landowners join on our side
Then will I sing
When the debt no more threatens us all
No more banks pushing us to the wall
Free at last?

We will be so happy to hear the song
Ring out once more
In your neighbor's eyes the signs of a friend
A kingdom for all

When mass destruction is ended
Torturers, jailers befriended,
Oh can I dream
Of efforts to end our oppression
Faith and honesty our sole possession
Oh I can dream
When the clear voice of truth is heard
Corrupters, deceivers deterred
Then will it be
A new era of justice for all
No more hatred, torture, or tears,
Free at last!

A sense of the spirituality of the New Age can be discerned from
the following poem written by the participants of an international conference of New Age management consultants and trainers (Roberts
1994):

A Deconstructive Prose Declamation (!),
or Joining Forces—A Conference Alphabet

A is for avatar, aura, arrogant, act, for ally, angels . . . and assertion

B is for beast, beauty, brute, babe, BMW, for birth . . . and beginning

C is for colleagues and crystals, for calm, cause, for circles and cycles, collision, collapse . . . and crisis!

D is for death, dance, delight, depths, decision, and the definition (we're always resisting)

E is for empathy, enlightenment (where?), exegesis (what's that?), eggs and eggheads, ENERGY!!! . . . and emergence

F is for failure, fear, for freak-out . . . and FUTURE

G is for goddess, gold, goodness . . . for gripes? . . . for your god (if you have one)

H is for hellhole (the company office?) . . . hugging and healing

I's for injustice, impotence . . . and incarnation

J is for justice, "judicious" (the bishop?), jealous and jinxed

K is for Kill! . . . kerygma (the company message!) and karma

L is for lucidity, lust . . . linkup and love

M is for money and mind, for magic, meditation . . . and the company mission

N is for neutral (participant observer)

O is for organ, organism, orgy, orgasm . . . the ORGANIZATION!

P is for peace pipe, for persons, persuasion . . . and PERFORMANCE!

Q is for quaking and quelling disturbance

R is for reach-out, rebellion, rights, revolution/resolution

S is for sincerity, sex, spirit, and SPIRITUALITY!

T is for terror and tyrants . . . and telling the story

U is for ultimate . . . and for use and utility

V is for voice, victim, values . . . and victor!

W is for WOMEN, for whales, work, weeping, and WARRIORS . . . and wimps

X is for exact, excitement . . . and X the Unknown

Y is for youth, for yodels, and Yuppies

Z is for zany, for zoo . . . and it's over to you!

REFERENCES

Azevedo, M. 1993. "Basic Ecclesial Communities." In *Mysterium Liberationis,* edited by Ellacuría and Sobrino.
Boff, L. 1986. *Ecclesiogenesis.* Collins.
———. 1992. *Good News to the Poor.* Burns and Oates.
Campbell, E., and J. Brennan. 1990. *The Aquarian Guide to the New Age.* Aquarian Press.
Ellacuría, I., and J. Sobrino, eds. 1993. *Mysterium Liberationis.* Orbis.
Gutiérrez, G. 1984. *We Drink from Our Own Wells.* SCM.
———. 1987. *On Job.* SCM.
———. 1990. *The Truth Shall Set You Free.* SCM.
———. 1991. *The God of Life.* SCM.
John Paul II. 1985. *Discursos y Homilías de Juan Pablo II al Perú.* Loyola.
Melton, J. G. 1993. "Whither the New Age?" *The Way* 33, no. 3 (July).
Northcott, M. 1992. *The New Age and Pastoral Theology: Towards the Resurgence of the Sacred.* Contact.
———. 1993. "New Age Rites: The Recovery of Ritual." *The Way* 33, no. 3 (July).
Peters, T. 1991. *The Cosmic Self.* HarperCollins.
Roberts, R. 1994. "Power and Empowerment." *Religion Today* 9, no. 3 (Summer).
Seddon, P. 1990. *The New Age: An Assessment.* Grove.
Woods, R. "New Age Spiritualities: How Are We to Talk of God?" (unpublished).
———. 1993. "What Is New Age Spirituality?" *The Way* 33, no. 3 (July).
York, M. 1994. "New Age in Britain." *Religion Today* 9, no. 3 (Summer).

7

Reasons of the Heart

Peggy Morgan

MODERNITY, RELIGION, AND SPIRITUALITY

The modernity with which I am concerned, and even more so the postmodernity which has followed in its wake, is characterized by rapid change, individual choice, and ever-increasing complexity (Berger 1979). Our knowledge of religious traditions, their history, and their contemporary practice is richer than it has ever been before, but with this increase in knowledge has come the challenge to discern amid the seeming contradictions of their teachings and the compromises of their histories where meaning and integrity are to be found. Current affairs as well as history illustrate the compromises that have been and are being perpetuated by religious groups whose activities do not match the ideals of the faith within which they stand. This knowledge has produced a natural, and to my mind wholly good, skepticism about religion and religions which stands side by side with the contemporary interest in dialogue with its affirmations of com-

Reprinted from the *Journal for the Critical Study of Religion, Ethics, and Society* 1, no. 1 (Winter/Spring 1996). By permission of the publisher.

monalities and harmony. This is one of the contexts in which one can locate the currently fashionable use of the term *spirituality,* a use which is exemplified in the orientation of this essay as well as in many other books and articles. From the perspective of someone teaching religious studies, an interest in talking about spirituality often indicates a discomfort with the word *religion* as well as with some of the facts about religious life. Religion is more often than not associated with institutions, with rituals, with the articulation of doctrines, and with what is external to individual experience. Using the word *spirituality* seems to allow us to emphasize what is deep, personal, inner, experiential, and authentic in people's lives. The term *spirituality* can also be linked to explorations of art and music, to the aesthetic sense, which widens access to the topic for those who locate themselves in secularity or are for other reasons unsympathetic to the discourses of religious traditions (Cupitt 1980; Robinson 1987).

A religious studies analysis of this emphasis on spirituality might also see it as the contemporary quest for the essence of religious life, for the heart of religions, for what really matters. It brings to normative status just one of the dimensions of religion in a way parallel to the traditional Western Christian equation of religion with belief or doctrine. This is in tension with academic attempts in recent years to implement the most rounded and multidimensional models of religion that are available and which seem to do justice to all the phenomena of religious life (Smart 1983; Smart 1989; Sharpe 1983). Against that background, talking predominantly of spirituality might be seen to tap only the experiential dimension of the total complex and organic reality that constitutes religions or other worldviews. This might be wholly in keeping with modernity's orientation on the individual, a fruit of the age or century of experience that followed the Enlightenment, but it can also be challenged by those working for an increase in our sense of community and interconnectedness, though their emphasis, too, can be seen to have grown from the individual's experience of alienation from both humankind and nature. If secularism continues to increase and modernity and postmodernity are in the end inimical to religion as we have traditionally known it, then it may be that concentration on the more sympathetic discourse of spirituality is the way forward.

I recently asked some final-year students what the word *spirituality* meant to them. They claimed that it is possible to think about or practice a spirituality without having anything to do with religions. Its characteristics, they suggested, are an emphasis on relationships with things (chairs), the earth (creation or, to use the more secular term, the universe), other people, and God (if you choose to speak of God). They emphasized moral values (the biblical emphasis on "by their fruits ye shall know them," which is also important to James 1902; Hick 1989) and the importance of starting with the individual, from what is personal and then working outward. They said that for a religion to be a true religion there had to be spirituality as well, but for a spirituality to be true spirituality, people don't have to have a religion.

BEING MODERN AND BEING BUDDHIST

The examples of modern spiritualities that I want to focus on are Buddhist. This seems to me to be appropriate in an enterprise such as this for a variety of reasons. If, as I have suggested, the word *spirituality* is being used in a context where people are uneasy with the word *religion,* then Buddhism, as a worldview that has not infrequently been disassociated from the word *religion,* provides a natural example. Secondly, although the term *spirituality* is not a natural one for Buddhists because it seems to imply an inner essence called a spirit or soul, the existence of which is challenged and denied in Buddhism, Buddhist teaching has always emphasized the test of experience in religious life. This is well summarized in the Pali words *ehi passika,* which Rahula translates as 'come and see' and which can be linked with the emphasis in the Buddha's teaching to the Kalamas where he says "when you know for yourselves," rather than depending on the authorities of texts or teachers (Rahula 1959, 2–3). Thirdly, the transplantation of Buddhism to the West is one of the most interesting phenomena of the modern and postmodern landscape of spiritualities. On

Saturday, March 5, 1995, during the weekend when I was writing this paper, its importance was noted in an editorial in the *Independent* entitled "Suburbia Turns to Buddha," and there was a report in the Sunday program on March 6 in which one young person stated that when she first encountered Buddhism, "Buddhism did not feel like a religion, it felt like a way of thinking." Unlike the transplantation of many of the other major religious traditions to the West, it is not linked as much to the continuing religious practice of migrant peoples as with the attraction of Westerners to a newly imported tradition, or rather traditions, since there are many kinds of Buddhism. It more often calls itself a practice or a way than either a religion or spirituality. Fourthly, I am able to describe some of the work of one very interesting Western Tibetan Mahayana group which I shall place alongside a set of articles by a Western Theravada Buddhist who is writing a book on *The Training of the Heart,* a theme parallel to that being used as the central focus by the Mahayana group.

The Mahayana group has pioneered a distance learning course, the Indestructible Heart Essence. The Theravadin's ideas have been aired to date in four articles on the Luminous Mind, which have appeared in the journal of the Buddhist Society, *The Middle Way,* during 1988. Initial concentration on one small group and then on an individual's work is an acknowledgment of the fact that spirituality in modernity and postmodernity is most characteristically to be seen in what is small-scale and individual and what might appear, at least at first glance, to be fragmented. The group that I shall concentrate on is very aware that what it is doing is transplanting a "foreign" tradition of teaching and practice to the Western world. To do that they are using language which gives very broad access to these spiritual teachings; they are tapping everyday concepts such as sensitivity and openness and using similes and metaphors and, in particular, they are using the language of the heart. This use of easily accessible language is, I think, essential for any modern spirituality to be successful because most people in the contemporary West have little natural access to and recall of the technical language world of Christianity, let alone of a religion that has but recently arrived. But I shall also show how the language that the group has chosen for teaching is very firmly rooted in the classical textual tradition of Buddhism and is therefore important for more than one of the major Buddhist schools. The individual whose work I shall quote is working on the Sutta material in the Pali Canon to unpack teachings there about the heart which she considers have been distorted by translators and other exponents. I shall also suggest that the use of the language of the heart, a terminology that is rich in its connotations in the English language, is entirely in keeping with the Buddhist claim that its teachings and practices are "the truth about the way things are." This is a common translation of the term *Dharma,* and emphasizes a harmony and continuity with ideas to be found elsewhere. Terms which might also have a wide cultural use or even a more technical meaning in other religious traditions can, on this basis, be used quite happily by Buddhists. I shall indicate that this is the case with the language of the heart.

The enterprise that is underway links with the use of metaphors in other cultures. Ruth Padel writes on the classical Greek metaphors of the body in her book *In and Out of the Mind* where she asks what we invoke when we say "heart" or "mind" and how our metaphors are formed. She asserts that,

> If we say someone had a "seizure" or a "heart attack," or was "on fire with love," we connect ourselves to an extraordinary complex train of physiological and religious imagery and scientific theory winding back through eighteenth-century medicine, Renaissance scholarship, mediaeval theology, Hellenistic philosophy, to Greek poetry and medicine. And, since tragic poetry is, after Homer, the largest and most public early body of poetry about feeling, very often to tragedy itself. But the origins of such phrases do not explain our use of them. On the contrary, the way we say them and what we mean by them has been changed by the very centuries that handed them on. . . .
>
> When tragic poets write about what is inside people, they are also writing about what is outside, as their culture represents it. Outside explains inside, and vice versa. The two-way connection between them is fluid, ambiguous, mercurial, transformative, and divine. (Padel 1992, 10–11)

We can now add to the complex heritage described by Padel the Buddhist use of the word *heart* for which there are various synonyms in Pali, for example, *vinnana, manas,* and *citta.* The English terms *consciousness* and *mind* are used as translations of *vinnana* and *manas,* but *citta* may be translated as either 'heart' or 'mind'. Padel reminds us (1992, 12) that Socrates, too, refers to a controversy about what part of the body we think with! Placing the Buddhist heritage in the pot with the classical, Christian, and general cultural meanings exemplifies the ongoing blending or interconnectedness of a variety of cultures which is what I read into the use of the words *global* or *world* whether for our theology, ethics, or spirituality. This is just a further and more acknowledged stage in a process that has always happened as cultures have met, blended, changed, enriched, and transformed each other (Smith 1981, 4–29; Eck 1994, 211–12).

Various modern spiritualities, as well as the example I shall use, see themselves as particular and rooted as well as being historically accumulative in the complex way described by Padel. They also see themselves as responding to the distinctive needs of the age. This seems to me to be true of both the New Age phenomenon (whatever we mean by that), as well as of Celtic and creation spiritualities. Certainly some of the emphases in the work of Matthew Fox overlap with some of those in the Buddhist group I am describing and can be seen as a response to the needs of modernity. Examples are the insistence that we need to harmonize body and mind; that confidence and a positive self-image need to be developed over against the common Western ethos of guilt, which is commonly linked with the doctrine of original sin; and that we also need to work in and from communities to counter the worst aspects of modern individualism.

The group whose work I am describing is also firmly planted in modernity in its use of distance and open learning. This, as well as the central images implemented in their teaching, is a good example of modern Buddhist skillful means in the service of Buddhist spirituality (Pye 1978; Hick 1994). My examples are taken from the pilot six-month run of the project, which involved meeting for four-day schools as well as forming local link groups where that was wanted.

TEACHING THE INDESTRUCTIBLE HEART ESSENCE

The distance learning materials on which I want to focus are produced by the Longchen Foundation whose headquarters are in Oxford. The Foundation is under the spiritual direction of Michael Hookham (now known as Rigdzin Shikpo after his completion of a three-year retreat at his home in Marston) who is assisted by Shenpen Hookham. Michael Hookham is the subject of one of the vignettes in Denise Cush's study, *Buddhists in Britain Today* (Cush 1990, 64–75). He was born in 1935, is a mathematician and mathematical physicist by profession, and has studied all forms of Buddhism. He practised Theravada meditation for many years before meeting the Tibetan Kagyupa Lama Chogyam Trungpa Rinpoche, who had left Tibet in 1959 after the Chinese invasion. In 1965 Michael Hookham took Trungpa Rinpoche as his teacher and practiced within the Tibetan tradition. In 1975 Trungpa Rinpoche asked him to begin teaching and he has established both the Nitartha School and Longchen Foundation, which teach the Kagyu-Nyingma (Dzogchen) tradition of Tibetan Buddhism. The organization of the teaching is done from his home. The tradition he teaches, Nyingma (Dzogchen), is the one which Trungpa Rinpoche thought most appropriate to use in Britain as it stresses lay life and has married lamas rather than monks as teachers. Shenpen Hookham is also a Kagyu and Nyingma trained teacher, having spent nine years as a Kagyu nun in India before returning to Oxford to complete a doctorate of philosophy thesis on the Tathagatagarbha Doctrine. This has been published as *The Buddha Within* (1991). Her principal teacher is Khenpo Tsultrim Gyatso Rinpoche. It is perhaps important to say at this point that behind the work of this group is the authority and confidence of several Tibetan lamas who consider their teaching to be wholly and authentically Buddhist and whose names and visits give support to the Foundation.

The Longchen Foundation describes itself as a circle of Buddhist teachers and students. Community is important. Its introductory pamphlet sets out its orientation:

> Underlying the external universe and our own minds is a single intrinsic ground of being. Because we do not realize the nature of this primordial ground, we are estranged from the basis of our own experience. The purpose of the Dzogchen tradition is to arouse this realization in oneself and others.

Even in these few lines some important themes emerge. The phrase *ground of being* is reminiscent of Tillich and the stream of post-Enlightenment theology which comes through him. There is also the emphasis on experience which links particularly with Schleiermacher and the so-called century of experience. It is indicated that what is needed is something that is in our own hands and within our potential, realizing what is there all the time. We have autonomy. This links with modernity's roots in Kant. And finally there is the assertion of an underlying reality that is both within and beyond us. Withinness is identified with the mind, but as has been pointed out earlier, in Pali the word *citta* can be translated as either 'mind' or 'heart'. This is explored later in the materials. Elsewhere the Longchen Foundation uses heart as the most powerful and immediately accessible image for its students, as for instance in the title of its three-year distance learning course, Indestructible Heart Essence (Longchen Foundation 1993–1994), and of a series of published talks by Michael Hookham called *On Freeing the Heart* (1985). There is also an emphasis on the natural resonance of words and cultural symbols and that the only prerequisites needed to follow the material are "a sincere and honest heart and an open, inquisitive mind" (Longchen Foundation 1993, 3). The four booklets for the first year of the three-year course, Shenpen Hookham's published thesis, and two volumes of talks by Rigdzin Shikpo are the material I have used for this study.

The very style of the Indestructible Heart Essence course is modern. Distance learning gives the student an autonomy in harmony with the orientation of the teaching. The overview booklet emphasizes this: "Students can determine for themselves where and when they study. . . . Students can also choose the pace at which they progress through the materials. . . . The emphasis of this teaching is on finding something within yourself" (Longchen Foundation 1993, 1–2). It is stated that the course aims to give the Western student the necessary equipment to understand the traditional Buddhist teachings such as the Four Noble Truths in the spirit in which they were meant (Longchen Foundation 1993, 5) and to awaken in them a heart response giving them increased confidence, a greater sense of connectedness, value, meaning, purpose, and direction in life (Longchen Foundation 1993, 8). Some of the important terms and ideas used that are easily accessible to students are *confidence, clarity, sensitivity,* and *openness.* Concepts with unfamiliar names and more obvious Buddhist content such as *mandala* and *meditation* are included, but are in the minority and are explained very carefully in nontechnical terms. Meditation is discussed with daily life practice and the section on mandala is placed after the other more accessible terms have been explored. The mandala principle is unpacked in this way.

> Many of the problems of the modern world arise because we lack a living experience of connection, belonging, and wholeness. Everything appears meaningless, fragmented, and too complex for us to handle. . . . Mandala principle is about the pattern and structure of everything that happens. Everything that happens has a center or a central point from which it emanates and a periphery or boundary where it peters out or where there is an interface with the next thing or the world outside it. All our experience is a mandala. . . . We begin with the idea of the heart essence in the center of our being which is expressed through body, speech, and mind. This is a mandala. . . . Is it intuition or an aesthetic sense of some kind that tells us that it is good to be centered, grounded, balanced, and integrated? Whatever it is, as time goes by, and we become more deeply involved in the awareness practice, this sense of being centered and having a center, almost like a physical center to our being, becomes increasingly important and subtle. (Longchen Foundation 1993, 16)

This passage expresses the teachers' self-consciousness in addressing some of the issues of modernity. The fragmentedness of life and our experience of it, which is one of the key characteristics of modernity, is a problem which can be solved in centeredness. We might point out that both our existence in and our creative use of modernity can be seen both in positive terms and as a part of the problem. This is where the modern person wants to tap continuity with a tradition that seeks to resolve problems which have always been a part of the human condition but which modernity has brought to a particular flowering. After the overview document, part one of the course gives the student a great deal of opportunity to explore the natural associations of heart language. The possible range of responses touches on the heart as part of our physicality, as an image for what is central ("Birmingham is in the heart of England"), a source of life and energy ("the heart of the countryside"), making a connection with people ("our hearts go out to them"), and then makes heart-image connections with the other general terms that have been introduced as important in the overview booklet. Confidence is linked to the phrase *to take heart* or *to be stouthearted*; openness with the phrases *openhearted* and *bighearted*; clarity with *to know in your heart* and *straight from the heart*; sensitivity with *tenderhearted,* to take some of the examples that are used. The language is seen to be a very powerful use of metaphor with resonances that

> go far beyond the English language and are to be found worldwide and throughout history. For these associations emanate from an underlying understanding of ourselves that we have as human beings, regardless of race, religion, or culture. They are found, for example, in the words *chitta* (Sanskrit, Pali) and *sem* (Tibetan) which are so important in Buddhism. (Longchen Foundation, vol. 1 [1994]: 24–25)

When the use of heart language is affirmed and linked with practice, students are encouraged to use phrases such as *downhearted* or *heavyhearted* rather than the word *depressed,* which, it is suggested, "might have the positive effect of reminding yourself and others that we have hearts and that they need uplifting and strengthening" (Longchen Foundation, vol. 1 [1994]: 33).

The material continues with an exploration of the differences and tensions between heart and mind imagery in our everyday language and an introduction to the Buddhist idea that mind and heart are one, together and integrated, which is illustrated in the use of the same term *citta* in Pali. The image of the mind here is particularly linked to the qualities of spaciousness and clarity, not to mental or intellectual activity as conventionally understood. Part two of the course focuses on confidence and heart wish. It addresses the need for confidence as it is linked with modernity.

> For many people these days a lack of basic confidence is a fundamental problem. People feel lost, unsure of their place in the world, unsure of what life is about, fearful of other people, ashamed and embarrassed at their own confusion, and swept this way and that by what other people might think of them.
>
> Traditional society protects its members from a great deal of this insecurity and fear by giving each individual a strong sense of their natural place in society. This gives them a certain basic confidence and self-respect. However, society never could and never will be able to protect us entirely from insecurity and fear. The confidence that arises from knowing one's place in society is useful up to a point, but since it is conditional and limited, ultimately it fails us.
>
> Over recent years, as a society we have become increasingly aware of the problem of a lack of this kind of basic confidence and all the psychological, social, and spiritual problems that follow from that. In response all sorts of therapies, counseling, assertiveness training, support groups, and "anonymous" groups of various kinds have sprung up. . . . A lack of this basic kind of confidence is symptomatic of a society undergoing rapid social change. In traditional societies one's sense of place, of dignity, of lineage, of worth, of role, of duty, and so on are socially defined. The price exacted for this security is that individuals lose their freedom to think and choose for themselves. Everything is prescribed for them from cradle to grave.
>
> More freedom means we need more basic confidence. In our society we greatly value our freedom to choose how we are to live our lives and with whom. We think ourselves lucky that we can choose our own friends, interests, role, religion, or career. So even though we are forced to live without the support of a traditional society, we value the freedom that the breakdown of tradition has

given us. Therefore we need much more of the kind of basic confidence that is also the basis for the path of awakening. We need this both to make up for the lack of basic confidence that a traditional society might have given us and also to cope with the insecurity that greater freedom brings us.

For the Buddhist practitioner this is an ideal situation. Even the lack of certainty itself can be a tremendous inspiration to deepen our awareness practice. So first of all we need to develop plenty of confidence. As mentioned above, this comes partly from being clear about our place, where we are, where we belong, and partly from being able to trust ourselves and our own power of discernment. (Longchen Foundation, part 2 [1994]: 5)

Following this passage there are various exercises to make the reader aware of areas where they are confident and developing confidence further. This is related to body posture, to different kinds of confidence, and to what confidence is not. Most importantly confidence is described as a person's capacity for openness, clarity, and sensitivity, which are seen as the intrinsic nature of their being—the Indestructible Heart Essence—all the way through the course.

The second section of part two is focused on the Heart Wish. This may well be seen as a parallel concept to the Christian phrase, "longing for God."

We have defined the "heart wish" in this course to include intention, volition, the heart's deepest wish, hoping, longing, aspiring, deciding, resolving, promising, giving our word, making a vow, and accomplishing it. (Longchen Foundation, part 2 [1994]: 49)

Even in the depths of depression there is a deep longing to be free of that feeling of dark, cold numbness. This is the heart wish. (Ibid., 64).

Part three of the introductory course explores the qualities of openness and clarity and the linking of those with mindfulness practice.

What do we really want? If in our hearts we want to be aware, awake, sane, open, sensitive, and alive; if in our hearts we long for deeper meaning, deeper peace, a deeper sense of well-being, then we should align ourselves with that wish. We should keep making that choice at every opportunity. The practice of mindfulness is aligning ourselves with our heart's wish. (Hookham 1992, 96)

THE HEART OF A TRADITION

What I have been describing is in many ways an innovative and modern spirituality in its mode of delivery and in its content. It is not, however, cut off from or a deviation from traditional Buddhist roots. I mentioned at the beginning the traditions within which the Hookhams, the Nitartha School, and the Longchen Foundation are located. Shenpen Hookham's thesis, published as *The Buddha Within* (1991), links the kind of language that is being used in their course with the classical texts and debates within Tibetan Buddhism. Her study focuses on the different interpretations of the Tathagatagarbha doctrine in Buddhism. She says that "wherever it occurs, the term *Tathagatagarbha* refers to the power within beings that enables them to become Buddha" (Hookham 1991, 94). It is imaged as the Clear Light of both the mind and the heart (Hookham 1991, xv). It involves the optimistic teaching that all beings have the Buddha Nature or Nature of Reality, but in an obscured, tainted state.

> The Sanskrit term *garbha* has many meanings, one of which is 'womb' or 'matrix'. . . . It can also mean 'embryo' or 'treasure in a mine'. In other words, it can mean something valuable or potentially valuable as well as its container or bearer. . . . In Tibetan . . . *garbha* is translated *snyng po* meaning 'heart essence', that is the valuable part of something, like butter from milk, sesame oil from seeds, and gold from gold ore. . . . *Tathagatagarbha* is translated in such a way that it means 'having the essence of Buddha'. (Hookham 1991, 100)

In his study of Mahayana Buddhism Paul Williams says that in the Gelugpa School of Tibetan Buddhism, which is not the one within which the Longchen Foundation is placed, there is the idea that the Buddha taught the Tathagatagarbha doctrine for the purpose of introducing non-Buddhists to Buddhism (Williams 1989, 106). It is in itself, in that case, a ready-made piece of skillful means. Williams also affirms that the teaching emphasizes that the true nature of things, what is elsewhere also called pure consciousness in the Cittamatra School, is discovered in meditation rather than in reasoned discourse. It is essentially a practice, which is the emphasis of the coursebooks. There is also a community dimension to the development of a person's spirituality. A great deal of effort was made during the days of group attendance for the pilot run of the Indestructible Heart Essence course to prepare an excellent meal for the students which was served with considerable attention to the pleasantness of being together and which people ate with a real sense of relaxed enjoyment.

TRAINING THE HEART IN THE PALI CANON

The other example that I want to link with my discussion of the materials from the Longchen course are taken from the articles on the Luminous Mind by John Frederick. These were published in *The Middle Way,* the journal of the Buddhist Society, during 1988. They are written under a pseudonym by a Western Theravada Buddhist who reads Pali. She begins with an examination of the meaning of *citta*:

> *Citta* (mind or heart) is a key word in the Pali suttas. One of the difficulties in trying to understand the teachings of the early Buddhist scriptures, however, is that we have no precise concept of the *citta,* and no word for it in Western languages. (245)

The *citta,* says the author, is what is trained, developed, and freed, but it is not a static entity. It is

> a series of events; notions, feelings, wishes, decisions, indecisions, judgments, and so forth. This is its natural mode in the phenomenal world. It is capable of other modes, and fleeting suspicions of these

are wonderful and intermittently draw it in that direction. . . . As it is presented in the Canon, the *citta* is a continuum which survives the death of the body. (250)

At the end of the training of the heart the *citta* is luminous and its main characteristic in the texts of the Pali Canon is a loving-kindness that is "far-reaching, widespread, immeasurable" (148). This is a very optimistic and positive teaching that is often missed in presentations of Buddhism which give a strong initial analysis of its teachings about the suffering or unsatisfactory nature of life. The Theravada author has explored the teaching on the luminous mind, or heart of loving kindness, in reaction not only to the neglect in her view in Theravada teaching of the texts which she discusses in her articles, but also as a balance to what she sees as an overemphasis on *anatta,* not-self, in Buddhist teaching. She sees this emphasis in particular as a characteristic of Sri Lankan Theravada, which for historical reasons and in terms of textual interpretation has been so influential in Britain. She links her emphasis to Westerners' problems with *anatta* in a footnote of an as yet unpublished chapter.

> Given our particular type of education, Westerners are inclined to address the problem of not-self intellectually and I am reminded of an observation of the Thai meditation master—the Venerable Acarya Maha Boowa—who said that Westerners are always talking about *anatta* (not-self) when they could not possibly understand it, and that it would probably be better for them if they were to regard the *citta* as belonging to them, for the time being, so that they could make a wholehearted attempt to train it. Having trained the *citta,* they would then realize that it was not 'self'. (John Frederick, *The Training of the Heart,* footnote 8)

THE HEART OF THE MATTER

There is in the material from the Longchen Foundation in particular a language of profound ordinariness which reminds me of the emphases in the work of Ludwig Feuerbach (1841). The metaphor of the heart is deliberately linked with our everyday use of language. There is also in the vocabulary of the heart a language of inwardness and intention which is used across religious traditions. Noting these resonances between religions, as well as having an awareness of deep differences in their discourse, is an important aspect of our modern spiritualities. In the "Long Search" series broadcast by the BBC in the 1970s, Ronald Eyre talks in Cairo to a Muslim sufi about his Islamic faith and practice and Islam's insistence on the use of the Arabic language. The sufi comments that Islam goes first of all "through the heart" and does not need a language ("Long Search: There Is No God But God"). This emphasis can be linked with Qur'anic teaching that

> We know what his soul whispers within him
> and We are nearer to him than the jugular vein

which the sufi also mentions, and that the person who goes to Paradise is

> whosoever fears the all-merciful in the unseen,
> and comes with a penitent heart.
>   (Qur'an sura 50 vv. 15 and 32)

Readers who assume that Islam is a religion of exteriority and transcendence are often surprised at what the sufi indicates to Ronald Eyre with a chuckle, that God is even "inside you." In the Christian religious tradition the language of the heart resonates in particular through a great deal of liturgy. The famous Celtic hymn that begins "Be thou my vision, O Lord of my heart" toward the end refers to this Lord as "heart of my own heart." Elsewhere God is addressed as the one "to whom all hearts are open, all desires known, and from whom no secrets are hid." Pleas are made for the "thoughts of our hearts" to be cleansed, for hearts to be planted with "that most excellent gift of charity," and the "flame of sacred love" to be kindled on "the mean altar" of the heart. This Christian emphasis can be seen to be rooted in a much older emphasis illustrated in Jeremiah's desire that the law (Torah) be written on the heart (Jeremiah 31:31). This is now taken to emphasize not just inwardness and individuality but the law as a natural and freely flowing part of the community's life, what a Buddhist might point to in the idea of spontaneity and naturalness.

The main part of this exploration has used two very particular Buddhist examples and then tried to link the imagery of the heart being used there with a smattering of the same imagery found elsewhere in religious traditions. The reader is now asked, because taking things in a personal and individual way is an important feature of modern spiritualities, to notice and to be mindful of heart metaphor and heart imagery in other places and to analyze its meaning and use.

REFERENCES

Arberry, A. J. 1964. *The Koran Interpreted.* OUP.

Berger, P. 1979. *The Heretical Imperative.* Anchor.

Cupitt, D. 1980. *Taking Leave of God.* SCM.

Cush, D. 1990. *Buddhists in Britain Today.* Hodder and Stoughton.

Eck, D. 1994. *Encountering God.* Beacon Press.

Feuerbach, L. 1841; 1957 ed. *The Essence of Christianity.* Harper.

Frederick, J. 1988. *The Middle Way* 63, nos. 1–4.

Hick, J. 1989. *An Interpretation of Religion.* Macmillan.

———. 1994. *Disputed Questions.* Macmillan.

Hookham, M. 1985. *On Freeing the Heart.* Longchen.

———. 1992. *Openness, Clarity, Sensitivity.* Longchen.

Hookham, S. 1991. *The Buddha Within.* State University of New York.

James, W. 1902. *The Varieties of Religious Experience.* Longmans, Green and Co.

Longchen Foundation. 1993. *Indestructible Heart Essence.* Overview Document. Longchen.

———. 1994. *Indestructible Heart Essence.* Parts 1–3. Longchen.

Padel, R. 1992. *In and Out of the Mind.* Princeton.

Pye, M. 1978. *Skillful Means.* Duckworth.

Rahula, W. 1959. *What the Buddha Taught.* Gordon Fraser.

Robinson, E. 1987. *The Language of Mystery.* SCM.
Sharpe, E. 1983. *Understanding Religion.* Duckworth.
Smart, N. 1983. *Worldviews.* Scribners.
———. 1989. *The World's Religions.* CUP.
Smith, W.C. 1981. *Towards a World Theology.* Westminster Press.
Williams, P. 1989. *Mahayana Buddhism.* RKP.

8

Islam and Muhammad Iqbal

Clinton Bennett

THE CLASSIC FORMULATION

Books on Islam often state that it makes no distinction between the spiritual and the secular. Its ideal is a religio-economic-political unit governed by a single legal code, the *Shari'ah*, which includes religious, criminal, and civil jurisprudence. This model is based on the early Muslim community, or *ummah*, under the leadership of Prophet Muhammad (570–632) at Madinah (622–632). Muhammad governed the community in every aspect of its life, according to the rules and precepts revealed in the Qur'an (Islam's scripture) as well as by his own inspired judgments (*hukum*). Muhammad's *sunna* (example) serves as the model for the whole of Islamic life. The ideal, for any Muslim, is not merely to imitate Muhammad's spirituality, how he prayed, fasted, or thought theologically, but to copy his behavior as a husband, lover, father, employer, businessman, soldier, judge, and ruler. What the Islamic ideal aims to do is to hold spiritual activities, such as prayer and fasting, in balance or harmony with work and leisure activities. No permitted (*halal*) act is essentially any less, or more sacred, or holy, than any other. The whole of life, if lived in harmony with God's will, is sacred. This is what being "Muslim" means: to live in conformity with the divine will, at peace with God and with one's neighbors. Islam, the noun, and Muslim, the participle, are both derived from the Arabic root *slm*, meaning "peace."

Another fundamental concept, *Tawhid* (unity, balance, harmony) also expresses the Islamic ideal—to hold the affairs of *din* (religion) in balance with those of *dunya* (world). Both Islam and *Tawhid* should be understood less as passive submission than as an active "making one"—as striving to bring the whole of life into a balanced, harmonious at-one-ness with God's own inherent nature. As God is in harmony within God's self, so harmony should be maintained within human society, between prayer, worship, work, and leisure. As God is just, so justice must be upheld within the *ummah*. As God rejects evil and chooses good, so must the *ummah*: "And there may spring from you a nation who invite to goodness, and enjoin right conduct and forbid indecency" (Q 3:104). In Muslim understanding, the *ummah* under the rule of the prophet was a perfect society. Not everyone, all the time, lived blamelessly. However, mechanisms were in place to ensure that wrongdoers were dealt with—either punished or forgiven—with least disruption of the common peace.

Traditionally, Muslims extend this golden, or ideal period, of Islamic history to include the reigns of the first four khalifs, or successors, of Muhammad. Their rule lasted until 661. Known as the "rightly guided Khalifs" (*al-Khulafa ar rashidun*) their friendship with the Prophet, their piety and personal sincerity, is understood to have peculiarly qualified them to govern the community. Their authority, however, was different from Muhammad's. The scripture was now complete, and considered definitive. No new revelation would be forthcoming. Nor did the khalifs share the *ilham* (inspiration) of the messenger. Thus, their role was to rule by interpreting the scripture, and the *sunna* (which was later codified into definitive collections, known as *ahadith*), in accord with the principles contained in these primary texts. The Islamic path, or way, was believed to be perfect and complete, suggested at Qur'an 5:3, "This day have I perfected your religion and completed my favor unto you." The majority of Muslims, the *Sunni,* believed that authority to interpret the tradition was now invested in the whole *ummah.* No single, individual Muslim could claim special or unique authority of interpretation. For them, the khalif's role was that of a first-among-equals. The khalifs did take the lead in military matters, in continuing the empire's territorial expansion. Their application of Qur'anic principles to new, or to unexpected situations, too, was generally accepted as valid due to their status as *sahaba* (companions of Muhammad). A minority group, the *Shi'a,* did think certain individuals peculiarly able to interpret the tradition, namely, male descendants of Muhammad, and broke away after 661 under the leadership of their imams. Neither group, however, differed on the question of the *din-dunya* relationship. In both *Sunni* and *Shia* Islam, the sacred and the secular are two sides of a single coin.

SPIRITUALITY IN THE CLASSICAL TRADITION

In practice, this conviction resulted in a holistic view of life as a spiritual-physical whole. Every permitted activity qualifies as worship (*ibadat*). Derived from the root word *abd,* "slave," this means that any act that harmonizes with God's will praises and glorifies the Creator. A business transaction in the marketplace is no less holy than prayer five times a day or fasting during the month of *Ramadan.* Indeed, interrupting other daily chores and tasks, ritual prayer helps to sacralize the time spent between the canonical hours of prayer. Similarly, as prayer can be offered anywhere, inside or outside a mosque, whatever space is used for prayer becomes sacred space and reminds Muslims that within Islamic society, all space is really sacred space. Islam is thus a this-world affirming religion. Upholding justice, ensuring a fair distribution of resources, and caring for the handicapped or disadvantaged are all as essential to Muslim obedience as prayer, fasting, or pilgrimage. All reflect God's own inherent nature as a just, merciful God. So, too, does maintaining balance between the natural world and the manufactured or "people-made" world; this also reflects God's *tawhid* nature. At creation, humanity was declared God's "vice-regent" (*khalifat*; literally, "deputy")—"custodians of the earth" (Q 6:165). Even birds have their modes of prayer and praise (Q 24:41). This is why traditional Islamic architecture integrates gardens and fountains into its buildings, courtyards, and public places. Islamic art—geometric forms, arabesque patterns, Qur'anic calligraphy—which covers the surfaces of domestic, commercial, and governmental buildings, as well as of "places of prostration" (mosques, or *masjid*), similarly indicates that any distinction between these is functional rather than intrinsic.

Islamic prayer, too, involving body, mind, and soul, says that all three are equally valuable and wholesome in God's sight. Thus, "He shaped you and made good your shapes" (Q 64: 3). Muslims have not hesitated to use quite erotic language to describe the felicities of paradise, or the ideal relationship between Creator and creatures: "the most intense and perfect contemplation of God is through women, and the most intense union in the world is the conjugal act," said ibn Arabi (1165–1240); "I do not wear a nightshirt when I sleep with my beloved," said Jalal ar-Rumi (1207–1273). Muslims have often found the attitude, expressed by some Christians, that "sex is evil" and celibacy the higher calling too this-world denying. Islamic spirituality, then, does not value inner devotion—soul-feeding activities—over wholesome physical activities. The effort to live justly, to trade fairly, to achieve the highest intellectual capabilities—*ilm*, "knowledge," is an attribute of God which *tawhid* demands people reflect in their own lives—are as essential as prayer, fasting, and pilgrimage for a balanced spiritual life. The outer *jihad*, or struggle, to uphold social justice goes hand-in-hand with the inner *jihad* for spiritual health.

HISTORICAL DEVELOPMENTS: RELIGION VERSUS THE WORLD

For the first three or four hundred years after Muhammad's death, the challenge of governing an ever-expanding empire according to the principles of Qur'an and *sunna* resulted in a dynamic, creative, imaginative, and progressive civilization. Pursuit of *ilm* led to high achievement in philosophy, medicine, theology, and mathematics especially. The *Shari'ah* was developed into a detailed and comprehensive legal code. As new situations arose, its content had to be extended. This was achieved by applying its principles (*usul*) to deduce new laws consistent with its ethos, as well as with earlier laws. We should perhaps note that the literal meaning of *Shari'ah* is "a path leading to a watering hole." However, after 661, with the creation of the hereditary *khalifat* and after the death of the last surviving *sahaba,* Muslim scholars became increasingly uneasy with this dynamic process, known as *ijtihad* (mental exertion, effort). While some khalifs were pious and godly, many paid Islam lip service only; they were emperors of a rich empire and wanted a lifestyle to match this status. By the beginning of the tenth century, the *ulema,* "scholars" (who now claimed the right to speak on behalf of the whole community), declared that the *Shari'ah* was complete. So far, they said, the dynamic process of extending its content had enjoyed divine oversight. That process was now complete. *Shari'ah* was now definitive, complete, and unchangeable. Hereafter, *bida* (innovation) was banned and *taqlid* (imitating) the past was elevated as the highest goal of Islamic excellence.

What happened was this: in order to bypass the strictures of *Shari'ah,* which usually did not suit their purposes, the khalifs, or their increasingly independent deputies, the sultans, simply set up their own secular courts. While this completely contradicted the classical view of the *din-dunya* relationship, those who wished to retain the traditional pattern were faced with a dilemma. Should they oppose the khalif, who they saw as a symbol of Muslim unity, even as divinely appointed? If so, who should they put in his place? On the one hand, this led to creative debate about who should rule; on the other, it resulted in the scholars standing by while the scope of *Shari'ah* was limited to domestic law, and to matters to do with the *fard* (obligatory) duties of Islam. Taxation and criminal and commercial law were entrusted to grievance courts. The khalifs justified this by saying that their duty was to uphold *Shari'ah* and in order to do this effectively they needed to introduce certain regulations to protect its impartiality. Thus, originally, the new courts were set up to adjudge cases concerning senior officers or relatives of the ruler, on the basis that the regular magistrates might be too intimidated to deal fairly with them. The rulers carefully avoided using the word *Law,* since lawmaking is God's prerogative and God had already given His definitive legal code. Instead, "regulations" were issued. Thus, in theory, *Shari'ah* remained the law of the land. This was usually sufficient to stay the hand of most would-be rebels.

Many Muslims, unable to exert much influence in public affairs, witnessing what they believed to be a decline in public morality, began to concentrate instead on *din.* Sufi Islam, with its emphasis on the *batin* (inner, esoteric) meaning of texts and ritual, attracted popular support. Sufi thought shall not be fully explored in this essay. Suffice it to say that its goal of *fana* (passing away) and of *baqa* (union with God) tended toward an introverted spirituality. This, though, cannot be called world-denying. As a way of realizing the falsehood of selfishness, Sufism encourages generosity and selfless service. However, its leaders have concentrated on spiritual teaching, on devotional techniques; they have, as it were, pursued the inner *jihad* of spiritual health, not the outer *jihad* of engagement with the political and social reality. The *tariqah,* or path to the center (union with God), has taken priority over the *Shari'ah*, the path around the circumference. Sufis have rarely taken part in public life. In Sufi thought, too, this world is but a manifestation of the Divine Reality, and the Sufi goal is to realize that only Ultimate Reality is really real. This world, and ourselves, must reunite with Ultimate Reality; merge into its infinite, undefinable Being.

During the eighteenth and nineteenth centuries, the Muslim world experienced a political crisis. Almost everywhere, colonial governments were in control, *Shari'ah* was not even nominally established, and Islamic power and prestige seemed a forgotten glory. What had gone wrong? Muslims, who interpreted Islam's initial success as a sign of divine approval, now interpreted its decline as a sign of God's disfavor. One popular response was to blame this decline on *Shari'ah*'s abandonment. It must be reinstated. Many also blamed Sufi thought and practice, seeing this as a corrupt expression of Islam, too concerned with the inner struggle to devote enough energy to upholding justice in the external world. Traditionalists wish to reinstate the *Shari'ah* as defined in the tenth century, without any change. Usually its interpretation would be entrusted to a body of pious and respected scholars, who may emerge by popular acclamation, or be elected democratically. Most prefer the former, since standing for election probably rules one out as a suitable candidate. Thus, the solution is to be found by replicating the past; the perfect society that once was can be realized again. The problem with this response, for some Muslims, as well as for some non-Muslims, is that tenth-century *Shari'ah* seems out of step with contemporary values. Even though the *hudud* (extreme) punishments are only last resorts and are hedged around with checks and balances, including the possibility of repentance and forgiveness, many people today believe that such measures should never be enforced.

THE CONTRIBUTION OF MUHAMMAD IQBAL

Sir Muhammad Iqbal (1876–1938), Muslim philosopher, thinker, and poet, offered an alternative response to Islam's crises. He shared the traditionalists' suspicion of Sufism. Like them, he wanted to reunite *din* with *dunya* but, unlike them, he rejected *taqlid* (imitation) in favor of *tajdid* (renewal) and *islah* (reform). In my view, Iqbal represents the most creative, potentially world-transforming Muslim contribution to human thought in this century, perhaps ever. Although now dead for over half a century, the impact of his thought, despite the proliferation of Iqbal societies, academies, and journals, has not really penetrated very far beyond the immediate circle of his admirers. His writing, too, has consequences for our thinking about "new spiritualities." As we shall see, while it rejects Sufi celebration of "unity," it also critiques—and challenges—the traditional Muslim view of the divine-human relationship. It offers a radical, alternative possibility.

Muhammad Iqbal was born into a Punjabi family not long converted from Hinduism to Sufi Islam. They belonged to the Brahmanical class. Iqbal attended a Scottish mission college at Sialkot, followed by the government college at Lahore where Sir Thomas Arnold (1864–1930) was then teaching. It was while at Lahore that his poetry began to earn him fame, and by the time he left to study in Europe in 1905 he had already become a national literary figure. There he qualified as a barrister at Lincoln's Inn, gained a degree in philosophy from Cambridge, and earned his doctorate from Munich (his dissertation was on Persian metaphysics). He found Europe exciting and vibrant, but thought its nationalisms and petty rivalries a fatal flaw. He later denounced nationalism and racism as "false idols." Traveling in Spain, he wept with pride while visiting the beautiful mosque at Cordoba, converted into a cathedral in 1236. He celebrated Islam's past achievements in his poetry, but what about the future? Could Islam again become dynamic, creative, holistic? Iqbal shared the general suspicion that something had gone seriously wrong with the Islamic enterprise.

Influenced by Hegelian confidence in human progress as an inevitable dialectic of history, he identified Islam's closing of the gates of *ijtihad* as its principal weakness. This not only hindered progress but also posited the past, not the future, as the ideal. Iqbal did not share the traditionalists' goal of replicating the Madinah that once was; instead, he looked to a Madinah yet to come. He called for a fresh, futuristic orientation, for a reconstruction of Islamic thought. Incidentally, he borrowed this concept from Sir Sayyed Ahmed Khan (1817–1898), whose influence he acknowledged:

> He was the first modern Muslim to catch a glimpse of the positive character of the age that was coming. . . . But the real greatness of the man consists in the fact that he was the first Indian Muslim who felt the need for a fresh orientation of Islam and worked for it. (Cited in Esposito 1991, 135)

Iqbal's classic *The Reconstruction of Religious Thought in Islam* was published in 1930.

IQBAL'S RECONSTRUCTED ISLAM

Islamically, how did Iqbal justify his vision? First, he argued that Muslims had wrongly called a halt to the dynamic process of *ijtihad* which had once creatively extended *Shari'ah*. Next, he said, Muslims have confused the real *Shari'ah* and its eternal, immutable principles with particular applications of these principles to tenth-century contexts. This had brought about a legal and dogmatic slumber, a preoccupation with the past which needs to yield to confidence in human ability to create an even better future: "A false reverence for past history," he wrote, "and its artificial resurrection constitute no remedy for a people's decay" (1930, 151). "Each generation," he said, "guided but unhampered by the work of its predecessors, should be permitted to solve its own problems" (cited in Gandhi 1986, 68). He argued that the "completeness" of the Qur'anic revelation, and of the Prophet's mission, was "potential" rather than "realized." Muhammad's message was "final" only in the sense "that it was," and remains, "eternally valid." Its function is to "awaken" in us consciousness of our real relationship with the universe. By assuming our God-given responsibility as *Khalifat,* we can actualize the ideal society which lies "dormant in our minds." "Man," insists Iqbal, can progress "onward to receive ever-fresh illuminations from an Infinite Reality which 'every moment appears in a new glory' " (1930, 123).

God—God's self—said Iqbal, is dynamic, not static. God's essence contains within itself unrealized potentiality; creation had lain dormant until actualized. As creation, aided by its *khalifat,* unfolds toward the perfection it can achieve, God's own potentialities will also unfold. Thus, "The Ultimate Ego [God] exists in pure duration wherein change ceases to be a succession of varying attitudes, and reveals its true character as continuous creation" (1930, 60). All life, and all creation, is in process—the process of becoming what it is intended, and capable, of being. Thus he disliked Sufism. It stifled, he believed, development of the human personality. The *khudi* (ego, self, personality) was central to Iqbal's thought. This drew on Nietzsche's concept of the "super man," but also on the "Perfect Man" (*insan-i-*

kamil) of the Sufis. Muhammad was the pototypal "Perfect Man" but all can realize this at-one-ness with the divine will by right effort and constant struggle. This also resonates with Muslim philosopher al-Farabi's concept of the "potential intellect"; a latent capacity to acquire eternal truths lies within us all. The prophets were born with this capability fully developed; others, through philosophical training, can realize this same potential (see Bennett 1994b, 127). It also resonates with such contemporary concepts of "becoming persons" as a process of constant change which Carl Rogers (1967, 1980), James W. Fowler (1981), and other writers have articulated. On a negative note, I should add that Iqbal excluded women from this dynamic; "even at his most poetic, his most progressive, his most inclusively utopian" moments, says Wilfred Cantwell Smith, "Iqbal left the women out of his dynamic new world (Gandhi 1986, 62).

Instead of celebrating *baqa* (unity) with God, Iqbal celebrated *firaq* (separation). Man needs God to maintain cosmic order, but as human society and humanity's relationship with the rest of creation begin to reflect the divine *tawhid,* God will be able to take a rest from being God;

> More blissful than a thousand pious acts
> Is for Thee and me to come a step nearer by way
> of friendship
> Come, rest a while in my bosom
> From the toil and weariness of Godhood.
>
> (Cited in Gandhi 1986, 60)

Sufism took people mistakenly along the radius to the center; the human task is to concentrate on the circumference. Here, not at the center, lies all we need to be fully human. In Iqbal's system, *din* and *dunya* are not two sides of a single coin; they are identical: "Basing himself upon the Prophet's saying , 'the whole of the earth is a Mosque,' Iqbal could assert that in Islam: 'All that is secular is therefore sacred in the roots of its being,' for 'All this immensity of matter constitutes a scope for the self-realization of spirit' " (1930, 155). For

Iqbal, then, the "kingdom of God" (a phrase he used), like that of the Hebrews, will be here on earth:

> this world of color and scent is your empery—grain by grain gather the jewels from its soil, falconlike seize your prey out of its skies, smite your axe against its mountain ranges, take light from yourself and set it all afire . . . hew out a new world to your own desire. (1920, 78f)

Like the Hebrews, he did not speculate overmuch about individual destiny. What is clear is that, for him, the "matter" "spirit" divide is false; heaven and hell are "states of perception," the resurrection will not be an external event "but the consummation of the life process within the ego" (1930, 126). This begs the question: Will self-realized individual egos exist eternally, or will they merge into a single cosmic human consciousness which then partners God in bringing creation to even greater fulfillment? Would Iqbal share Carl Rogers's prediction that as "tomorrow's people" emerge, "evolution" may "lead us to a supraconsciousness and supermind of vastly more power than mind and consciousness now possess" (1980, 344)? Certainly, Iqbal seems to speak about the individual "losing his self in the community" (Esposito 1983, 177). Thus:

> The link that binds the Individual
> To the Society a Mercy is,
> His truest Self in the Community
> Alone achieves fulfillment. (1953, 5)

What is clear is that, in his system, the God "out there" becomes a God "alongside"; either alongside us individually or, as true community evolves, corporately. Wilfred Cantwell Smith comments that Iqbal put "God back in the world, now, with us, facing our problems from within, creating a new and better world with us and through us" (1946, 105).

Before adding a word about Iqbal's "spirituality," it should be noted that while his vision (if sexist) was universal—the kingdom would be for all regardless of color, creed, or race—its law and government would be Islamic. He admired the West's achievements, but thought both capitalism and communism equally bankrupt. He condemned respectively their materialism and their godlessness. Pragmatically, the new world order should begin locally, and expand out by means of example and persuasion:

> the humanitarian ideal is always universal in poetry and philosophy, but if you work it out in actual life you must start with a society exclusive in the sense of having a creed and a well-defined outline, but ever enlarging its limit by example and persuasion. (Cited in Gandhi 1986, 65)

This is why he lent support to the call for the creation of the Muslim state of Pakistan. Eventually, when authentically ordered and governed, the Muslim nation-states should form an international League of Nations. This might also lead to a resurrection of the khalifate. How would these states be governed? Iqbal's answer lies in his view that the earliest form of Islamic government, after the Prophet's death and before 661, had been democratic; government by a process of *ijma* (consensus) and *shura* (consultation) with the khalifs as respected first-among-equals. Thus, in his system, the dynamic process of applying the *usul* to the needs and contexts of today would be entrusted to a democratically elected assembly. Iqbal still believed in a comprehensive *Shari'ah*, but not in a "fixed" or "sacrosanct" code. His dynamic approach allows for change. However, although he looked to Islam and not to Europe for the "model of his new world," he never expressed the total negativity toward and rejection of everything non-Islamic that we find in the writing of some Muslim revivalists (represented also by the anti-Western activities of some Islamic organizations). Instead,

> it is necessary to examine in an independent spirit what Europe has taught and how far the conclusions reached by her can help us in the revision and, if necessary, reconstruction of religious thought in Islam. (1930, 8)

IQBAL AND SPIRITUALITY

Finally, what about our focus on spirituality? Iqbal's spirituality looks to human responsibility in, and toward, planet earth, for its fulfillment. An ego-sustaining life, as opposed to an ego-dissolving life, is his aim. Within this, all acts which sustain our role as *khalifat,* which nurture our progress toward fuller humanhood, are *ibadat* (worship). His view of the human person is holistic, not divided into matter, mind, spirit. It resembles Carl Rogers's concept of tomorrow's person, who will "not like to live in a compartmentalized world—body and mind, health and illness, intellect and feeling, science and common sense, individual and group, sane and insane, work and play." Instead, they will "strive for a wholeness of life, with thought, feeling, physical energy, psychic energy, healing energy, all being integrated in experience" (Rogers 1980, 350–51). Iqbal thought Christianity mistaken to separate the "spiritual from the temporal"; it had, he said, "uncritically accepted the duality of matter probably from Manichean thought" (cited in Zakaria 1988, 6).

The goal, not only of Sufi but also of classical Islam, is separation from the universe; Iqbal's goal is an eternal divine-human partnership. Morality, too, might be less rigidly prescriptive than traditional Islam's strict division into *halal* (permitted) and *haram* (prohibited)—whatever sustains ego is right, whatever does not is wrong (see 1930, 119). Above all, Iqbal's new world would be humanitarian. What, in Iqbal's view, is always wrong is a religion-politics division. He rejects out-of-hand any religious life and worldview which does not engage with the political reality (see Esposito 1983, 184). Here, he practiced what he preached; he served on the Punjabi Legislative Council, took part in the London roundtable talks on India's future (1931–32), and served as president of the All India Muslim League. He was knighted in 1922. Spending almost everything he earned on promoting his vision, he died almost penniless.

There is, I think, some resonance between Iqbal and New Age thought. In New Age thinking, a "turnabout in consciousness of a critical number of individuals" will "bring about a renewal of society"

(Barker 1989, 189), "a new age of peace, prosperity and enlighten-ment" (Woods, 3). This resembles Iqbal's vision of a renewed human awareness of our proper role; of our potential to become "perfect peo-ple," which will in turn lead to the perfect society. Carl Rogers has similarly spoken of how development of our understanding of "the person and the world which he or she perceives" may "constitute a 'critical mass' that will produce drastic social change" (1980, 347). Iqbal's confidence in evolution toward a better future, embracing yet unrealized potential, is also shared by much New Age thought. The New Age God, like Iqbal's—if anywhere—is with us in our process of becoming what we are meant to be. In this "process of progressive change God becomes a co-worker" with us, provided we "take the ini-tiative" (1930, 12).

This also resonates with process thought (Iqbal often cited A. N. Whitehead, 1861–1947), which expounds "a dipolar panentheism in which the universe belongs to the 'actuality' of God but not to his 'essence', thus elucidating the meaning of God as a living God actively responsive to the universe of his creation" (Cunliffe-Jones 1970, 163). Iqbal also drew on the writing of Henri Bergson (1859–1941), whose influence

> continues amongst existentialists who borrow his distinction between conventional and "higher" morality and continues within various process theologies that abandon classical theism to find both divine and human creativity at work in an evolving world (Eliade 1987, 2: 114).

Teilhard de Chardin (1881–1955) both "borrowed much" and "de-parted from" Bergson (Eliade 1987, 2: 114), which suggests that Mus-lim Iqbal and Catholic de Chardin may have some common roots.

Iqbal's cosmology—like de Chardin's—too, respects the natural world; we have responsibilities toward the whole creation. This also resonates with contemporary concern for a spirituality that embraces all life, not just the human. Similarly, Carl Rogers has predicted that the person of tomorrow will "feel a closeness to, and a caring for, elemental nature." They "will be "ecologically minded, and . . . get their pleasure from an alliance with the forces of nature, rather than in the conquest of nature" (1980, 351). Humankind's destiny, and creation's, are inseparably intertwined. It has been said that Iqbal's God was supremely a "poet, the supreme creative artist, incessantly creating out of a grand passion of self-expression," while humanity is "God's apprentice and helpmate in this creative enterprise, always adding to his Master's work and daring even to improve it. . . . His universe is that perfect poem yet to be written, which God and man are writing in collaboration" (Gandhi 1986, 77). Humankind, says Iqbal, is not reading from a prewritten script, or moving toward a predetermined destiny. Instead, we are cowriting the script and determining our own destiny. Iqbal's spirituality may not be "new," but it does offer an interesting alternative to more dualistic (otherworldly) options that place, ultimately, more value on human existence elsewhere (in a spiritual realm, perhaps) than here, on planet earth.

ANNOTATED BIBLIOGRAPHY

Barker, Eileen. *New Religious Movements: A Practical Introduction.* London: HMSO, 1989. I consulted this for references to the New Age movement. It is a useful guide to alternative religious traditions written by a value-free social scientist.

Bennett, C. "The Din-Dunya Paradox: Contemporary Debate About the Nature and Scope of Islamic Law," *Bulletin of the Henry Martyn Institute of Islamic Studies* 12, no. 1/2 (1993): 58–73. In this article I survey how the relationship between religion and politics in Islam has been differently interpreted at different times, with consequences for the role and scope of Islamic Law. I drew on this earlier research in preparing this essay.

————. "Islam," in *Sacred Place,* ed. Jean Holm with John Bowker, pp. 88–114. London: Pinter, 1994a. In this chapter I explore the relationship between the secular and the sacred in Islam through Islamic art, architecture, the role of prayer, traditional city planning, as well as theologically. It uses some anthropological data. I also drew on this earlier research in preparing this essay.

Bennett, C. "Islam," in *Picturing God,* ed. Jean Holm with John Bowker, pp. 113–41. London: Pinter, 1994b. Surveying Islamic concepts of God, I also discuss Sufi metaphysics, including references to the Perfect Man in the thought of ibn Arabi (1165–1240) and other mystics. For al-Farabi (870–950) on the intellect, see page 127.

Cunliffe-Jones, H. *Christian Theology Since 1600.* London: Duckworth, 1970. This book, by my former professor, charts trends and developments in Christian thought, including a very brief but useful précis of process theology.

Eliade, M. (ed.). *The Encyclopaedia of Religion.* 1987. I consulted various entries; see especially under Bergson and Iqbal.

Esposito, J. L. *Islam: The Straight Path,* rev. ed. Oxford: Oxford University Press, 1991. In this much-acclaimed introductory text on Islam, Esposito's brief but useful discussion of Iqbal locates his thought within the context of modern interpretations of Islam.

Esposito, J. L. (ed.). *Voices of Resurgent Islam.* Oxford: Oxford University Press, 1983. Chapter 8, by Esposito, discusses Iqbal and the Islamic state. He explores this aspect of Iqbal's thought more fully than I have.

Fowler, James W. *Stages of Faith: The Psychology of Human Development and the Quest for Meaning.* New York: Harper and Row, 1981. This seminal work applies W. C. Smith's verbal understanding of religion to the concept of faith development as a continuous process of becoming self-actualized persons.

Gandhi, R. *Understanding the Muslim Mind.* London and New Delhi: Penguin, 1986. The Mahatma's grandson discusses eight prominent Muslim thinkers in nineteenth- and twentieth-century India against the background of the independence movement and Hindu-Muslim relations. Chapter 3 is an insightful analysis of Iqbal's contribution, including examples of his poetry.

Iqbal, Muhammad. *The Secrets of the Self.* London, 1920. Iqbal's concept of personality, ego, selfhood—translated by his Cambridge friend Reynold A. Nicholson—widely known for his work on the mystical tradition.

———. *The Mysteries of Selflessness.* London: Oxford University Press, 1953). More of Iqbal's Persian poetry on self, and on the realization of self in societal involvement and humanitarian action.

———. *The Reconstruction of Religious Thought in Islam.* 1930. Reprint. Lahore: Muhammad Ashraf, 1968. This represents the most accessible and systematic prose presentation of Iqbal's thought. It was written in English.

Rogers, Carl. *On Becoming a Person.* London: Constable, 1967. In this widely influential book, depth-therapist and adult educationalist Carl Rogers develops his concept of personhood as a process of becoming.

————. *A Way of Being.* Boston: Houghton Mifflin and Co., 1980. Rogers speaks about learning, which embraces feelings as well as ideas; predicts what will characterize the person and the world of tomorrow; and continues to expound his person-centered philosophy of life.

Smith, W. C. *Modern Islam in India.* Lahore: Minerva, 1946. Smith surveys trends and developments among India's Muslim community, focusing on social and political contexts. Marxist analysis distinguishes this from most of Smith's later writing.

————. *Islam in Modern History.* Princeton, N.J. Princeton University Press, 1957. After an overview of Islamic history, Smith identifies and discusses issues which Muslims face as they respond to the contemporary reality. Islam, he says, is faced with a choice: to look backward into history or forward into the future. Smith argues, like Iqbal, for a dynamic understanding of Islam.

Woods, R. "New Age Spiritualities: How Are We to Talk about God?" I consulted this unpublished paper by the Blackfriars Dominican scholar for more insight into New Age spirituality.

Zakaria, R. *The Struggle Within Islam: The Conflict Between Religion and Politics.* London: Penguin, 1988. While the author's own preference for a secular Islam does not resonate with Iqbal's vision, this carefully researched historical survey of the religion-politics dynamic by an Indian Muslim politician, and former Congress party deputy leader, represents a valuable resource and contribution to scholarship in this field.

Masowe Spirituality: The Case of Central and Southern Africa

Isabel Mukonyora

r·ᴄᴘᴜᴀᴜᴇᴛ·ᴄ

HISTORICAL BACKGROUND

The Masowe church has representative communities in Zimbabwe, where it emerged in 1932 under the leadership of Johane Masowe; Port Elizabeth, in South Africa, where the Masowe community flourished as the Korsten Basketmakers (Dillon-Malone 1978); Zambia; Tanzania; and Kenya. The European term *independent churches* means churches that either break away from the European mother churches or, as is the case with Masowe, are indigenously led and distinguished by the fact that questions of belief in God are addressed through vernacular religious idioms. I define Masowe-type churches as heterodox Christian because the use of vernacular idioms has led to questions about the Christian value of Masowe teaching, not so much from my own perspective, but from that of European studies that precede my own (Daneel, Oosthuizen, Sundkler, and others). However, Masowe spirituality is not as far removed from what is comprehensible in a Christian framework.

MASOWE SPIRITUALITY

I have loosely defined the word *spiritual,* for purposes of this essay, as a descriptive term for being awakened to the reality of God. This is a condition whereby the individual becomes conscious of God and, being in the world, lives accordingly. "Being in the world" for a Masowe believer is given a special meaning here against the background of Shona traditional beliefs about God as the source of life who first creates a place where all creatures live harmoniously.

The following quotation from a Masowe sermon delivered at Lusaka (Zambia) in 1974 helps us understand the Masowe view of the human being as a symbolic representation of God.

> Baba Johane came. Baba Johane was there. Even today, he is there. He is also the one who used to talk about our forefathers. They are the ones who heard the voice from the tree. The voice used to say "Come here" but nobody knew that it was God who was speaking. People used to say it was the spirits of the earth who were speaking. Our forefather used to say that "we were given porridge, we were given rice, we were given milk, we were given everything." They never knew that it was God who was giving these things to them. They used to say that these were the wonders of the earth, and that they were caused by the spirits of the earth. But you understand now what it was. The voice (word) has taken flesh, the voice has appeared as a person. It has become a person who has lived among you. Gloria, Gloria. You have gathered to hear him. You have gathered to hear him.

There are three lessons in this sermon. First, God speaks and provides "everything" that is good including what is sometimes interpreted to be "the wonders of the earth." God is benevolent. Second, God takes on flesh and lives in the world, thereby communicating divine truths in a way that is intelligible to humanity. Third, God is a "wonder"—God fills the adherents of the Masowe church with awe by inspiring the feeling that only through others can God be heard and understood.

The key to understanding Masowe spirituality lies in the concept of God as the being who is by nature intimately related to creation as the source of life in all living creatures.

In the Shona myths of creation, God is portrayed as a transcendent and hidden power that is impossible to comprehend except through descriptive terms concerned with the creation process and the position of humanity in the created world. Shona mythical language reinforces a view of God as power through which all human beings are enabled to live in the world.

MYTH ONE: MUTANGAKUGARA (THE FIRST TO EXIST)

Mutangakugara's name is also God's name. He begins as a spirit who lives in the heavens with God until God opens the sky and "gently" drops his servant Mutangakugara "into the dark water beneath the sky." God said, "Take my walking stick and the stick will fulfill all your wishes." Mutangakugara wished that there be light to break the darkness (associated with ignorance of God) and the sun (*mwenje wezuva*) rose in the morning and set at night. In the Shona language both the sun and daytime are called *zuva. Mwenje* (light) coming from the sun is associated with knowledge of the divine manifested in the creative powers of the "stick." Mutangakugara wished for land, living creatures, mountains, plants, and a female companion with whom to bear children—and all this happened. All the living creatures lived in harmony, and there was no death. (Source: Aschwanden 1987.)

We can interpret this myth in two ways. First, God is not what we see in the creation process taking place from within earth, but a divine agent named after God that is sent to earth to create with matter that already exists (not a creator ex nihilo). According to this interpretation, God, called by the Shona name Mwari, is the supreme light of knowledge that remains hidden in the heavens. According to Aschwanden, "the first to exist" can only be the transcendent God who exists in relation to humanity. In humanity we have God's creative power and this power is exercised as much through procreation as it is through another exercise of human creative power in the construction of a peaceful society. In this case, the matter that already exists is the world in which human beings exercise a God-given creative power symbolized by the descent of Mutangakugara (the first human being to exist).

Human beings can be said to be made in the image of God according to the myth of Mutangakugara. Mutangakugara reminds us of humans when he produces children through a female companion, thereby beginning procreation. The interest in childbearing among the Shona can be seen as following the divine will first expressed by Mutangakugara for there to be a human society.

It is also possible to interpret the myth in a second way, by saying that the creative power of God is manifested in the creator god who descends from the heavens as a symbolic representation of God on earth, rather like the biblical logos. Here the divine agent is God incarnate and not any human being. A study of Masowe Christology is possible along these lines.

MYTH TWO: MUSIKAVANHU
(THE CREATOR OF HUMANITY)

Musikavanhu also descends from heaven. He is portrayed as a man who is not fully aware of his role to fulfill the divine purpose. Musikavanhu has to be awakened from within the world by the voice of God telling him to approach a beautiful woman standing by the pool. The woman is unable to move and speak until she is also awakened by God to become the mother of the first children. (Source: Aschwanden 1987.)

Musikavanhu as portrayed in the first myth is a divine agent, named with God's own name. In myth one, Mutangakugara also uses God's name (the first to exist). It is clear from Musikavanhu's story that God is transcendent and that God is revealed to the world through a "voice" and/or the spirit of awakening heard in the creation process, Since Musikavanhu does not seem to be fully aware of God's will, he cannot be the supreme being on earth, but someone used by God to fulfill a divine purpose. Here the divine agent is a human being.

Attracted by the gender dimensions of Shona myths of creation, Aschwanden tries to remind us of man's creative power. As he understands it, "man is also creative through his phallus, through which he begets life" (Aschwanden 1987, 19). Aschwanden designates Barth as the womb in which life is generated. This way, humanity becomes a symbolic representation of God in whose image the male and female are made.

Aschwanden's anthropomorphic interpretation of God's creative power experienced from within the world, while limited to the generation of life on earth, helps us to understand a Masowe spirituality as having to do with existing in the world. As indicated in the quotation above on the God of the forefathers, God's power is experienced in other ways, especially through providence (e.g., milk and thick porridge [*sadza*]). Also important is the encounter with awe-inspiring phenomena reminding us of the idea of God in terms of a transcendent power that intervenes in history.

To recognize the importance of the transcendence of God in Masowe teaching, let as turn to the myth of Samututu as a final example of the way God and humanity are indissolubly linked through creation.

MYTH THREE: SAMUTUTU
(THE POSSESSOR OF THE WIND OR SPIRIT)

Samututu is of unknown origins. He exists in the heavens and creates the world using matter that already exists. It is said in another myth that God first created the firmament (sun, moon, stars) and dwelt upon them. Samututu is a divine agent from the heavens who is distanced enough from the supreme being to not know his own origins. Nonetheless, through God's creative power Samututu creates the earth. Again the pattern of descent can be discerned whereby God is linked to humanity as a spirit of life in all living creatures. When two intelligent human beings appear Samututu exclaims, *"Ah tunhu"* (Oh, little humans). As he does with all living creatures, Samututu proceeds to blow his spirit into the humans, and is pleased with creation. He breathes over the whole creation to firm the soft rocks, to bring about life, and to strengthen the feeble.

God (Mwari) is the source of all life and Samututu, who breathes over the whole creation, helps us to understand the suggestion that God is immanent. Hence, "He was and is here, like a wonder of the earth."

It can be concluded from Samututu's story and the other two myths that God is revealed in the created world as a life-giving power that is manifested in all living creatures, especially in humans, who are gifted with intelligence.

Anthropologists who have written about the concept of God among the Shona on the basis of ritual activities that focus mainly on ancestors raise for us questions about a spirituality derived from the Shona traditional god, which has a lot to do with living on earth generally. They suggest that Mwari is a *deus remotus.* Van der Merwe, Bourdillon, and Murphree, for example, argue that God among the Shona is "far removed" from people, "exalted so high that he becomes irrelevant." Daneel adds that it is mainly through Christianity that the Shona have the idea of a personal God. Against the background of the three myths, I disagree and argue instead that the use of the name *Mwari* to refer to the biblical God reinforces the idea of a transcendent God who is also a personal God.

Using public rituals among the Shona that are usually performed collectively as the starting point for the investigation into Shona religion has led to a misunderstanding reviewed through this investigation of Shona mythology. It is interesting that scholars who suggest that the traditional concept of God among the Shona is a *deus remotus* overlook the theological significance of Mwari rituals where the *Mbonga-svikiro* (the female medium of revelation) pronounces God's will in the world. Her voice is interpreted among the Shona as the voice of God addressing humanity from the supernatural realm. God (Mwari) must, therefore, be *mutatis-mutandis,* involved in the world and certainly not remote. Masowe spirituality fits into this scheme with the prophet Masowe (Baba Johane) as the intermediary who symbolizes God's presence in the world.

THE PERSONAL GOD

Nhume yaMwari is a title used to describe the Masowe leader. Masowe states in B55: "I was sent to Judaea as a white messenger but now here in Rhodesia, I am a messenger to the Africans (*nhume yavatema*)." The role of the *nhume* in A5 is to "tell people to throw away their witchcraft medicines, not to commit adultery or rape"—all which disrupt peace in the community. In B46 the message is: "Repent and cease from your evil ways and be baptized by water because the world will come to an end."

Masowe is a messenger of God, a prophet carrying out a mission similar to that of John the Baptist. Just as John the Baptist announced the coming of the Messiah, Masowe does something similar by announcing the second coming of Christ and challenging the believer to repent from sin. At the top of the list of aims for the church is: "To believe in the Coming of the Lord Christ or Messiah (Mal. 3:1–2, Isa. 19:19–20; 60:8; 11:6 . . . Rev. 10:1–6, 14:6–9, 7:9, 19:1–9, 21:3, 22:4, 12: 7:15). Biblical references are used to legitimate a belief in God known in the world through the intermediary Christ. That God as a transcendent being who is known by becoming manifested in the world is already comprehensible in Shona culture.

Munhu waMwari means "an agent or messenger of God" whose role is to voice God's will. In B71 Masowe says, "I went into it [a pool in which there were an evil creature called *njuzu*—a mermaid who makes people disappear under the water—and the crocodile] and baptized many people there and the crocodiles there did not devour me. When the people saw this wonder, they knew that I was a man of God (*munhu waMwari*)." In B69 and B70 Masowe states that "I ate poison did not affect me," and saw people possessed by evil spirits who complain out of fear, "Where shall we go now that you have come to earth?"

These quotations show that Masowe is victorious over the forces of evil. Being a messenger means more than imparting information or knowledge about God. It also means taking part in the opposition to and the defeating of evil through the power of God encountered from within the world.

Mbonga-svikiro means "the female medium of revelation." Sometimes she is called the "wife of God." In the Mwari religion her presence is crucial at Mwari shrines. According to Daneel, in rituals she represents God because it is through mbonga-svikiro's role as divine agent that the Voice (Izwi) of God is heard in the church.

Dillon-Malone writes that Masowe would not marry in the early part of his ministry because of a belief that "may have been based on his awareness of himself as Mbonga-svikiro who was looked upon as the 'wife of God' " (Dillon-Malone 1978; cf. Daneel 1971, 70). In the text of *Vadzimai vaBaba Johane Masowe,* Masowe does not draw our attention to himself but to the female virgins of his church, among whom the senior woman, Mai Meggi, fulfills the role of Mbonga-svikiro. Masowe says, "The woman Meggi is the senior woman, the great representative of the house of God." "The house of God" associated with the virgins means the church because Masowe says, "Wherever the sisters are is the church."

The sisters are the female virgins who are comparable to *zenderes* and *mbongas* in the Mwari belief system. In short, the female virgins referred to as "sisters" led by Mai Meggi are looked upon as a symbol of the presence of God on earth, clean and pure. In Gos. God 3:81 it states, "The role of the sisters is to work as intermediaries between God and people." Other terms taken from the Bible and used to describe the mediatory function of the "sisters" are in Gos. God 3:77: "the ark" (like Noah's ark); Gos. God. 3:76: *chitenderano* (covenant); and Gos. God 3:85: "the holy city of Jerusalem."

The following quotation not only helps to understand the awe-inspiring nature of God, but also Masowe spirituality against the background of a traditional belief in God as a supreme being represented in the world by human beings living in obedience to God. It is an extract from a sermon by Cyprian, one of the early disciples of

Masowe. Cyprian makes useful qualifying remarks to help understand the significance of Masowe as an example of what is possible for other believers:

> God loved us, we in Africa, and he descended to Africa himself . . . [God] sent his messenger to Africa just as it happened in the land of the Jews where Jesus Christ had been sent. . . . Now when we talk about God, we mean the spirit of God. The spirit descends on whomsoever it wishes because everyone has been created by God.

In B22, the coming down of the Holy Spirit from heaven is described thus, reminding us of the awe-inspiring dimension of God which compels Masowe followers to pray:

> At midnight, there was a roar of thunder on earth from east to west. Cattle bellowed as they looked toward the east; cocks crowed as they looked toward the east. There was noise everywhere. People were awakened by the sound. The spirit said that the word of God had fallen somewhere in the east.

Then James Gore, another close follower of Masowe, said, "Then in 1932, we heard that Baba Johane had come. I know immediately that he was the word of God . . . and was compelled to pray to God."

In conclusion, the assertion that God in Masowe's background culture is a *deus remotus* sounds misleading in the light of Masowe spirituality. God in Masowe's cultural background brings everything into being through mediators who operate both from above and from within the realm of earth (including the ancestors). While God remains hidden in transcendence, God is not remote. The coming of, or rather, the descent of Christ, the ultimate revealer of God, in Masowe teaching can be understood against the background of the Shona religious and biblical idea of God as the source of life on earth.

Masowe spirituality as having to do with a humanity to be awakened to the reality of the Life-Giver whose original aim is to have all creatures live together in harmony is comprehensibly African and Christian.

REFERENCES

Aschwanden, H. 1989. *Karanga Mythology: An Analysis of the Consciousness of the Karanga in Zimbabwe.* Gweru: Mambo Press.

Bourdillon, M. F. C. 1987. *The Shona Peoples: An Ethnography of the Contemporary Shona, with Special Reference to Their Religion.* Gweru: Mambo Press.

Dillon-Malone, C. J. 1978. *The Korsten Basketmakers.* Manchester University Press.

van der Merwe, H. 1957. "The Shona Idea of God." *NADA* 34:42.

10

The Gospel, Secular Culture, and Cultural Diversity

M. M. Thomas

From the beginning, modern Western Christian missions held together in their concept of mission the understanding of the Gospel as means of spiritual salvation of the peoples of the non-Christian world and of Western culture informed by Christianity as the agent of civilizing them. William Carey's book *An Enquiry into the Obligation of Christians* (1792) with its call for evangelistic mission to non-Western peoples proves it. Since the civilizing function went along with Western colonial domination over non-Western peoples, and had in its goal the displacement of non-Western cultures by the Western culture, such civilizing brought the missions a bad name, and they were often referred to as an appendage of imperialism by later historians of missions.

However, the 1993 bicentenary celebration of the arrival of Carey in India in 1793 has brought out that, though a child of his age in his characterization of non-Western peoples generally as "heathens" and "destitute of civilization as they are of true religion," Carey was aware of the destructive aspects of the global Western colonial expansion, as is shown by his reference in the *Enquiry* to "the accursed slave trade in the coast of Africa" and to his participation in the movement in Britain to boycott West Indies sugar because of "the iniquitous manner in which it is obtained," that is, slave labor. He also spoke from India against the denial of education for blacks and the prohibition of their religious meetings in an African colony as "a most lamentable decision," and warned Britain of the divine judgment that awaits "nations whose trade is maintained by robbery and cruelty" (Pearce Carey, *William Carey,* p. 210). In the bicentenary celebration, the Calcutta newspapers hailed Carey as the creator of Bengalee prose and the Serampore mission under Carey for its contribution to the Bengal renaissance. Not all missions were aware as Carey was of the positive and negative in the dialectics of global colonial expansion of the West.

The educational missionaries and the Christian colleges of higher education conceived the teaching of secular Western knowledge as intellectual and cultural preparation of their non-Christian students for the gospel of Christ. Alexander Duff of Calcutta, John Wilson of Bombay, and William Miller of Madras were enthusiastic in imparting education in Western culture and modern science with the teaching of English literature at the center of secular courses and in spiritually interpreting them in the light of the Christian faith in their Scripture classes. So as William Miller said, "Very largely, especially when contrasted with the tendencies in Hinduism, European thought is Christian thought." Hence, "Scriptures were to be the spearhead, all other knowledge the well-fitted handle; Scriptures were to be the healing essence, all other knowledge the congenial medium through which it is conveyed." Duff, of course, thought that this process would result in supplanting the Hindu civilization by the Western. But the results were different, namely renaissance of the Hindu religion and the secular ideologies of Indian nationalism. So C. F. Andrews modified Duff's idea of Christian education as preparation of the gospel, by affirming that, and not cultural substitution by cultural assimilation, was the goal. "The wealth of English literature, science and culture" should be grafted onto the "original stock" of Indian thought and experience. Here cultural renaissance, social reform, and ideology of democratic nationalism produced by the spirit and values of Western secular humanism was seen as humanizing society. It may not lead people inevitably to accept Christ, but the moral problems of humanization of society would shift the Indian emphasis from the metaphysical to the moral, which would make the peoples' grappling with the person and teachings of Jesus Christ relevant and inescapable. For this, indigenization of Christianity by grafting it to traditional culture and contextualization of Christianity to the new national aspirations of the people was considered important. In all these the intimate relation between Western culture and the Christian gospel was assumed.

Christian missions among the tribal, outcaste, and other traditionally depressed classes also found the secular culture their ally in making their dent into the traditional spirituality that kept the people enslaved. Traditional religious spirituality, which divided the people into the ritually pure and the impure, had to be weakened before outcastes of India enslaved by untouchability and other oppressions of the caste structure could be awakened to their selfhood and to its rights of equal participation in society. The Lord's Supper in which converts from the different caste and outcaste groups participated did make the first dent into the traditional spirituality, but the secular awakening of the people was also a help. The traditional primal spirituality that saw nature, humanity living and dead, and the gods as one undifferentiated continuity had to be weakened to release the tribal people from a life conformed totally to the cycle of natural seasons into a consciousness of self-identity as peoples with a sense of history and historical destiny. Here also Western secularism was an ally of the Christian mission.

Asian nationalism fought Western domination in the name of Western secular values. Its opposition to colonial power had as its goal the building of independent Asian nation-states on the Western pattern. The hope was that nationalism would serve as an instrument in promoting the assimilation of Western secular humanism in the indigenous cultures as part of its planned national development. One may be surprised to see "liberty, equality, and fraternity" from the French Revolution and "justice" from Western socialism finding a place in the Preamble of the Indian Constitution as the bases of the new society which "We the People" of independent India wanted to build. The national movements of religious and cultural reform were efforts to assimilate these values into the traditions of Asia.

Secular ideologies like liberal capitalist democracy, socialism, and Marxist communism sought to mould Asian nationalism. There were also movements of militant, defensive nationalist reactions against such alien values. For all these, the modern global secular culture provided the framework of debates and struggles, and it was necessary to distinguish between the creative and the destructive not only in the Western cultural and political impact but also in the nationalist responses to it.

Ever since indigenous churches took over from Western missions their role as prime agents of evangelization in Asia, they have been emphasizing the Christian obligation to encourage a discriminating Christian participation in nation-building and social development through the process of modernization. There was thus in Asia a realistic recognition that globalization created by modern secular culture had come to stay, and that it had in it the potential for a fuller and richer human life for Asian peoples, but also that the creative potential could not be realized without fighting the destructive forces inherent in the situation. Along with this was the recognition that the church had a mission to cooperate with peoples of other religions and secular ideologies to build up and strengthen the idea of a secular state based on the fundamental rights of the human person for freedom of religion and freedom from religious discrimination in social and political life. In fact, the East Asia Christian Conference (now the Christian Conference of Asia) in its inaugural Assembly in Kuala Lumpur in 1959 called the Christian churches of Asia to this task within a secular framework of cooperation with adherents of other faiths, as it was assumed that this was the best framework of Christian witness to the gospel of the New Humanity in Christ.

The Dutch theologian Arend van Leeuven in his *Christianity and World History* (1964) saw that Asian opposition to Western colonial power was meant to assimilate Western technology and culture more fully into Asian life. He formulated a theology of mission according to which the impact of Western technology, social revolution, and secularism on Asian cultures would break their ontocratic character (i.e., conformity to an eternal order) and open them for the prophetic messianic tradition of historical movement towards a future with its eschatological goal of the Kingdom. This was seen as a necessary cultural preparation for the church's mission of humanization and evangelization. Van Leeuven's Gifford lectures interpreted Marx himself as a kind of negative theologian. The assumption was that the secular culture, which emerged in the framework of Western Christendom, had its inner spiritual connection with the Christian faith and the Christian interpretation of the human being and human history, even though that emergence was in a secularized form and in protest against the Christian religion. Even when Hitlerism was seen as a "modern paganism" totally severed from Christian humanism, the hope remained that the culture of modern secularism would retain and even strengthen its original Christian humanist roots. Van Leeuven's positive theological evaluation of technology, social revolution, and secularization was that they were carriers of the Christ *in cognito*.

But the situation today is very different. With the dehumanizing effects of modernization on the Western and non-Western peoples becoming stronger, Van Leeuven's positive theology of modern secular culture as an ally of the Christian mission in the world has got weakened considerably. Bert Hoedemaker, who teaches mission and ecumenism in the Netherlands, says, "The core of the problem is that the project of modern rationalization seemed to have reached its limits, at least the limits of its humanizing effects. It is widely experienced as dehumanizing" (*Costly Unity*, WCC 1993).

Illustrative of this change in the interpretation of the relation between Christ and Western civilization is the change in the theology of Bishop Lesslie Newbigin. In the fifties, when he was Bishop in Madura (Church of South India), he wrote about the "tremendous surge of new life" in independent India:

> I believe that this new upreach of vital power which is expressing itself in the whole life of the country—in rural development, in industry and technology, in politics and social change—is in the last

analysis the fruit of the meeting of the Gospel with the soul of India. I do not mean only the gospel as missionaries have brought it, but the gospel reflected and refracted in a thousand ways—yes, and distorted too—in the civilization of the West, within its literature, its service, its jurisprudence, its political ideas, and in many other ways. India is responding to that contact now for the first time with her whole strength. And that means both vast opportunity and vast danger. The coming of Christ always means mercy and judgment (*Revolution in Missions,* ed. Blaise Leval, 1957).

Here Western culture in its secularized form making its impact on Indian culture and the national Indian response to it are both seen as having their inner unacknowledged connection with Christ releasing creative energies to enrich human life. Newbigin was of the view that the Christian doctrine of creation was supportive of the idea of secular state and society:

The secular field of politics, economics, science, and so forth belong to this created world . . . God wills to preserve here a sphere for the free decision of faith . . . the Christian has responsibility to safeguard the real though provisional autonomy of a secular order wherein men of all religions can cooperate in freedom.

He also defended the autonomy of the secular because it is "the true antidote to the temptation of the church to absolutize itself . . . I do not believe that we shall go back on this insight" (*A Faith for This One World,* pp. 67, 83).

Newbigin moved back to Britain in the eighties and found himself in a cultural milieu that had undergone radical changes. In his *Unfinished Agenda: An Updated Autobiography* (1993) he gives the story of his wrestling with the relation between Christian faith and public issues:

I was only beginning to understand the dimensions of the changes that were being forced through under the leadership of Mrs. Thatcher. . . . Things which had been simply taken for granted in the years after the war had been swept aside. The idea that we have obligations to fellow-citizens, that public service is a good way to spend one's life and that public consensus is something to be sought—all these were swept contemptuously aside in favor of commitment to private gain. Market forces were to have final sovereignty over our lives. People would only work effectively if they were subject to the pressures of a competitive market. Teachers, doctors, nurses, social workers, and others in public service could not be trusted to acknowledge good professional standards; they had to be bribed or threatened. . . . We were out of the era of pragmatic politics and into an era of ideology. We were seeing (at a less violent level) a replay of what happened in the 1930s when British people with their long liberal tradition could not grasp the dimensions of what was happening in Italy and Germany. We had been thinking of Britain as a secular liberal democracy. It was only slowly that one began to see that the terms of the Church's mission had to change. We were dealing not with a political Programme but with an idolatry. We were coming into a confessional situation. (p. 250)

It was within this understanding of the British situation that he wrote the book *The Other Side of 1984* outlining his critique of modern global culture and its secularism which posited a division between the public world with its certainty of knowledge of value-free "facts" on which the common life was based and the private marginalized uncertain world of a plurality of "values" to which decisions of religious faith were relegated without reference to the totality of common culture. He comes to the conclusion that if dehumanization of modernization is to be overcome, faith in Christ must become the focal point of cultural reintegration, without, however, returning to the Christendom pattern. The book was widely discussed.

Today's globalization seems to underline the separation of secularism from its earlier humanism to which Newbigin draws our attention. Richard Barnett who earlier coauthored *Global Reach* has now coauthored the new book *Global Dream*. In its introduction the authors say, "Global integration has many positive aspects. But in the late twentieth century there is strong evidence that as national economies become increasingly intertwined, nations are breaking up in different ways and no alternative community is yet on the horizon." They affirm that "unparalleled prosperity" for one transnational class will go with "crushing poverty" for others. But their forecast on culture is most significant. "As traditional communities disappear and ancient cultures are overwhelmed, billions of human beings are losing the sense of place and the sense of self that give life meaning. The fundamental political conflict in the opening decades of the new century, we believe, will not be between nations or even between trading blocs, but between the forces of globalization and the territorially based forces of local survival seeking to preserve and to define community" (p. 22).

The January 1996 issue of the *International Review of Mission* is on the theme "Gospel and Identity in Community." The editorial by Christopher Doraisingh, after pointing out how the present globalization through market, media, and technology abjures the very idea of nations or any other parochialism that limit it in time and space, says, "However, it is important to ask ourselves how we as Christians exercise our prophetic Calling in witnessing to a free and reconciled human community in justice and peace in the face of the dehumanizing forces of globalization that destroy identities and freedom of local cultures and groups."

Charles West of Princeton in his recent essay "Gospel and Culture: An Anglo-Saxon Report" (published in *Mission and Evangelism in India: A Historical Appraisal*, ed. Jesudas Athyal [Madras, 1996], pp. 34–57) speaks of a contemporary Gospel and Culture movement in Britain and America initiated by Bishop Newbigin. It recognizes that the Anglo-Saxon culture had "two contending pillars: Christian and Humanist," but that the shift through the years had led to culture being "dominated by secularist assumptions" without Christian correction, leading to the erosion of the human values and purposes which were present earlier. So Christianity must now consider its mission to the modern culture founded on the Enlightenment faith as "mission to a pagan culture." Lesslie Newbigin with his books *Nineteen Eighty-four, Foolishness to the Greeks, Gospel as Public Truth,* and others, and David Bosch through his massive missionary work *Transforming Mission* (1981) and the posthumous essay *Believing in the Future* (1995) have been, according to Charles West, giving theological direction to this contemporary Christian mission to modern secular culture.

I welcome this challenge to the pietist who sees the gospel simply as a private experience of personal forgiveness of sins and leaves the world of power and money to the demons (as the Lausanne follow-up Willowbank consultation characterized the pietist) and to the liberal who shapes his Christianity to suit the culture of the Enlightenment. But with a note of caution: I have the feeling that Newbigin has gone too far when he opposes the very idea of secularism as related to state and other institutions of public life rather than seek to redefine it in the light of the gospel of Christ.

There is no doubt that the church and Christian believers should interpret the message of the gospel of Jesus Christ as the faith-basis of all rational understanding and present it for consideration in dialogue with people of other faiths in a pluralistic society. This is necessary for the renewal of modern secular culture. But to ask that the public worlds of the state, the university, or culture as a whole should make a public commitment to Christian faith or Christian dogma would mean denying people of other faiths—religious, ideological, or philosophical, their right as human persons to do the same from their faith-angle. The right of human persons to religious freedom requires a secular framework for public life which, though it was a product of the Enlightenment and is liable to be distorted when absolutized as a call to persons not to make decisions in the light of the ultimate challenges of truth, is an achievement of a cultural tradition informed by Christianity. It is significant that it has been fought for by free churches and accepted at last even by the Roman Catholic church during Vatican II in that light. It needs continual reinforcement by the Christian faith to maintain it as a humanizing factor in the life of peoples. But it is to be done not by rejecting the public framework of secularism but by supporting and maintaining a tension with Enlightenment rationalist struggles for a postmodern idea of secular humanism open to Christian insights. Otherwise we shall be surrendering ourselves to the ideologies of religious or antireligious theocracies and give up the Enlightenment's "unfinished agenda" (as Newbigin puts it) with respect to Islam, Hindutva, communism, or other public philosophies which reject or restrict the fundamental right of persons to religious freedom and other freedoms arising from it.

The *Postscript* by Wesley Ariarajah from the Sri Lankan angle to Newbigin's book *The Other Side of 1984* is very relevant here. He says,

> When one analyses the structure of societies that depend on dogma for their fiduciary framework, it becomes evident that dogma is interpreted and applied, not least by the priests and prophets of a given religious tradition, to enslave larger sections of the people. This was true of Christianity in the Middle Ages, and it is still the case in many societies today. There is little room for confidence that it will not happen again, perhaps in more subtle and sophisticated ways, when the dominant role of dogma is restored. We cannot evade the issue of power; those who interpret dogma and apply it to the ordering of social life will be subject to the insidious temptation to control and dominate people. (p. 69)

Newbigin's old defense of an autonomous secular order as necessary to keep any religion from playing god has relevance still for all religiously pluralistic societies.

From any angle the rejection of an autonomous secular order in culture and the promotion of integration of culture with any one religious faith reflect too negative a judgment of secularism, based on a nonrecognition of religious and cultural pluralism. No doubt, closed secularism, which does not have a transcendent reference, soon becomes idolatrous. Open secularism involves public commitment to values of reverence for the human person and to freedom and justice in relationships between persons and peoples expressed in the constitution and laws. There must certainly be open public recognition of the religious dimension of the human selfhood if these values are to find constant spiritual reinforcement, nourishment, and renewal. The public philosophy of a secular state or society must recognize what E. F. Schumacher has called "a hierarchy of levels of being" in reality; the I-It and I-Thou levels of Martin Buber; the mechanical, the organic, and the personal levels of John Macmurray; or the levels of matter, life, consciousness, and self-awareness of Schumacher (Schumacher, *A Guide for the Perplexed*, 1977, pp. 37f).

That is, it needs a culture of dialogue among religions, secular ideologies, and the sciences to evolve a common holistic anthropology, at least a common body of anthropological insights on the basis of which they can undertake public actions for social and ecological justice. Christian anthropology has a significant contribution to make in this dialogue to evolve ideologies informed by a realistic idea of the relation between love, power, and justice. Christianity has a great deal to contribute to this common understanding of being and becoming human. Not only Christianity, but perhaps other religious cultures may even correct certain attitudes toward nature or some ideas of historicism which have come to be associated with Western Christianity. Especially in the situation of ecological crisis humanity faces today, Leonard Boff, Jyoti Sahi, and Gabriele Setlione see the relevance of incorporating the primal spirituality of panentheism (God in nature) as different from pantheism (nature as God) to enable the development of a human reverence for nature. A syncretism at the level of culture as different from a syncretism at the level of faith should be welcomed. The Christian contribution can be made within the dialogue only if the Christian laity involved in public life are more informed in theological anthropology than at present, which calls for a new type of theological education.

In the present situation with its threat of globalization to all particular local cultures, it is necessary to emphasize the need of the local traditional cultures in a renewed form for the protection of the humanness of people. It is inherent in the Christian and social anthropology's idea that human persons find human fulfillment in interaction with persons. It gives priority to preserve and develop small-scale social institutions which enable face-to-face relations to develop personal values and humanize people. A papal encyclical calls it "human ecology."

Hannah Arendt writing on the human condition speaks of three elements that make the lives of people truly human, namely, "social life in its plurality . . . relationship with the earth . . . and a relationship with time," i.e., the encounter with the other, earthliness, and sense of participation in a movement of historical future. The former two have been preserved by the traditional cultures. It means that politics and economics should be seen as means of the social, that is, as means of the development of peoples' organic relations with nature, family, and local neighborhood communities rather than ends in themselves for which these relations can be sacrificed.

The ethical significance of the indigenous traditional cultures for providing the roots of the self-identity of every human individual and people and as the basis of further self-development toward a fuller human life is a relatively recent recognition in modern history. There was a time when it was believed to be possible and desirable to displace traditional cultures with modern culture with its more universal values. Today we realize that it is neither possible nor desirable. No people can attain human identity without the memory of their past history as a people and no people can grow in their humanity without reinterpreting that past for the future.

The need is to evolve a genuinely human pattern of development integrating tradition and modernity. The present pattern of integrating the two is criticized by the people at the bottom as a choice between two inhuman alternatives. One alternative is where the traditional oppressive hierarchies and patriarchies are sought to be strengthened by the introduction of modern technology without any change in the traditional value system. This amounts to suppression of their awakening to their tights of responsible and equal participation in society. Vandana Shiva and others of the women's movement interpret the increasing atrocities on women in Asian societies today as the result of modern technology having strengthened the patriarchal structure further. The other alternative uproots them totally from their community culture by a mechanical individualism or collectivism that does not recognize the organic dimension of human relation with nature or the web of mutual relations of human society. Traditional primal and village peoples thrown into the whirlpool of modern globalization tend to lose their organic patterns of life in community and its harmony with nature, and the uprooting has led to widespread mechanization of life and demoralization. Of course there is no possibility of turning back from modernity, but it may be possible to go forward to a new cultural reintegration. The question is, Can these traditional patterns be renewed and reintegrated with modernity in a postmodern humanist framework informed by the gospel and supported by the witness of the local church congregation? Can the ecumenical movement and local congregations become the nucleus of a movement of counterculture (as the late Fr. Sebastian Kappen SJ has been urging) for the defense of human beings as persons called to responsible existence in community, among peoples who are victims of modern development? Can the fellowship (koinonia) in Christ be realized in the experience of the congregational life of the church to the extent that it becomes extended into a mission of secular koinonia in the larger pluralistic neighborhood? They can. The church's local congregations and the larger ecumenical movement have to show in all continents the power of the gospel of Christ and the fellowship in Christ to resist homogenizing tendencies of modern global secular culture, and to renew traditional cultures and open them to each other and to the universal human values.

Part Four
Spirituality and Persons

11

Anthropomorphism

J. E. Barnhart

For whatever reason, the human species around the globe has for thousands of years demonstrated a proclivity to populate the world with spirits and various forms of more or less conscious life. It may be that *religion* is to be defined as the activities and behaviors employed to come to terms with those beings who, while perhaps not publicly observable, are nevertheless taken to be not only real in some sense but more or less personlike.

Religions differ considerably among themselves as to how far they go in extending personlike qualities in the universe. Modern Christians, Jews, and Muslims are disinclined to attribute personlike qualities to trees, brooks, thunderclouds, or insects. They are unbelievers or skeptics regarding such claims made by the Oglala Sioux Black Elk that qualified agents can converse "with the Thunderbeings who came with hail and thunder and lightning and much rain."[1] Some religious scholars demythologize by suggesting that extended animism and anthropomorphism are sometimes a more or less poetic way of referring to the *numinous,* that is, a sacredness and holiness that manifest the ultimate being, Great Spirit, or divine presence.[2]

Animism and anthropomorphism can be seen in the Gospel of

Mark's story of Jesus' rebuking the wind and saying to the sea, "Peace! Be still!" The disciples, according to Mark, "were filled with awe, and said to one another, 'Who is this, that even the wind and sea obey him?' " It is perhaps possible to save Jesus from blatant animism by interpreting the story so that Jesus rebuked the disciples and told *them* to be still lest they in their excitement overturn the boat. In any case, the disciples themselves in the story appear to be highly anthropomorphic. According to Matthew 14, during the night some of the disciples in a boat saw Jesus walking on the sea. But not knowing that he was Jesus, they grew terrified, saying, "It's a ghost!" Mark 6 indicates that Jesus had intended to pass by them unseen. Matthew omits this, but both Gospels add that Jesus, once he was seen, identified himself and told the men to take heart and have no fear.

According to a story in Luke 4:38–39, Simon's mother-in-law "was taken with a great fever." When Jesus stood over her and "rebuked the fever," it left her. In verse 41, Jesus rebukes a demon. In Luke, disease and demon seem sometimes to be one and the same, which suggests a variant of anthropomorphism. Indeed, Jesus is represented in the Synoptic Gospels as conversing with demons.

In visiting Oral Roberts's City of Faith in Tulsa, Oklahoma, I had a fruitful talk with a psychologist who knew the Reverend Roberts quite well. I asked the psychologist why Roberts seems to proliferate demons, so that each disease or behavioral problem seemed to be the manifestation of a distinctive demon. The psychologist answered that Oral Roberts did not possess a psychological vocabulary. His tradition uses demon-talk to refer to behavioral problems.

There are various theories purporting to explain the human tendency to populate the world with personlike traits. One theory suggests that in the early stages of human species' development, animism enjoyed a certain survival value. Anthropologist Stewart Elliott Guthrie points out that even today "it is better for a hiker to mistake a boulder for a bear than a bear for a boulder."[3]

There is perhaps some advantage to treating human infants as persons even though they have not yet developed into persons. By treating them as persons in so far as possible, the parents and others help create the second womb or social environment necessary to the eventual emergence of personhood. To say that the newly born are not yet persons is not to say they are not human beings. There are, of course, certain disadvantages in treating infants as morally responsible persons since their intellectual equipment has not yet sufficiently formed to make moral choices. It is quite likely that much of the controversy over abortion has to do with the extension of anthropomorphism, that is, viewing the fetus as if it were a person.

Although we learned over the centuries to revise some of our animistic conjectures, we did not give up all animism. Rather, on the one hand, we refined it so that we could not only distinguish degrees of animation but eventually conjecture that many things were inanimate. On the other hand, we invented all sorts of other animated and anthropomorphic beings. Wind became spirit, and spirit became spirits of staggering diversity of intentions, strengths, and needs. Some religions seemed to be virtually shackled to the service of the putative needs of spirits, gods, and demons.

One of the earliest negotiators with these spirit beings was the shaman. In time, as the shaman's alleged skill developed, other members of the species became quasi-shamans serving the gods and spirits as priests, oracles, and prophets. Many of these spirits and gods were believed to require food and appeasement, which is perhaps the origin of offering sacrifices to the gods and spirits. In the Hebrew Bible, the god required blood as well as bread, incense, spices, and other things that kings and royal personages were accustomed to receiving. And of course homage along with fear and trembling were demanded by the gods.

Theists find themselves in the position of having to draw the line on runaway anthropomorphism. According to the Hebrew text of Genesis 8, the god Yahweh smelled the sweet savor or pleasant aroma of Noah's burnt offerings on the altar. Interestingly, the evangelical translators of the Tyndale House Living Bible demythologize the passage to read: "And Jehovah was pleased with the sacrifice." In a footnote, they say: "Literally, 'and Jehovah smelled the delicious odor and said. . . .' " Presumably, evangelicals are more comfortable with a god who hears and speaks than one who smells aromas and odors.

That much of the Hebrew Bible has deep anthropomorphic roots is difficult to deny. In Genesis 3, Adam and Eve hear the sound of the god Yahweh as he walks through the garden in the cool of the day. Theologians have dealt with this passage in various ways, some suggesting a theophany or a kind of walking docetic being appearing as a kind of representative of the Creator of the universe. It is difficult to determine to what extent this anthropomorphic representation was conceived to be more than a hologram that could speak. Did the J writer in Genesis truly think that Yahweh did not know where Adam and Eve were hiding and therefore had to call out and ask where they were? Or was Yahweh only pretending not to know?

Some of the Hebrew prophets came to believe that their god had more interest in justice and mercy than in burnt offerings and rituals. The moral importance of this shift cannot be exaggerated. It represents a link between religion and ethics. The philosopher of the Enlightenment—Immanuel Kant—went so far as to insist that it would be immoral to give homage to a putative divine being whose behavior and commands were less than highly moral. Ironically, some theists who have allowed their god to manifest all manner of anthropomorphic traits have protested against Kant's insistence that elementary humanlike decency—respect for persons—become a part of the divine being.

The debate about the specifics of anthropomorphism will doubtless continue among theists for decades to come. English philosopher F. H. Bradley in *Appearance and Reality* writes:

Religion prefers to put forth statements which it feels are untenable, and to correct them at once by counterstatements which it finds are no better. It is driven forwards and back between both. . . . We may say that in religion God tends always to pass beyond himself. He is necessarily led to end in the Absolute. . . . If you identify the Absolute with God, that is not the God of religion. If again you separate them, God becomes a finite factor in the Whole. . . . Hence, short of the Absolute, God cannot rest, and, having reached that goal, he is lost and religion with him. . . . We may say that God is not God, till he has become all in all, and that a God which is all in all is not the God of religion.[4]

This is perhaps another way of saying that theistic religion in particular cannot easily come to terms with its own anthropomorphic tradition. On one front, it must fight off those who would swallow up their god in the maw of nature or the Absolute; on the other front, it must fight off zealous believers who would turn their god into a company of genies, angels, returning relatives and saints, and mediums of every stripe. At the same time, theists must determine whether to allow their god to suffer heartache but not heartburn, whether he is personlike and therefore takes on new experiences (including surprises), or whether he or she is the Eternal Now and therefore is, as Spinoza saw clearly, personlike only in the most abstract and remote sense.

Early Christians debated as to whether God the Son *really* suffered. The orthodox concluded that he did. But later they debated among themselves as to whether God the Father suffered. Some of the most powerful of the Church concluded that he did not. In the Second Person of the Trinity, the Church tried to make room for anthropomorphism while keeping it at bay in the First Person of the Trinity. In time, the Virgin Mary entered to satisfy the demand for a more personlike being. Eventually, in popular Christianity, anthropomorphism prevailed with the proliferation of commuting saints and angels. The Reformation was in part a secular movement to trim back some of the runaway anthropomorphism.

Actually, centuries before Christianity, runaway anthropomorphism had already begun among Native Americans and others of the Old World who populated the universe with talking animals, flowers and birds delivering wisdom, and wind taking on conscious personality.

At the other end of the continuum is the tendency to reduce human beings to machines and reactions. Ironically, theism has always had a heavy strain that tended to reduce human beings to instruments and tools of Heaven. Paul in Romans 9 insists that Jacob and Esau are of the same lump of clay. Individuals like Esau and Pharaoh who were elected to be menial tools of the deity are said to have no basis for complaint since they are clay and since the Creator is the potter. (This image of the Creator as the potter has deep roots in the ancient Egyptian religion, which was highly anthropomorphic.)

Fundamentalists who forcefully reject the theory of evolution contend that it robs human beings of their dignity. It is not clear as to how Romans 9 and similar biblical passages improve over the view that the human species evolved from simpler forms of life and through earlier primate species. Indeed, the evangelical and Catholic doctrine of eternal damnation is perhaps the most ruthless form of dehumanization concocted by the most twisted of human minds.

Some theists advance a version of human evil that is quite similar to the psychopath's view that everyone is corrupt and vile. The psychopath justifies cheating and deceiving others on the ground that they deserve to be treated in this way and that they would do him great harm if they were not restrained by their weakness or stupidity. Some theists hold that because the human race is corrupt and vile, each and every person deserves damnation. If the word *spiritual* functions to call attention to human dignity, then it would appear that the doctrine of original sin would be more unspiritual than spiritual. Some theists who hold to original sin are prepared to recognize human dignity but contend that such dignity cannot take effect in practice until the individual adopts a certain version of theism and submits to its salvation requirements.

Another version of original sin, which may or may not be tied up with various notions of salvation, simply stresses that human beings have a radical evil strain in their nature. It is not always clear, however, as to whether the descriptions of radical evil apply to each and every individual or whether they apply to collective interest groups struggling for power. In practice, the descriptions seem to refer more to one's opponents or enemies than to one's own interest group. The point is that too frequently the charge of original sin functions to justify dehumanizing certain members of the human race if not all members.

Secularists are frequently accused of robbing the human species of its dignity and humanity by failing to acknowledge the reality of both the human *spirit* and *spirituality*. In response, those of us who are secularists must openly acknowledge that there are secularists who are far from being humanists. Joseph Stalin was a secularist of sorts but no more a humanist than was the savage-minded author of the

New Testament Apocalypse. There are secular views of humanity that portray the human species as scarcely more than complex machines lacking creativity, genuine compassion, and dignity. Ironically, those secularists who grossly degrade and dehumanize others tend to make gods of themselves. Usually, this kind of self-deification takes the form of viewing oneself as intrinsically superior to most members of the human race. Joseph Stalin's drive to make himself into a god took the inevitable course of turning himself into a vicious human monster.

There seems to be nothing gained morally in attributing to oneself and others a *spirit* or a *soul* that survives the body. Indeed, there is ample reason to conjecture that cruel, inhuman deeds can be perpetrated equally by those who believe in an immortal spirit and by those who do not believe in immortality.

There is one area in which the secularist can and should acknowledge that the human race might enjoy quite an advantage if there were a cosmic person or god who, as William James suggested, is friendly to the highest values to which we human beings devote ourselves. Goodness, decency, kindness, creativity—these are worthy of anyone's support, including the support of whatever gods might exist.

On the other hand, there is no moral imperative to believe what one cannot in good faith believe to be the case. Naturalists and secularists who are devoted to a humanistic morality can focus on the values dearest to them and often find themselves happily working side by side with theists who daily exemplify the highest human values and morality. It may be that morality has its roots in alliance making. Immanuel Kant, who spelled out the principle of treating each individual as an end rather than a means only, has in effect advanced alliance making by proclaiming the human race to be a family. This means that no group or individual is an alien and that each person deserves the respect and dignity that we expect to be extended to ourselves.

Some may wish to regard the Golden Rule as the highest of *spiritual* rules. Others of us prefer to regard it as one of the greatest challenges of humanistic morality. The debate as to whether Jesus, Confucius, or someone else became the first individual to cast the Golden Rule in language is not an important issue. What is important is that the rule did emerge in the development of the human species and has survived for many generations. The challenge for us is not to see human qualities in events and in invisible gods. Rather, the moral challenge is to *create more humanness* in the world as well as more respect for the worth of other species. As the noted secularist Jeremy Bentham pointed out, a part of morality must inquire into whether other beings can *suffer.* If they do suffer, then it is perhaps a moral imperative to ask how we may help relieve some of that suffering without in the process creating more. Whether some call this a *spiritual* duty or others call it a *human* duty is less important than our seeking to carry out that duty together.

NOTES

1. Black Elk, through Joseph Epes Brown, "Hanblecheyapi: Crying for a Vision," in *Teachings from the American Earth: Indian Religion and Philosophy,* ed. Dennis Tedlock and Barbara Tedlock (New York: Liveright Publishing Corporation, 1975), p. 34.

2. Ibid., pp. xviii, 41 n. 4.

3. Stewart Elliott Guthrie, *Faces in the Clouds: A New Theory of Religion* (New York: Oxford University Press, 1993), p. 6.

4. F. H. Bradley, *Appearance and Reality* (New York: Oxford University Press, 1946), pp. 395–97.

12

Becoming Spiritual:
Learning from Marijuana Users

Bernard C. Farr

INTRODUCTION

This title was chosen with great care. The reasons for the exact choice and order of words will be explained in a moment. A number of people have approached me with comments about the likely contents of this essay, clearly misunderstanding what it is about. Three sets of expectations have been revealed in these comments.

Firstly, a number of colleagues have come to me in some degree of excitement saying, "I didn't know you were into that," or using some similar phrase. I assume they were meaning that to write an essay which includes in its title the words "marijuana user," or even that for me to be interested in adverting to the topic of marijuana use, indicates that I either do or have used marijuana or would like to do so, that I keep company with those who use marijuana, or that I have an unhealthy interest in the uses of marijuana—unless, of course, they are indicating that their own secrets can now be shared with me! So let me say right now that I have not, do not, and do not intend to use

Reprinted from the *Journal for the Critical Study of Religion, Ethics, and Society* 1, no. 1 (Winter/Spring 1996). By permission of the publisher.

marijuana. I have, to my knowledge, no friends who use it and have no personal interest in its use per se.

Secondly, I do not intend to write about the spirituality of marijuana users. I have no idea whether marijuana users are spiritual in any special way from which others could learn, or even whether they are at all spiritual.

Thirdly, I received a letter (together with some articles) as follows:

> I see that you are giving a talk at the conference on "Modern Spiritualities" about learning from marijuana users on how to become spiritual. I am intrigued to know what you will say with such a title. I am a member of the International Cannabis Research Society, and am an expert in this field. . . .
>
> I have spent many years of daily contact with cannabis users as a Christian minister in caring and therapeutic work. I have never noticed any spiritual illumination I would want to learn from them. Those many young drug abusers converted to Christ in the "Jesus movement" in the 1970s all testified to the vast change and improvement the Christian faith had made to them. I met lots of such people and had a colony of the Children of God living in my house for a while (that was before they became degenerate with a probably psychotic leader M.B.). Perhaps you would be so good as to send me a copy of your talk.

I have no idea whether it is possible to learn from marijuana users on how to be spiritual. It may well be the case, as this writer claims in one of his enclosed articles, that scientific evidence shows that marijuana use has the following adverse effects on the human person:

- it retards learning;
- it affects the reproductive system and production of sex hormones;
- it has the capacity to affect every organ of the body and can affect individual cells;
- its constituents are stored in fat cells and the brain is one large mass of fat;

- it affects lung functions;
- it interferes with psychomotor functions and heart functions;
- it contains 50–70% more carcinogenic compounds than a tobacco cigarette;
- it affects memory;
- it decreases motivation; and
- it interferes with the immune system.

Indeed, of all the points put to me in response to my title a concern with the known and unpleasant aspects of marijuana use is the only one which is relevant, since it will be part of my argument that "becoming spiritual" and "becoming a marijuana user" both present a problematic for explanation. There are reasons for not becoming either—that is, for not becoming spiritual and not becoming a marijuana user.

So what is this essay about? It is only and precisely about what my carefully chosen title indicates, namely what might be learned about people becoming spiritual from giving careful attention to what is involved in people becoming marijuana users. To make my purpose absolutely clear, my paper might be fully titled, "Becoming Spiritual: What Can Be Learned about Spiritual People Becoming Spiritual People from Studying What Is Involved in Marijuana Users Becoming Marijuana Users." This is, therefore, a study of parallelisms in experience between two distinct sets of people—those who are spiritual and those who use marijuana.

What, then, is involved in marijuana users becoming marijuana users? I turn to Howard S. Becker's account of his research on this topic and present this by listing in a series of points the gist of his argument as he developed it in 1953 in his paper "Becoming a Marijuana User."

There is a large number of marijuana users in the United States in spite of its being both illegal and disapproved. Research by psychologists and law enforcement officials accepted that such behavior is deviant, and has been concerned with the question: Why do they do it? Explanations from those sources lean heavily on the premise that there must be a behavioral trait which predisposes or motivates this behavior. The trait often suggested is the need for fantasy and escape from psychological problems the user cannot face.

These theories are inadequate, says Becker, because they do not account for the way in which deviant motives actually develop along with the deviant activity. Thus, it is not that deviant motives lead to deviant behavior but rather that deviant behavior in time produces deviant motivations. Curiosity, or some other vague impulse, becomes transformed into a definite pattern of action through the social interpretation of an ambiguous physical experience. Thus, marijuana use is a function of how a marijuana user conceptualizes marijuana and the uses to which he/she thinks it can be put—and these conceptions themselves change over time. The marijuana user, therefore, has a "career" as a user, made up of a sequence of changes in attitude and experience which lead, through a process which will shortly be described, to *the use of marijuana for pleasure*. Such uses are predominantly thought of by users as recreational, occasional, casual, noncompulsive, and pleasurable.

Psychological approaches to marijuana use run, however, into two great difficulties that are avoided, Becker claims, by attending to marijuana use in terms of an achieved "career" rather than as a result of a psychological trait. Firstly, psychological theories that are based on the existence of some predisposing psychological trait(s) have difficulty in accounting for the sizeable numbers found in every study who do not exhibit the trait(s) claimed to be a cause of the behavior.

Secondly, psychological theories (in any case) have difficulty in accounting for the great variation over time in an individual's use of marijuana. For example, whereas it is difficult for such theories to account, by an appeal to the "need for escape," for an individual's attitude to vary over time as to whether marijuana use is pleasurable, this variation in attitude is easily accounted for as a consequence of changes in a marijuana user's conception of the drug and its effects. Therefore, Becker asserts, we have no difficulty in understanding the existence of psychologically "normal" users, if one thinks of the marijuana user as someone who has learned to view marijuana as something which can give pleasure.

Becker's research was interview-based and focused on the history of a person's experience with marijuana, seeking major changes in attitude toward it, in the pattern of its use, and the reasons for those changes. His theory starts with a person who (a) knows others who use marijuana to "get high," (b) does not know what this actually means, (c) is curious about that experience, (d) is ignorant of what it may turn out to be, (e) is afraid that the experience may be more than was bargained for, but (f) is at the point of willingness to try.

Such persons, therefore, have the following career path as users of marijuana. They will (a) learn the technique, (b) learn to perceive the claimed effects, and (c) learn to enjoy those effects and thus become persons who can use marijuana for pleasure.

Learning the Technique

(1) Novices do not usually "get high" at the first attempt but need instruction in the proper technique. At the beginning, the novice learns that perhaps the drug has not been smoked "properly," i.e., with a technique that ensures symptoms of intoxication. Marijuana inhalation is not like tobacco inhalation and a new technique has to be mastered or else the drug will produce no effects and there will be no "high." Without this mastery of technique the user cannot develop a conception of the drug as an object which can be used for pleasure, so that that career can begin. The use of the drug must be such that the expected effects occur, as a result of which the user's conception of the drug will change.

(2) Correct technique is achieved as the result of participation in the groups in which marijuana is used. A group may offer direct teaching or, where a novice is ashamed to admit ignorance, provide a basis for observation and imitation. Becker comments, "No one I interviewed continued marijuana use for pleasure without learning a technique . . . only when this was learned was it possible for a conception of the drug as an object which could be used for pleasure to emerge. Without such a conception marijuana use was considered meaningless and did not continue."

Learning to Perceive the Effects

(1) Being high involves two elements: (a) the presence of symptoms caused by marijuana use, and (b) the connection of those symptoms by the user with their actual use of the drug. The user must be able to identify the symptoms for himself and consciously and deliberately connect them with use of the drug—otherwise the user considers that the drug has had no effect. Such persons might believe that their experiences are illusory and that it is the wish to be high, rather than the use of the drug, which is effective and that other users deceive themselves into believing that something is happening when in fact nothing is. In that case they cease to use marijuana.

(2) Typically, however, the novice believes (based on observation within a group experience) that the drug will produce effects and persists in its use until it does. Failure to achieve a high is a source of worry, and recourse is made to advice and guidance from more experienced users. That advice may be of two kinds: (a) pointing out details in the experience which had escaped notice or (b) helping to identify certain experiences as instances of being high. One such symptom is an intense hunger. An awareness of this helps the novice conceptualize the experience of being or getting high. Another might be to have "rubbery" legs. Whatever the symptoms are, the novice picks up concrete referents of the term *high* from others and applies those notions to their own experiences. These new concepts make it possible for the symptoms to be located among their own sensations and also enables the user to point to something different in their experience that can be connected with marijuana use. Only when this can be done is it possible to be high. There is still, of course, the further necessary step of identifying being high as pleasurable. Becker observes, "In every case in which use continued, the user had acquired the necessary concepts with which to express to himself the fact that he was experiencing new sensations caused by the drug. That is, for use to continue, it is necessary not only to use the drug so as to produce effects but also to perceive these effects when they occur. In this way marijuana acquires meaning for the user as an object which can be used for pleasure."

(3) As users become expert they become "connoisseurs" who can examine succeeding experiences closely, looking for new effects and making sure the old ones are still there. Gradually, a stable set of categories emerges so that a delight in being able to offer a commentary on the experience also develops. As with an expert in fine wines, the high is commented on in terms of the source of the drug, the time of its harvest, and so on. Part of the career is, therefore, for the connoisseur to be able to relate kinds of high to the particular features of the marijuana used.

(4) An ability to perceive the drug's effects must be maintained if this use is to continue. To be always high, or to be high because of the use of other drugs, interferes with the essential element of a noticeable difference between feeling high and feeling normal. Marijuana use may, in these cases, be temporarily or permanently discontinued.

Learning to Enjoy the Effects

(1) The last condition for continued use is learning to enjoy whatever effects the user has already learned to experience. This taste for marijuana use is socially acquired as are a taste for oysters or dry martinis. To continue marijuana use is to have decided that feeling dizzy, being thirsty, having a tingling scalp, and misjudging time and distance are pleasurable rather than unpleasurable. A novice may find those experiences unpleasant or ambiguous, confusing or frightening. Redefinition as "pleasurable" is, then, essential for continued use. Such redefinition typically occurs in interaction with more experienced users who in various ways teach the novice to find pleasure in an experience that is at first frightening. Steps on this path involve advice that the unpleasantness is temporary or not serious, and not to be compared with the later pleasures. Reassurance is the order of the day, especially if it is based on personal testimony. Also, the reality of the connoisseur's continued use and knowledgeable pleasure is an important source of reassurance. Improvement in techniques that control unpleasant experiences plays a part, but especially important is the advice offered by connoisseurs that the novice can get to like it

after a while. Thus Becker observes, "In short, what was once frightening and distasteful becomes, after a taste for it is built up, pleasant, desired, and sought after. Enjoyment is introduced by the favorable definition of the experience that one acquires from others."

(2) Experienced users also, however, may from time to time have frightening experiences. Again, a redefinitional process comes into play, or else marijuana use ceases. The likelihood of such a redefinition occurring depends on the degree of an individual's participation with other users. Where the community of use is intensive, an individual is quickly talked out of the temptation to backslide.

BECOMING SPIRITUAL: LEARNING FROM MARIJUANA USERS

In contradistinction to the approaches to spirituality that are premised on there being an inner personal reality, broadly categorizable as "spirit," such "spirit" being both the possibility and to some degree the determinant of the trait known as "being spiritual," I propose:

- that "spirituality" might be better understood, as mentioned above, as a kind of human performance rather than a state of (human) being. That is to say, spirituality is a matter of "becoming" that category of person who has learned to act in certain ways termed "spiritual" rather than a matter of "being" the kind of person who possesses certain traits characterizable as "spiritual."
- that Howard S. Becker's article, "Becoming a Marijuana User," provides, through parallel analysis, key insights into the process of "becoming spiritual."
- that Becker's sociological approach (and his rejection of psychological approaches) is better fitted to understand any social process whereby we "become" something we once were not, or whereby we cease to maintain ourselves as this newly achieved category of person. In this regard, I note that the second and third misappropriations of my title already mentioned were made by people whose self-definition was as psychologists of some kind.

Perhaps that is why they assumed that I am interested in the state of being of marijuana users and why they were wrong in that assumption. But on this point, I will have more to say when emphasizing Becker's comments on his research methodology.

Let me summarize my argument. Firstly, as a basis for my argument I have set out the substance of Becker's account of "becoming a marijuana user," to provide a parallel from which I wish to comment on "becoming spiritual."

Secondly, and in the light of Becker's argument, I wish to note the unsatisfactory nature of philosophical and other definitional approaches to a believable and workable account of "spirituality." I suggest that the general unease with such philosophical and definitional approaches is the reason why there is commonly a gap between the willingness of people to use the words "spiritual" and "spirituality" (and their cognates) in ordinary language, and their unwillingness to give specific account of their use of those words. Further, given the extent of disagreement among philosophical experts, and the parallel lack of clarity among the common public as to the proper usage of these words (which varies, for example, from the strongly theistic to an avowedly atheistic, from strongly ontological to an avowedly epiphenomenal understanding, and from a clearly religious to a vaguely emotional ambience), I suggest that it is safer to treat the "spirituality" family of words only as signifiers of a distinctive form of human activity, namely the "spiritual" form of activity, that signification having neither an inward nor external ontological reference.

Thirdly, and turning to the actual practice of spirituality for the real-time support of my argument, I note that in the practical life of religious communities there is an assumption that "spirituality" is not something which is simply "given" in the personalities of community members, but is something that needs to be "formed" within the daily living of the community through observation, imitation, courses of instruction, and regimes of discipline. There is also, it seems, an apprehension in religious communities that there is something either difficult or unpleasant in the processes of spiritual formation, spiritual instruction, and spiritual discipline since both instruction and discipline are given rule-based foundations and the formation is achieved under direction. Just as education was once seen by educationists as having the task of driving out ignorance and instilling discipline, so a spiritual formation within religious communities achieves the same twofold purpose of bringing the novice through to spiritual maturity by driving out their spiritual ignorance and instilling in its place a spiritual discipline.

In the light of these comments I return to Howard S. Becker's account of becoming a marijuana user, to consolidate my basic claim that spirituality is better understood as a form of human activity than a state of human being. Becker contrasts, as I showed above, a sociological against a psychological account of becoming a marijuana user. I now use this analysis to throw light on what is involved in *becoming* spiritual. By this parallelism of analysis, the same steps are retraced in understanding how a person becomes spiritual as were detailed with regard to a person becoming a marijuana user. These steps, I suggest, are true for any religious community which is seeking to engage in spiritual formation among its members. To make my point, however, I have chosen one kind of modern spirituality, namely the charismatic, to demonstrate the process by which a person becomes spiritual within a given community of practice.

Learning the Technique of Charismatic Spirituality

(1) Spiritual novices may not "get charismatic" at the first attempt but may need instruction in a proper technique. The spiritual exercises of prayer, speaking in tongues, and the like, are undertaken by the novice but without the desired outcomes since, in the first stages of becoming a charismatic, these spiritual exercises may not have performed "properly," i.e., with a technique that ensures the real symptoms of charismatic spiritual "intoxication." The model of charismatic spirituality is not like that of ordinary spirituality: the novice has to learn and new techniques have to be mastered or there will be no "signs," no "wonders," no charismatic effects, no spiritual high. Without this mastery of technique, without conformity to the

model, the novice worshipper cannot develop a conception of charismatic spirituality as a source of spiritual pleasure and so a charismatic career cannot begin. Participation in a charismatic experience for a novice must be such that effects occur as a result of which the novice's conception of the spiritual can change.

(2) Correct charismatic techniques in prayer, song, and worship are the result of participation in a group in which charismatic experiences occur. This group may offer direct teaching or, where the novice is ashamed to admit ignorance, provides the basis for observation and imitation. Recall Becker's comment:

> No one I interviewed continued marijuana use for pleasure without learning a technique . . . only when this was learned was it possible for a conception of the drug as an object which could be used for pleasure to emerge. Without such a conception marijuana use was considered meaningless and did not continue.

One may make a parallel observation about charismatics. Continuation with joy in the charismatic career requires the worshipper to find and continue to find pleasure in the experience. Without such an attained spiritual performance, attendance at charismatic services is found to be meaningless and the novice does not continue the career.

Learning to Perceive the Spiritual Effects

(1) Attaining a spiritual high consists of two elements: (a) the presence of symptoms caused by a charismatic experience, and (b) the connection of these symptoms by the worshipper with becoming spiritual. The charismatic worshipper must be able to point to those symptoms for themselves and consciously connect them with becoming spiritual, otherwise the worshipper considers that there is no spiritual experience. In the latter case, the person believes the whole thing is an illusion and that it is the wish to have a spiritual high rather than any reality to the spiritual experience that is causing the effects. In that case, the worshipper deceives himself into believing that something is happening when in fact nothing is. In that case the charismatic wor-

ship ceases. (It is this lack of ability to "connect" which may explain why it comes about that disagreements may arise as to whether a miraculous healing has occurred. Prima facie, such a physical event should not be the source of disagreement, but in fact commonly is. I have myself been present at a charismatic service where praise was given for the miraculous lengthening of a leg which had been short from birth. I could see nothing but the same limping walk as I had known before, but, in the Spirit, the congregation saw a different state of affairs and were moved to rapturous hallelujahs.)

(2) Typically, however, the novice charismatic has faith (based on observation within a group experience) that charismatic spiritual experience does produce effects and so persists in this form of worship until he also experiences the effects. Failure to achieve a charismatic high is a source of worry for the novice and recourse is had to advice and guidance from more experienced worshippers. This advice may be of two kinds: (a) pointing out details in the experience which had escaped notice or (b) help in identifying certain experiences as experiences of being on a spiritual high. One such symptom of being high is, for example, swooning (or being "slain by the spirit"). An awareness of this connection helps the novice charismatic conceptualize the experience of what it is to be on a spiritual high and thus to get to this high. Another symptom might be speaking what outside this context might be thought to be gibberish (glossolalia). Whatever those physical expressions are, the novice charismatic picks up from others concrete examples of the term *spiritual high* and applies these to his own experience. Those new concepts make it possible to locate the sought-for symptoms among one's own sensations and to be able to point out something different in experience that is connected with being a charismatic. Only when this connection between physical and spiritual experience can be made is it possible to attain a spiritual high.

There is still, of course, a further necessary step before identifying being high as pleasurable and therefore to be desired. Paralleling Becker's observation that in every case in which marijuana use continues, the user has acquired the necessary concepts with which to express to himself (firstly) and to others (secondly) the fact that he is experiencing new sensations caused by the drug, one may say that in every case in which a charismatic spirituality continues, the worshipper has acquired the necessary concepts with which to express to himself (firstly) and to others (secondly) the fact that these forms of experience and new sensations are caused by charismatic spirituality. That is, for charismatic worship to continue, it is necessary not only to engage in charismatic practices, so as to produce the desired effects, but also to be aware of these effects as having significance with regard to becoming spiritual and thus to perceive them as spiritual whenever they occur in an appropriate context. In this way, charismatic worship acquires meaning for the charismatic worshipper as a form of spiritual practice that leads to spiritual pleasure.

(3) As charismatics become expert they become "connoisseurs" and gain status in a charismatic community on account of their spiritual performance. Such connoisseurs examine succeeding charismatic experiences closely, looking for new effects and making sure the old ones are still there. Gradually, a stable set of categories emerges and delight in being able to offer a commentary on them arises. As with an expert in fine wines, the spiritual high is commented on, and the commentary typically involves the interpretation of tongues and the uttering of prophetic words. There is a career, therefore, for a charismatic connoisseur in being able to relate kinds of spiritual high to the particular interests and needs of the community in which they occur.

(4) The ability to perceive physical experiences as spiritual effects must be maintained if charismatic worship is to continue. To be always spiritually high, or to be high because of noncharismatic factors, interferes with the essential element of a noticeable difference between feeling the spiritual high and feeling normal. Charismatic practice may, in these cases, be temporarily or permanently discontinued, though I would be interested to know if this is in fact the case.

Learning to Enjoy the Charismatic Effects

(1) The last condition of a continuing charismatic experience is that of learning to enjoy the effects the worshipper has learned to expe-

rience. Such a taste is socially acquired within a religious community, and is similar in kind to the "acquired tastes for oysters or dry martinis" to which Becker referred, or for a taste for marijuana use. As noted above, to continue marijuana use is to have decided that feeling dizzy, being thirsty, having a tingling scalp, misjudging time and distance are pleasurable rather than unpleasurable. A novice charismatic may find some charismatic experiences initially unpleasant or ambiguous, confusing or frightening, and perhaps above all acutely embarrassing. Redefinition of these experiences as pleasurable is essential to continued charismatic practice. This redefinition typically occurs in interaction with, and support from, experienced charismatic worshippers who in various ways teach the novice charismatic to find pleasure in an experience which might at first have been frightening or embarrassing. Steps on this path comprise advice that the unpleasantness is temporary or not serious, the embarrassment inappropriate—and certainly not to be compared with the pleasures to come. Reassurance is the order of the day, especially if it is based on personal testimony from those who have successfully gone through the same passage before. Also, the actuality of the connoisseur's continued use and knowledgeable pleasure is an important factor in this process of reassurance. Improvement in technique to control unpleasant experiences plays a part, but it is especially the advice that the novice charismatic will get to like it after a while. Thus it is for the charismatic worshipper, as for marijuana users, that what once might have been frightening and distasteful becomes, after a taste for it is built up, pleasant, desired, and sought after. Enjoyment is introduced by the favorable definition of the experience that one acquires from others.

(2) Experienced charismatic worshippers may also have frightening experiences. Again, a redefinitional process comes into play or else charismatic practice ceases. The likelihood of such a redefinition occurring depends on the degree of the individual's participation in the experiences along with other charismatics. Where this experience is intensive and present in the community, an individual is quickly talked out of his temptation to backslide. An aspect of this restoration to grace is, not infrequently, admonition of the potential backslider,

this admonition being based on the superiority of the common experience of the community of marijuana use for pleasure over the occasional contrary experience of the individual

Although I have illustrated my argument from charismatic spirituality, I suggest that the parallelism holds for many if not all forms of spirituality within religious communities. The same threefold experience, within a supportive social context, of learning the technique, learning to perceive the effects, and learning to enjoy the effects is the basis of spiritual formation—that is to say, this threefold process is the way in which members of religious communities "become spiritual." Thus, the argument of this paper focuses on the *steps* through which a person "becomes spiritual" and it emphasizes spirituality as a problematic kind of performance within human activity.

CONCLUSION

I would finally draw attention to a possible counterpoint to my thesis in the possibility of writing a paper entitled, "Becoming a Marijuana User: Learning from Religious Communities." Marijuana use depends crucially, as has been shown, on the role of the "witness" in communities of marijuana use. Becker records the testimony of one experienced marijuana user who described how he handles newcomers (converts) to marijuana use:

> Well, they get pretty high sometimes. The average person isn't ready for that, and it is a little frightening to them sometimes. I mean, they've been high on lush (alcohol), and they get higher that way than they've ever been before, and they don't know what's happening to them. Because they think they're going to keep going up, up, up till they lose their minds or begin doing weird things or something. You have to like reassure them, explain to them that they're not really flipping or anything, that they're gonna be all right. You have to just talk them out of being afraid. Keep talking to them, reassuring, telling them it's all right. And come on with your own story, you know: "The same thing happened to me. You'll get to like

that after awhile." Keep coming on like that; pretty soon you talk
them out of being scared. And besides they see you doing it and
nothing horrible is happening to you, so that gives them more confidence.

Or as Mother Julian witnessed in the face of the religious believer's
negative experiences of the world: "But all shall be well, and all shall
be well, and all manner of thing shall be well."

The place of "witness" in both spiritual communities and communities of marijuana use is thus an essential part of becoming a member of either type of community. "Conversion" to any specific form of
human activity is achieved through learning the right techniques,
learning to perceive in a particular way the effects associated with
those techniques, and learning to enjoy those effects.

These three steps are the "gateway" through which a person sets
himself or herself within any community of self-understanding, be
those communities mainstream, marginal, or even undesirable. They
are all that is necessary to understand what is referred to when the
word *spirituality* is used. There is no need when seeking to understand
spirituality to appeal either to ontological spiritual realities or to psychological traits, but only to specific experiences and achieved actions
which have been perceived in a particular way.

REFERENCE

Becker, H. S. 1953. "Becoming a Marijuana User." *American Journal of
    Sociology* 59 (November): 41–58.

13

Becoming Persons:
Neglected but Prior Concerns

Robert N. Fisher

The question of meaning is a question of "total context";[1] meaning is perceived when a person's awareness of particular events and individual experiences is merged into a more inclusive awareness of a whole. It is an activity that continually seeks to provide a unified framework and horizon within which a person orders and makes sense of life. Thus meaning is generated within a holistic context which makes sense of the diversity of experiences we encounter in the course of daily life. Our convictions and beliefs are "deposited" out of a continual "stream of experience," which the mind forms into meaningful wholes; our knowledge is "strained" out of a number of experiences and fused by the mind into "significant totalities." It is "total" because we seek a comprehensive framework of interpretation; it is "significant" because we bring whatever is going on in our experience into relationship with our own interests and values.[2] The creation of these contexts of meaning is not necessarily a matter of volitional control; it is part of an ongoing responsiveness to the world that operates on a variety of levels. Meaning is generated through the continual interaction of the person with the situations and events in the world that are perceived as being relevant to the realization of his or her own life.

The world in which we live as persons is encountered under two aspects: the world of persons, whose interpersonal relationships create a dynamic and highly creative social organism, and the natural physical world, whose complex forces and at times forceful coerciveness form the horizon within which human beings have to live. Both aspects merge with each other to create the total situation with which at any juncture the person has to deal. Meaning is thus culled from two levels of experience: from our relationship to the world, and from our relationship to the social organism that is constituted by other human persons. And persons, at all times, have to deal with both as providing the determining context and framework for the accumulation of knowledge.

The question of spirituality, the question of human awareness of God or divine reality must, then, be located within this "total context." To understand human spirituality, we must concern ourselves with the world as a whole; awareness of divine reality does not come purely through participation in the social world alone, nor is it given through the physical world alone. It comes through both, as they form a single world, but within which, at any moment in time, one may have more emphasis than the other. Awareness of God is, in fact, a fusing of two awarenesses given through the two aspects of the world in which we live. Neither exists apart from the other; they are both awarenesses of the same world context.

However, given that it is possible to identify an area of human experience as "spiritual," i.e., as having to do with divine reality, we cannot therefore suppose that it is possible to be concerned with spirituality alone—as something that exists and is a proper object of inquiry in its own right. Such an attitude neglects the persons with whom spirituality has to do. It is, or at least it should be, impossible to study spirituality without also having to study the persons whose spirituality it is.

Indeed, I want to go further; it is only insofar as we belong to human community that spirituality becomes possible at all. Only insofar as we are persons, and as we have become persons within the context of interpersonal community, can there be any sensible talk of spirituality. It is only when the individual can enter into and maintain personal relations with other human persons that the possibility even arises of encountering and forming relations with God.

This does not necessarily preclude the possibility of solitary mystical experience or deny the reality of a hermit's relationship with God; after all, in both cases the experiencer has already been to some extent conditioned by the interpersonal and social relationships into which he was born and brought up. Even if a person subsequently chooses to leave a particular society or social group, his identity has been shaped by the experience of interacting with and responding to other persons; in other words, they know what it is to be a person and enter into personal relationships.

The point being made is that in seeking to study the spiritual nature of human beings, attention has inevitably focused on spirituality to the detriment of focusing on persons. Following Martin Buber, we must insist that relationship with God is inseparable from relationship with other persons. Indeed, it is a mistake to see relationship with God as being something different from our relationships with other persons. The individual comes to exist as a personal being by entering into relationships with other persons; indeed, it is only insofar as there exists such a sphere that he can learn and know what it is to form relationships—can grow to recognize the characteristic elements that constitute personal relations. And only insofar as we can do this *first,* i.e., learn what it is to enter into relationships with other persons, can we then learn and know what it is to enter into a relationship with God. The awareness of God as personal is thus closely bound up with human I-Thou relations since these latter provide the structure and conditions within which awareness of the former can arise. Relationship between persons, and between persons and God are not two separate relations but dual aspects of a single relation. The former relationship is prior to, and forms the basis for the awareness of, the latter.

Why is it, then, that a prior concern with persons has, by and large, suffered neglect? I suggest such neglect can be traced to the prevailing academic spirit which unfortunately haunts education in the English-speaking world. It is an arrogant spirit (at times) of analytic empiricism which is as tyrannical as it is exclusive in its relations with everything it encounters. Not only does it ignore, but what is worse, it appears not even to be capable of understanding the call to be concerned with persons. Such concern, when exercised, attempts to be definitional or stipulative in nature. Such a response not only attempts to deal with persons in an unnaturally detached and generalized manner (with persons in a "universal" sense), but also gradually reduces the concern with persons to a matter of casual indifference.

Yet concern with persons arises in three important respects. In the first place, it arises from the experience of meeting with and reacting to other persons. It is a basic first-order everyday experience of the pleasure, enjoyment, frustration, and puzzlement of being encountered by and forming relationships with the people who surround us. Questions about the nature of persons arise within the context of interpersonal relations, and are indicative of the concerns and interests which stem from living in that context. As such they belong more to the process of continual engagement of what it is to be a person in relation to other persons.[3]

A second source of our concern with persons arises from our involvement with particular persons. Our concern with persons in general is invited in and through our participation in a close circle of those with whom we have friendly or intimate relations. We do not take or treat the people we know as generic exemplars of humanity "in general"; we address them as particular individuals who possess specific characters. And it is precisely their particularity or individuality which is obscured through the adoption of an objectively descriptive stance which treats people as members of a general class. Such a stance invariably creates depersonalizing conditions resulting in the breakdown of relationships and the manner in which members of such a class may be treated. A wider concern with persons naturally emerges from the concern I have toward those with whom I am in relation.

A third source, reflected in the other two, is with myself. In attending to others, I am attending at the same time to what it is to be me. In developing and exploring personal relationships with others, I am engaging in a lifelong process of understanding what it is for me to be a unique personal being. This is probably the dominant reason why we refuse to be treated as anything less than persons. For as David Jenkins rightly notes, if "we really belong in the same categories of classification and description as can be given to all the animals in the zoo, then our uniqueness is gone. And it is not merely our uniqueness as a race which is gone; it is our uniqueness as ourselves."[4]

Clearly much is at stake in the exploration of what it is to be a person; the need to reflect on the nature of personal being and the need to reaffirm the centrality of persons in modern thought possesses a sense of poignancy and urgency that should underpin our efforts. Even at a most basic level, some conception of personal being is necessary if we are to say anything of worth about human societies or practices. Yet as Trigg points out, all too often such conceptions "are merely implicit in the work of various intellectual disciplines."[5] Pittenger points to a similar problem; contemporary society abounds with a multitude of implicit definitions of persons—as economic consumer, political voter, psychological archetype of a national or cultural group, or a spiritual being. All possess an element of truth; but as Pittenger argues, all are "viciously inadequate" when taken in isolation, for that neglects the fact that in our human experience there is no such thing as the "wholly" spiritual, "wholly" political, "wholly" economic.

> The only human nature we know is an embodied humanity. Man in his own experience is neither an animal or an angel; he is no more "spiritual man" exclusively than he is "materialistic man" exclusively. In fact he is just *man*.[6]

The inadequacy of all such definitions lies in a failure to do justice to our experience of persons in everyday life—a failure to take a more holistic view of persons.

Given the significance of what rests on an understanding of persons, it is remarkable that what may be termed the "personalist tradition" in philosophy and theology has apparently made little or no headway in addressing these concerns. Three reasons for this fact can be identified. The first is what can be termed the mysteriousness of persons. Reinhold Niebuhr reflects that one main source of anxiety has been the fact that the human being has constantly been a problem to himself:

> Man has always been his own most vexing problem. . . . Every affirmation which he may make about his own stature, virtue, or place in the cosmos becomes involved in contradictions when fully analyzed. The analysis reveals some presupposition or implication which seems to deny what the proposition intended to affirm.[7]

The atmosphere of vagueness fostered by the assumptions and pre-suppositions with which most people and the majority of academic disciplines proceed is not aided by the apparent indefinability that accompanies talk of the personal. Berdyaev adamantly maintains that "personality is like nothing else in the world, there is nothing with which it can be compared, nothing which can be placed on a level with it."[8] Modern philosophy cannot cope with such an outlook! The uniqueness and distinctive complexity which appears to attach to personal being tends to negate attempts to sharply focus on what is involved in the constitution of persons. This sense of inscrutability is preserved through the supposition that persons are *sui generis* and necessarily mysterious.

Yet this apparently "vague" and "unfocused" view of persons forms the basis of the second reason for the decline of personalism. Such an approach to persons paves the way for a philosophical reductionism that claims to be able to dispel the "mystery" involved in being a person by applying appropriate physical, social, or psychological methods. Stemming primarily from the Anglo-Saxon empiricist tradition, it is argued that the features that constitute personal life can be reduced to nothing but the various factors and forces which are the domain of the relevant discipline. Thus materialist, behaviorist, and functionalist accounts seek to explain the person in exclusively physical terms—persons are complex organizations of matter who function according to the causal interaction of various physical processes.[9] Sociological theories offer an account of persons as being comprised by the network of family and social relationships within which the individual emerges and assumes an identity. Persons are a cumulative product of social forces.[10] Drawing on these ideas, psychological theories emphasize the psychodynamic and subconscious mechanisms responsible for the growth and development of personality.[11]

These reductionist tendencies in turn create theological difficulties. McFadyen passes the judgment that

> talk of human being in our society has been so completely secularized that we find it increasingly difficult to talk of humanity with reference to God in a way which is meaningful in our contemporary situation.[12]

Indeed, it is perhaps no coincidence that in historical terms at least, the emergence and rise of the analytic empiricist tradition in philosophy was accompanied by an equal and corresponding decline in the personalist position. McFadyen's judgment assumes greater poignancy with the recognition that the personalism of the first half of this century was conducted within the context of a metaphysical and ethical theism.

Consequently, the effect on theology has been both deeply felt and widespread in its influence. In particular, two reasons for the decline of personalism in modern theology can be cited. On the one hand, the content of recent theological thought, under the influence of philosophy, no longer finds the concept of the "personality of God" to be significantly important. Writing in 1966, Ramsey observed that to take such concepts as the subject of an academic paper "makes one inevitably old-fashioned, if not entirely out of date. One needs to go back fifty years or more . . . before the subject becomes interesting."[13] Ramsey is sure "the topic is more significant than it might appear to be at first sight," and attempts to reexpress the central insights that lie behind the term's usage. But nevertheless, his efforts have fallen on largely deaf ears.

Yet on the other hand, where theology has been interested in persons, modern philosophy has viewed with widespread suspicion the kind of person being encountered. In particular, such suspicions are directed at what are seen as the largely discredited Cartesian assumptions underlying much modern theology. Kerr levels the charge that "modern theologians are well aware of the difficulties that the modern philosophy of the self has created." However, his suspicion is that

> versions of the mental ego of Cartesianism are ensconced in a great deal of Christian thinking, and that many theologians regard this as inevitable, and even desirable. The appeal of some theological writing also seems inexplicable unless it touches crypto-Cartesian assumptions which many readers share.[14]

Thatcher also believes that too often "the credibility of theism suffers from a close association with Cartesian dualism," attempting to show that "neither the Christian concept of God nor the Christian understanding of the human person requires such a dualism in order to be credible."[15]

But in avoiding an unfashionable Cartesian dualism, and in response to or as a consequence of a prevailing mood of philosophical cynicism and reductionism, theology has mistakenly retreated behind what might be termed a confessional view of persons. Indeed, this third reason for the decline of personalism has created an anthropology that is remote from our everyday experience of persons and dogmatic in its dialogue with other disciplines. Thus Schwöbel argues that theology is confronted both with the challenge to "clarify what is *distinctively theological* in its accounts of personhood" and with the "task of finding criteria for what is *authentically Christian* in theological concepts of the person."[16]

Yet this project is conducted on the assumption that "Christian faith is irreducibly trinitarian in character," and consequently, an authentic response to and engagement with secular views of personhood must be "necessarily trinitarian." He concludes that trinitarian thinking "determines what can be theologically said about God as well as what can be stated about the world and humankind."[17] However, the effect of seeking to be distinctively Christian in relation to persons is a failure to take seriously the reality of persons as experienced in daily life.

Schwöbel denies this is the case, asserting that "reflection starts from the personal particularity of persons as it is constituted in their person in personal communion."[18] Yet we must question to what extent this is true, given the explicit acknowledgment that such "reflection" is already conditioned by a priori trinitarian considerations which subsequently determine the nature of what is found in the world. Indeed, this suspicion is affirmed when Schwöbel continues by arguing that

> the question is not primarily how reflection on human personality can offer grounds for the affirmation of divine personality, but rather how the insights concerning the character of divine personhood can be creatively applied to elucidate the understanding of human personhood.[19]

This approach does not start from the "particularity of persons"; rather, the nature of the persons being discerned is already delimited by a framework of theological assumptions. Personal reality is made to conform to an agenda that does not in fact stem from what we experience in our relations with other people. Schwöbel confesses that both approaches—from human to divine personhood or vice versa—cannot be "ultimately incompatible if it is the created destiny of human persons to be in the image of God and their eschatological promise to participate through the Spirit in the personal relationship of the Son to the Father."[20] This confessional stance both motivates his anthropology while at the same time removing it from the arena of modern debate.

A theological approach to persons does not need to be confessional. Nor, in keeping with the spirit of contemporary philosophy, does talk about persons have to represent either a certain looseness of thought (a charge leveled by those firmly situated within the analytic tradition[21]), or deal with a subject that is ultimately focused on a linguistic fiction.[22] The need to rethink at the most basic and fundamental levels what it is to be a person; how persons relate to each other on a social, national, and international level; the structure of relationships that exist between persons, and between persons and God—all need careful, yet creative attention. Once these questions have been addressed, then we can come back to the question of spirituality.

What it is to be a person is a becoming rather than a being. Over the course of a life in time, and in interaction with those who surround us, we become persons. Persons are always open to what they will become; they are in a process of ongoing creation in and through the relationships they form and develop. The living person is a stage in a process of becoming, a process which realizes the potential already possessed, but which itself becomes the next stage and resource for further development. The process of becoming a person is never complete and never finished.

The quality of incompleteness—the recognition of the unfinished character of the project that we as persons are—necessarily entails the continual need for exploration of and reflection on the nature of personal being. At no stage will it be possible to arrive at the "essence" of a person, or to fix on a timeless, noncontextual truth that applies to all persons and at all times. Exploration of persons, whether it is philosophical, theological, sociological, psychological, anthropological, or literary in character, means the acceptance of having to live with unresolved mysteries, tensions, paradoxes, and even contradictions; the study of persons demands the continual questionableness of what is said about them, and the perpetual need to revise, rethink, and restate what we imagine to lie at the heart of personhood.

Like the process of becoming characteristic of persons, discussion about persons is also an unfinished process, one which leaves us feeling uneasy in its incompleteness, unsatisfied that we have in any sense captured the heart of what it is to be a person, but spurred on to continue the exploration and sustain the conversation. Part of that conversation will doubtless include the spiritual "nature" of persons, or the spiritual "dimension" of personal existence; but it will be a conversation that is at least properly grounded in the context of a holistic enterprise to discover our personhood, and not based on the assumption that spirituality is a phenomenon other than and of equal status to personal being. For it is in the latter that we must ground any attempt to explore spirituality.

NOTES

1. The phrase is used by M. Polanyi, *Personal Knowledge: Towards a Post-Critical Philosophy* (Chicago: University of Chicago Press, 1962).

2. For a more detailed account of the way this process operates, see H. H. Farmer, *The World and God: A Study of Prayer, Providence and Miracle in Christian Experience,* The Library of Constructive Theology (London: Nisbet and Co., Ltd., 1935), ch. 2.

3. David Jenkins captures this sense well in *What Is Man?* (London: SCM Press Ltd., 1970), ch. 1.

4. Ibid., p. 11.

5. R. Trigg, *Ideas of Human Nature: An Historical Introduction* (Oxford: Basil Blackwell, 1988), p. 3.

6. W. N. Pittenger, *The Christian Understanding of Human Nature* (London: James Nisbet and Co. Ltd., 1964), p. 16.

7. R. Niebuhr, *The Nature and Destiny of Man: A Christian Interpretation,* vol. 1 (New York: Charles Scribner's Sons, 1941), p. 1. Pittenger holds a similar position—see *The Christian Understanding of Human Nature,* p. 13.

8. N. Berdyaev, *Slavery and Freedom,* trans. R. M. French (New York: Charles Scribner's Sons, 1944), p. 21.

9. See D. M. Armstrong, *A Materialist Theory of the Mind,* International Library of Philosophy and Scientific Method (London: Routledge and Kegan Paul, 1968); P. Churchland, *Matter and Consciousness* (Cambridge, Mass.: MIT Press, 1984); H. Putnam, *Mind, Language and Reality,* Philosophical Papers, vol. 2 (Cambridge: Cambridge University Press, 1975), ch. 16.

10. See G. H. Mead, *Mind, Self and Society from the Standpoint of a Social Behaviorist* (Chicago: University of Chicago Press, 1934); J. Ogilvy, *Many Dimensional Man* (Oxford: Oxford University Press, 1977); R. Harré, *Social Being* (Oxford: Basil Blackwell, 1979).

11. See R. Harré, *Personal Being: A Theory for Individual Psychology* (Oxford: Basil Blackwell, 1983); J. Glover, *I: The Philosophy and Psychol-*

ogy of Personal Identity (Middlesex: Penguin Books, 1988); S. Stich, *From Folk Psychology to Cognitive Science: The Case Against Belief* (Cambridge, Mass.: MIT Press, 1983).

12. A. McFadyen, *The Call to Personhood: A Christian Theory of the Individual in Social Relationships* (Cambridge: Cambridge University Press, 1990), p. 10.

13. I. T. Ramsey, "A Personal God," in *Prospect for Theology,* ed. F. G. Healey (London: James Nisbet and Co. Ltd., 1966), pp. 55–71, quote on p. 55.

14. F. Kerr, *Theology After Wittgenstein* (Oxford: Basil Blackwell, 1988), p. 10.

15. D. Thatcher, "Christian Theism and the Concept of a Person," in *Persons and Personality,* ed. A. Peacocke and G. Gillett, Ian Ramsey Centre Publication No. 1 (Oxford: Basil Blackwell, 1987), pp. 180–96, quote on p. 180.

16. C. Schwöbel, *Persons, Divine and Human,* ed. C. Schwöbel and C. Gunton (Edinburgh: T and T Clark, 1991), p. 9.

17. Ibid., p. 11.

18. Ibid., pp. 12–13.

19. Ibid., p. 13.

20. Ibid.

21. For example, see the following remarks made by Richard Swinburne: "It is one of the intellectual tragedies of our age that when philosophy in English-speaking countries has developed high standards of argument and clear thinking, the style of theological writing has been largely influenced by the continental philosophy of Existentialism, which, despite its considerable other merits, has been distinguished by a very loose and sloppy style of argument. If argument has a place in theology, large-scale theology needs clear and rigorous argument" (*The Coherence of Theism* [Oxford: Clarendon Press 1977], p. 7).

22. This is a position adopted by D. Parfit (*Reasons and Persons*) and S. Collins (*Selfless Persons*) among others.

Part Five
Spirituality and Science

14

Teilhard and Tipler: Critical Reflections

H. James Birx

In this century, one of the great spiritualists was Pierre Teilhard de Chardin (1881–1955), a remarkable human being who has had a profound influence on the religious thought of our time.[1] He especially appealed to those liberal religionists who interpreted this cosmos in terms of evolutionary science and process theology. To understand and appreciate this great thinker, it is necessary to consider those major events that helped form his unique interpretation of the place our species occupies within this dynamic universe. Teilhard's worldview represents a challenge to traditional religious beliefs grounded in the ideas of Aristotle and Aquinas but, at the same time, his vision offers a new framework for those believers who take science seriously and concern themselves about the future of humankind.

During his formative years, Teilhard was greatly influenced by both of his parents: his father was an avid naturalist while his mother was a devout mystic. Therefore, at an early age, Teilhard became interested in both science and religion. Throughout his life, this dual interest would remain with him. In fact, Teilhard spent his mature

Reprinted from the *Journal for the Critical Study of Religion, Ethics, and Society* 1, no. 1 (Winter/Spring 1996). By permission of the publisher.

years in a bold attempt to present a personal interpretation of our species within this universe that he thought did justice to both modern science and traditional faith (at least in terms of the basic religious beliefs of the Judeo-Christian tradition).

Shedding light on Teilhard's devotion to religion, one recalls that as a youngster he admired his so-called secret genie of iron, which he hid and, from time to time, would seek out as an assurance that in nature there is something that remains permanent. One day after a rainstorm, the young Teilhard discovered that his piece of iron had rusted and he tells us that he then threw himself on the ground and cried the bitterest tears of his life. Following this event, he would look elsewhere in his personal search for one essential thing in reality that is free from change and finitude.

In order to become "most perfect" as he put it, the adolescent Teilhard chose to become a Jesuit priest. He entered this religious society at the same time that he was developing a deeper interest in both geology and paleontology. As a novitiate in the order, he was sent to Egypt, where he spent several years teaching and doing research (he even had several scientific articles in geopaleontology published during this time).[2] While working at the Holy Family College in Egypt, Teilhard remained a devout believer in Roman Catholicism. Certainly, the exposure to multiple cultures broadened his perspective and prepared him for the worldwide journeys he would take during his lifetime as a scientist and Jesuit priest interested in rocks and fossils and, eventually, anthropology.

While completing his theological training in England, Teilhard happened to read Henri Bergson's major work, *Creative Evolution* (1907).[3] It was this book, and not the writings of Charles Darwin,[4] that convinced Teilhard of the truth of evolution. As a result, the young Jesuit and scientist would devote the rest of his life to a personal attempt at reconciling science and theology within an evolutionary interpretation of this dynamic universe. This unorthodox believer now focused special attention on the unique position he believed our species still occupies within this unfolding cosmos. Surely, his holistic synthesis grounded in both a scientific and religious framework would require him to reinterpret the basic traditional beliefs of Roman Catholicism in particular, and Christianity in general, in terms of the fact of evolution. To do so, it is understandable that Teilhard would come to see spirit pervading the entire universe and the process of evolution as being both progressive and directional. Furthermore, he envisioned the end of humankind partaking in some mystical unity involving a personal God and the unifying power of spiritual love reaching its end-goal at the completion of teleological evolution on our earth.

After his theology studies, Teilhard returned to France to finish his doctorate in geopaleontology and to serve as a stretcher-bearer in World War I. Again, we get a significant insight into this remarkable man in terms of his spiritual development when we read about the three mystical experiences he had while participating in the global war.[5] It is to Teilhard's credit that he emerged from his participation in battle even more optimistic than ever, for he saw the evolving earth from his geological perspective and held that developing humankind as a whole was preparing to unify this planet in terms of a collective consciousness focusing more on the survival and fulfillment of our species in terms of the religious values of Christianity.

During his first visit to China in 1923, Teilhard gave his mystical "mass on the world" in the Gobi Desert. Later, in his spiritual quest to unite science and theology, he boldly wrote a personal essay on Original Sin in which he dealt with the problem of evil from both a cosmic and human perspective. He saw evil as a necessary component of an evolving but unfinished universe which, through time and change, is perfecting itself from matter through life and thought to a spiritual end-goal in terms of a collective consciousness. Copies of this unorthodox interpretation of Original Sin fell into the hands of Teilhard's superiors. Fearful that this personal belief might be interpreted as heretical and therefore result in his removal from the Jesuit order, the society found it best to both silence and exile Teilhard before any further controversy might require more drastic measures. Consequently, Teilhard was sent back to China where he wrote his first book, *The Divine Milieu* (1927).[6] Unfortunately, he was not allowed to teach and only his scientific works could be published.

Teilhard the Jesuit evolutionist now found himself a geologist at the Cenozoic Laboratory of the Peking Union Medical College. With appropriate irony, he participated in excavating the Western Hills near Zhoukoudian, where the fossil hominid remains of *Sinanthropus pekinensis* were being discovered. This unique opportunity extended Teilhard's interests to physical anthropology, and brought him world fame as a result of his popularizations of this important discovery for understanding and appreciating human evolution.[7]

These years spent isolated in China not only gave Teilhard unique opportunities to do further scientific research, but also provided time in which he could read and think as well as write down his own reflections on cosmic evolution in general and the future of our own species in particular. The quintessential outcome was his masterpiece, *The Phenomenon of Man* (1938–1940).[8] This book offered a synthesis of science and theology which would, Teilhard thought, clearly show that humankind still occupies a privileged place and central position within this dynamic universe in terms of spirit and a theistic framework. Unfortunately, like his first book and the later *Man's Place in Nature* (1950),[9] this major work was never published during his lifetime. Therefore, the Jesuit evolutionist never had an opportunity to answer his critics, many of whom found his work vague or ambiguous or even erroneous.

Teilhard struggled with his devotion to science and theology, wishing to do justice to both empirical evidence and his religious beliefs. Clearly, Teilhard's life was a way of the cross for he accepted the fact of evolution as a spiritualist during a time when this scientific theory was a threat to traditional religionists who rightly maintained that it contradicted their deepest commitments to orthodox faith. Although Teilhard would never live to see his three books in print, he nevertheless anticipated that his ideas and beliefs would be published after his death and that they would, in turn, have an enormous influence on those who read them. During his life, Teilhard was exemplary of a religionist devoted to science and a scientist devoted to religion. In an age of analysis, he demands our respect for his bold attempt at a synthesis.

The Teilhardian synthesis is grounded in four basic ideas which mediate between science and religion. Under rigorous scrutiny, it can be seen that these concepts are used to interpret evolution in such a way as to give preference to spirit over matter while maintaining the uniqueness of our species despite advances in the special sciences (e.g., astronomy, biology, and anthropology) and rigorous reflection that strongly suggests atheistic materialism or at least philosophical pantheism.

As a pervasive monist, Teilhard always maintained that the whole universe is evolving spirit (since matter is energy and, for him, all energy is ultimately spirit). He distinguishes between the mental within-of-things (radial energy) and the physical without-of-things (tangential energy). Nevertheless, one way or another, he tells us that there is only one energy operating throughout this dynamic universe and it is, in the last analysis, spiritual energy that is evolving from the elementary particles of this cosmos to that final end-goal yet to be reached in the distant future. Furthermore, evolving reality is a cosmogenesis, i.e., this dynamic cosmos is ultimately a personalizing universe. In sharp contrast, secular humanists assert that this universe is obviously grounded in matter and energy.

By examining the entire sweep of cosmic history, Teilhard argues that a law of evolution has been operating throughout the entire history of this universe. He held that it is the accelerating law of complexity/consciousness that gives direction and purpose to cosmic evolution. As things evolve, they become both more complex and more conscious so that the most highly evolved object in this universe is the human being as a self-conscious person. Consequently, this teleological process of convolution or involution will result in the formation of a unified humankind in terms of a collective consciousness. As such, this spiritual unity of our species on the earth will be the end-goal of this personalizing universe. In short, this spiritual universe exists to produce persons who, in turn, will find their fulfillment at the end of planetary history in a spiritual unity. For the secular humanist, this argument to design ignores cosmic chaos as well as the pervasive chance and awesome inefficiency throughout the evolution and extinction of life (not to mention its glaring anthropocentric stance).

Throughout cosmogenesis, Teilhard argues that there have been critical thresholds crossed resulting in the advancement of spirit from matter through life to consciousness. Unlike the philosopher Henri Bergson, who saw creative evolution as a diverging process, the Jesuit priest and scientist Teilhard saw evolution as a converging process due to the finite sphericity of this planet. Geogenesis, biogenesis, and noogenesis have formed the geosphere, biosphere, and noosphere, respectively. Or, like a pyramid, evolution is moving from its material base through life toward an end-point of collective consciousness as the ultimate goal of teleological evolution grounded in the "directed chance" throughout the unfolding of complexity/consciousness within cosmic evolution in general and earth history in particular. The crossing of the latest critical threshold resulted in the emergence of the unique human zoological level that has stayed a single species physically reflexing around this planet while mentally reflecting as a result of self-consciousness grounded in the centralized complexity of its nervous system and brain. For Teilhard, it also resulted in the immortal soul. Briefly, the teleological evolution of spirit has finally produced persons who now represent the ongoing direction of consciousness on the earth. As such, the still emerging and spiritually converging noosphere is more and more a global envelope of immortal souls focused on a Supreme Person as the loving center of all reality.

Teilhard uses these critical thresholds to argue for both the uniqueness of life and the special place of thought within this evolving universe. Secular humanists, however, acknowledge the historical continuity and contingency throughout organic evolution as well as the tenuous existence of life and thought in material reality.

One is not surprised that, as a religious mystic, Teilhard saw the end of evolution in terms of an Omega Point, which, in the final analysis, is a mystical unity of a collectivity of persons on the earth with a personal God as the creator, sustainer, director, and end-goal of spiritual evolution. At the completion of human evolution on this planet, the collective consciousness of our species will detach itself from the earth, transcend space and time, and merge with the loving God-Omega at the Omega Point. This last creative unity or collective synthesis is the end-goal of human evolution in terms of spiritual existence that results in a process panentheism becoming a true pantheism (although one wonders what happens to the rest of this universe which does not participate in the final spiritual synthesis). In short, the Teilhardian cosmology is only a planetology.

It is puzzling that Teilhard as a geologist and paleontologist who thought of earth history in terms of many millions of years would, in considering the ultimate end of human evolution, see this Omega Point being formed only a few thousand years in the future. No doubt, this is due to Teilhard's giving eschatology a privileged position in his interpretation of this dynamic universe and the place of humankind within it. He never seriously considered a plurality of universes, the possibility that intelligent life exists elsewhere, or the probability that our species will populate other planets and perhaps venture to the stars and other galaxies.[10]

It is obvious that there is an enormous difference between the fact of evolution on the one hand and the various interpretations of this process in the scholarly literature.[11] Fortunately, Teilhard is no comfort to biblical fundamentalists or so-called scientific creationists. Yet, his interpretation of evolution does give priority to Christian theology and cosmic mysticism rather than to science and reason. As a result, it is not surprising that his spiritual synthesis was unconvincing to materialist scientists and, at the same time, unacceptable to rational philosophers and traditional religionists.

Nevertheless, one may easily admire Teilhard's moral fiber and intellectual acumen. He was deeply religious, and had a profound concern for the survival and fulfillment of our species on earth. One may certainly respect his dedication to scientific research and a holistic outlook. The lasting value of Teilhard's search for a cosmic phenomenology and an ultra-anthropology is his steadfast acknowledgment of the fact of evolution and its far-reaching implications for science, philosophy, theology, and mysticism.

For the secular humanist, it is not theology and mysticism but science and reason that will judge whether a synthesis of facts and beliefs represents a plausible system for understanding and appreciating the world and our place within it, or if the synthesis is merely a serious attempt to deceive oneself in order to save outmoded religious commitments despite scientific progress and rigorous reflection.

During the last decade of this century, the mathematical physicist and self-proclaimed atheist Frank J. Tipler has also presented a personal interpretation of this dynamic universe that focuses on the final outcome for our species at the end of the world. His major work is *The Physics of Immortality* (1994).[12] Like Teilhard de Chardin, Tipler offers a sweeping synthesis of science and religion which he claims supports a cosmology that offers personal immortality for all human beings before the big crunch brings about the end of life and consciousness within this physical universe. Of course, the promise of eternal life appeals to any human being who values existence against the background of inevitable death on the individual level and the future end of this physical universe on the cosmic scale.

Unlike Teilhard, however, Tipler's vision extends billions of years into the future and takes the whole universe into consideration when it deals with the ultimate destiny of all life and all consciousness at the end of this world. Rejecting both the heat death of Hermann von Helmholtz and the eternal recurrence of Friedrich Nietzsche as likely outcomes of evolving life in this material universe, Tipler makes an outlandish speculation that offers us a physical cosmology as a natural theology. Inspired by Freeman Dyson, who suggests the possibility of infinite life in an open-ended expanding universe, Tipler has imagined a cosmic model from global general relativity that is concerned with the ultimate future of organic evolution in a closed and contracting universe. Furthermore, his mixture of scientific concepts and theistic language is very confusing.

For Tipler, the next stage of advancing evolution will be the emergence of a robotic life form that will spread throughout this cosmos. In fact, billions of years from now, it will be necessary for these super-intelligent robots as information-processing machines to carefully control the collapse of this universe. According to Tipler, the final anthropic principle as the correct boundary condition maintains that this evolving universe exists only because all life and all consciousness will exist forever in infinite subjective time at the end of finite objective time. Immortality will happen in a cosmic computer of the far future. This desired result will be a perfect computer simulation (true emulation) of all possible visible universes as an eternal unity in cyberspace or virtual reality, resulting in personal immortality for all previous self-consciousness so that everlasting existence will be accomplished despite the end of this physical universe. Of course, it is possible that cosmic civilization will fail to become united or to control the collapse of this universe.

Instead of Teilhard's collective spiritualism, one has Tipler's emulated collective consciousness. As did Teilhard, Tipler refers to God-Omega as the end-goal of cosmic evolution. However, Teilhard's distinct God-Omega merges with humanity at the spiritual Omega Point as a final transcendent event of mystical significance while Tipler's material Omega Point is an emergent cosmic event that becomes the loving God-Omega at the end of this dying universe.

Tipler's interpretation of human evolution is grounded in the anthropic cosmological principle:[13] this universe is the way that it is so that human beings can exist or, if this universe were not the way that it is, then human observers could not exist. For an evolutionist, this sounds more like a tautology than any profound statement about cosmic reality. Obviously, neither trilobites nor dinosaurs could have existed if the universe were different than it was during their evolutionary success. But as we know, all trilobites and all dinosaurs are now extinct. And it is certainly anthropocentric in the extreme to maintain that the entire history of this cosmos was merely a preparation for the emergence of human life on this planet. Furthermore, there is absolutely no guarantee in evolution that our own species will survive long enough to create superior robots or, for that matter, that superior robots will survive long enough to guarantee our resurrection as emulations in a computer at the end of this universe. Even if robotic life or their distant descendents spread throughout and engulf this entire universe, why would superior robots billions of years from now even care any more for us than we now care about a bacterium that lived billions of years ago? Clearly, a long and complex series of predictions and assumptions is necessary to get to a point where cosmic life as infinite knowledge and infinite energy does in fact become a God-Omega Point capable of emulating all of us and all possible life forms for immortality in a virtual reality. For some, this vision sounds more like science fiction than serious speculation.

Surely, there is no guarantee that the laws of physics and principles of reason as we understand them today will remain unchanged over the billions and trillions of years to come. Neither Teilhard nor Tipler take seriously the possibility that superior beings with awesome technologies could now exist among the galaxies. In fact, such sidereal aliens may be utterly indifferent to or even evil toward the future evolution of our species.

Of course, our scientific knowledge of nature is incomplete and therefore rational speculations are often necessary. Yet the frameworks of Teilhard and Tipler are ultimately grounded in beliefs, wishes, and desires that support an unwarranted anthropocentric view of this universe. In their writings, what science and theology converge on is a pseudophilosophy that satisfies neither rigorous naturalists nor orthodox religionists. In the face of inevitable death, one can easily sympathize with a human being who desires personal immortality. However, the desire for personal immortality in terms of spirit is no guarantee that everlasting life will be given to any human being in a physical universe indifferent to its existence. One consequence of the fact of evolution is crucial: this physical universe exists without a personal god or conscious observers. In the last analysis, material reality preceded the emergence of our species and, no doubt, will continue to endure long after the human animal has become extinct.

For secular humanists,[14] the challenge of evolution is to save and enrich and fulfill human life, despite pervasive problems and the inevitability of death. The ongoing quest for truth needs free, open, critical, and responsible inquiry. It is science and reason, not theology and mysticism, that offer human beings a long and fulfilling and joyful life within a cold and violent universe uninterested in our emerging species with its personal goals and entrenched illusions.

NOTES

1. For an introduction to Teilhard's life and thought, refer to H. James Birx, *Interpreting Evolution: Darwin and Teilhard de Chardin* (Amherst, N.Y.: Prometheus Books, 1991), esp. pp. 178–222. See also Mary Lukas and Ellen Lukas, *Teilhard* (New York: McGraw Hill, 1981).

2. Concerning Teilhard's impressive scientific publications, refer to Nicole Schmitz-Moorman and Karl Schmitz-Moorman, eds., *Pierre Teilhard de Chardin: Scientific Works,* 11 vols. (Olten und Freiburg im Breisgau: Walter-Verlag, 1971).

3. Refer to Henri Bergson, *Creative Evolution* (New York: Modern Library, 1944). See also "Henri Bergson: Creative Evolution," in H. James Birx, *Interpreting Evolution: Darwin and Teilhard de Chardin* (Amherst, N.Y.: Prometheus Books, 1991), pp. 167–76; and Gilles Beleuze, *Bergsonism* (New York: Zone Books, 1991).

4. For an introduction to Darwin's life and thought, refer to H. James Birx, *Interpreting Evolution: Darwin and Teilhard de Chardin* (Amherst, N.Y.: Prometheus Books, 1991), esp. pp. 112–65. See also John Bowlby, *Charles Darwin: A New Life* (New York: W. W. Norton, 1991); and Adrian Desmond and James Moore, *Darwin* (New York: Warner Books, 1991). Of related interest, see also H. James Birx, "Ernst Haeckel," *New Zealand Rationalist and Humanist* (September 1994): 2–4.

5. Refer to Pierre Teilhard de Chardin, *Hymn of the Universe* (New York: Harper and Row, 1968), pp. 41–55.

6. Refer to Pierre Teilhard de Chardin, *The Divine Milieu,* rev. ed. (New York: Harper Torchbooks, 1968).

7. For an introduction to human evolution, refer to H. James Birx, *Human Evolution* (Springfield, Ill.: Charles C. Thomas, 1988). See also Donald Johanson, Lenora Johanson, and Blake Edgar, *Ancestors: In Search of Human Origins* (New York: Villard Books, 1994); and Richard Leakey, *The Origin of Humankind* (New York: BasicBooks, 1994).

8. Refer to Pierre Teilhard de Chardin, *The Phenomenon of Man,* 2d ed. (New York: Harper Torchbooks, 1965). See also "Teilhard de Chardin," in Julian Huxley, *Evolutionary Humanism* (Amherst, N.Y.: Prometheus Books, 1992), pp. 202–17.

9. Refer to Pierre Teilhard de Chardin, *Man's Place in Nature: The Human Zoological Group* (New York: Harper and Row, 1966).

10. Refer to H. James Birx, "The Challenge of Exoevolution," *Free Inquiry* 15, no. 1 (Winter 1994/95): 32–34.

11. Refer to H. James Birx, *Theories of Evolution* (Springfield, Ill.: Charles C. Thomas, 1984). The four major interpretations of evolution are: mechanistic materialism, creative vitalism, finalistic spiritualism, and cosmic mysticism. Of course, these interpretations may overlap as they do in the evolutionary worldview of Pierre Teilhard de Chardin.

12. Refer to Frank J. Tipler, *The Physics of Immortality: Modern Cosmology, God and the Resurrection of the Dead* (New York: Doubleday, 1994). See also John D. Barrow and Frank J. Tipler, *The Anthropic Cosmological Principle* (New York: Oxford University Press, 1986). Of related interest, see also Victor J. Stenger, "Scientific Nitwit Atheist Proves Existence of God," *Free Inquiry* 15, no. 2 (Spring 1995): 54–55.

13. Refer to Reinhard Breuer, *The Anthropic Principle: Man as the Focal Point of Nature* (Cambridge, Mass.: Birkhauser Boston, 1991); and F. Bertola and U. Curi, eds., *The Anthropic Principle* (New York: Cambridge University Press, 1993). For an introduction to theoretical physics, see Stephen W. Hawking, *A Brief History of Time: From the Big Bang to Black Holes* (New York: Bantam Books, 1988) and *Black Holes and Baby Universes: And Other Essays* (New York: Bantam Books, 1993). Of related interest, see also Freeman Dyson, *Infinite in All Directions* (New York: Harper and Row, 1988); G. F. R. Ellis and D. H. Coule, *Life at the End of the Universe* (University of Cape Town, 1992); Marvin L. Minsky, *Computation: Finite and Infinite Machines* (Englewood Cliffs, N.J.: Prentice-Hall, 1967); and Roger Penrose, *The Emperor's New Mind: Concerning Computers, Minds, and the Laws of Physics* (Oxford: Oxford University Press, 1989).

14. Refer to David Goicoechea, John Luik, and Tim Madigan, eds., *The Question of Humanism: Challenges and Possibilities* (Amherst, N.Y.: Prometheus Books, 1991); and John Ryder, ed., *American Philosophic Naturalism in the Twentieth Century* (Amherst, N.Y.: Prometheus Books, 1994). Of special interest, see also Marvin Farber, *Naturalism and Subjectivism* (Albany: State University of New York Press, 1968); and Paul Kurtz, *Eupraxophy: Living Without Religion* (Amherst, N.Y.: Prometheus Books, 1989).

REFERENCES

Barrow, John D., and Frank J. Tipler. 1994. *The Anthropic Cosmological Principle.* Oxford: Oxford University Press.

Berra, Tim M. 1990. *Evolution and the Myth of Creationism: A Basic Guide to the Facts in the Evolution Debate.* Stanford, Calif.: Stanford University Press.

Birx, H. James. 1989. "Darwin and Teilhard: Some Final Thoughts." *Proteus: A Journal of Ideas* 6, no. 2 (Fall): 38–46.

———. 1991. *Interpreting Evolution: Darwin and Teilhard de Chardin.* Amherst, N.Y.: Prometheus Books.

———. 1994. "The Challenge of Exoevolution." *Free Inquiry* 15, no. 1 (Winter): 32–34.

———. 1995. "Friedrich Nietzsche and Humanism." *Ethical Record* 100, no. 4 (April): 20–25.

Cunningham, Suzanne. 1996. *Philosophy and the Darwinian Legacy.* Rochester, N.Y.: University of Rochester Press.

Cziko, Gary. 1995. *Without Miracles: Universal Selection Theory and the Second Darwinian Revolution.* Cambridge, Mass.: MIT Press.

Dawkins, Richard. 1995. *River Out of Eden: A Darwinian View of Life.* New York: BasicBooks.

de Duve, Christian. 1995. *Vital Dust: Life as a Cosmic Imperative.* New York: BasicBooks.

Dennett, Daniel C. 1995. *Darwin's Dangerous Idea: Evolution and the Meanings of Life.* New York: Simon and Schuster.

Farber, Paul Lawrence. 1994. *The Temptations of Evolutionary Ethics.* Berkeley: University of California Press.

Gould, Stephen Jay. 1990. *Wonderful Life: The Burgess Shale and the Nature of History.* New York: W. W. Norton.

Haeckel, Ernst. 1992. *The Riddle of the Universe.* Amherst, N.Y.: Prometheus Books. Refer to the introduction by H. James Birx, pp. ix–xiv.

Huxley, Julian. 1992. *Evolutionary Humanism.* Amherst, N.Y.: Prometheus Books, esp. pp. 202–17. Refer to the introduction by H. James Birx, pp. vii–xii.

Leakey, Richard, and Roger Lewin. 1995. *The Sixth Extinction: Patterns of Life and the Future of Humankind.* New York: Doubleday.

Madigan, Timothy J. 1996. "Humanism and Human Malleability." *Free Inquiry* 16, no. 2 (Spring): 51–52.

Margulis, Lynn, and Dorian Sagan. 1995. *What Is Life?* New York: Simon and Schuster.

Mayr, Ernst. 1991. *One Long Argument: Charles Darwin and the Genesis of Modern Evolutionary Thought.* Cambridge, Mass.: Harvard University Press.

Nietzsche, Friedrich. 1993. *Thus Spake Zarathustra.* Amherst, N.Y.: Prometheus Books. Refer to the introduction by H. James Birx, pp. 13–27.

Plotkin, Henry. 1994. *Darwin Machines and the Nature of Knowledge.* Cambridge, Mass.: Harvard University Press.

Rachels, James. 1991. *Created from Animals: The Moral Implications of Darwinism.* Oxford: Oxford University Press.

Richard, Robert. 1992. *The Meaning of Evolution.* Chicago: University of Chicago Press.

Ridley, Mark, ed. 1996. *The Darwin Reader,* 2d ed. New York: W. W. Norton.

Stenger, Victor J. 1995. *The Unconscious Quantum: Metaphysics in Modern Physics and Cosmology.* Amherst, N.Y.: Prometheus Books.

Tattersall, Ian. 1995. *The Fossil Trail: How We Know What We Think We Know About Human Evolution.* New York: Oxford University Press.

Vitzthum, Richard C. 1995. *Materialism: An Affirmative History and Definition.* Amherst, N.Y.: Prometheus Books.

Ward, Peter. 1994. *The End of Evolution: On Mass Extinctions and the Preservation of Biodiversity.* New York: Bantam Books.

Weiner, Jonathan. 1994. *The Beak of the Finch: A Story of Evolution in Our Time.* New York: Alfred A. Knopf.

White, Michael, and John Gribbin. 1995. *Darwin: A Life in Science.* New York: Dutton.

Wilson, Edward O. 1992. *The Diversity of Life.* Cambridge, Mass.: Belknap Press.

Wyller, Arne A. 1996. *The Planetary Mind.* Aspen, Colo.: MacMurray and Beck.

15

Spiritualism, Neospirituality, and the Paranormal

Paul Kurtz

The term *spirituality* has been carefully analyzed and dissected. Like "justice," "truth," "beauty," or "virtue," it has meant all things to all men and women. More often than not it is used in a vague and ambiguous way. Some writers use the term metaphorically; they extol "spiritual growth," which means the development of "higher" moral, aesthetic, and intellectual qualities of experience, as contrasted with "lower" material interests. Traditionally, the term *spiritual* was considered to be the special domain of religious institutions, which cultivated prayer, devotion, and piety, as distinguished from purely secular interests. The proponents of spirituality have usually related the spiritual to the "mystical" dimensions of experience, which, it is alleged, open us to a sacred, divine, or transcendental realm. Some people have identified the "spirit" with the "immortal soul," or "the self," which, they have held, is separable from the body and can exist before and after death. Some have used "spirits" to denote ghosts, apparitions, or other occult entities. There are many other meanings: in America, "spirituals" refers to hymns sung by African Americans in Baptist churches; in Scotland, "spirits" refer to Scotch whiskey, which is distilled from malted barley.

The term *spirituality* has become very popular today. Some think we are undergoing a new wave of spirituality. They point to the recrudescence of fundamentalist and evangelical movements worldwide. But there is another aspect of the growth of neospirituality, and this relates to the apparent increase in belief in paranormal phenomena outside of and often in opposition to the traditional churches, temples, and mosques. This has often been called the "New Age."

Actually, this sociological trend goes back to the nineteenth century. Its precursor was known as "spiritualism." In North America, the land where bizarre cults are wont to sprout up and thrive, it began in Hydesville, in upstate New York (known as the "burnt out district") fifty miles east of Buffalo and not far from where the Mormonism of Joseph Smith was spawned. The immediate founders of spiritualism in 1848 were the Fox sisters, two young girls of eight and ten, who were allegedly able to communicate with discarnate spirits by receiving messages rapped from the "other side." The Fox sisters were heralded as mediums, and they were exhibited worldwide. In a period of ten years, thousands of mediums appeared in America; the same phenomena occurred in Britain (D. D. Home was perhaps the most famous) and in Europe (no doubt the most notorious medium was Eusapia Palladino). Spiritualism held that departed spirits were able to communicate with the living by means of physical manifestations such as table-turning, rapping, levitation, and voice transmission. Mediumship became so widespread in North America and Europe that many scientific researchers, such as Michael Faraday, resolved to investigate the mediums' claims and see if they were genuine or if alternative physical explanations could be given. The Society for Psychical Research (SPR) was established in England in 1882, led by Henry Sidgwick of Cambridge and many eminent philosophers and scientists, and the American Society for Psychical Research in 1885, headed by the noted philosopher William James, founder of the first psychological laboratory at Harvard.

Spiritualism offered a unique interpretation of reality. Given the challenge of Darwin's theory of evolution, spiritualism provided some comfort to those who felt their religious faith challenged; and the founders of the SPR were excited because they believed that for the first time, scientific confirmation of these phenomena was possible. William James reported that he and his colleagues expected, when they founded the Society, "that if the material were treated rigorously, and, as far possible, experimentally, objective truth would be elicited, and the subject rescued from sentimentalism on the one side and dogmatic ignorance on the other."[1] According to James, both he and Henry Sidgwick had hoped for prompt results. However, after twenty years, Sidgwick confessed to James that he was in the same state of doubt and balance that he started with. And James revealed that after twenty-five years he was "theoretically no further" than he was at the beginning. It was not possible to obtain "full corroboration." There were "so many sources of deception" that the entire lot of reports, he said, "may be worthless." The same disquietude has been expressed by other inquirers throughout the history of the field.

Since that time, the spiritualist movement had been so thoroughly discredited by the uncovering of fraudulent mediums that it went into decline. For example, Margaret Fox had revealed in 1888 that the mysterious rappings were caused by the cracking of toe knuckles on a wooden floor or bedstead. William James believed that he had found one white crow in a field of trickery, Mrs. Leonora Piper, who allegedly could communicate with the dead—though her psychic powers had been seriously questioned by skeptics. John Beloff, current editor of the *SPR Journal,* however, still believes that although Eusapia Palladino was caught cheating by scientific investigators on innumerable occasions, she still evidenced some remarkable psychic powers. He refers to the Feilding Report,[2] which undertook sittings on behalf of the SPR with Eusapia Palladino in Naples, and concluded that she was a genuine medium. In any case, by the 1920s, most scientists had become very dubious of these first efforts to establish a scientific basis for the claims of spiritualism.

In my judgment, there is in this field a mixture of spiritualist or psychic credulity and scientific skepticism; and there has been an ongoing battle between believers and skeptics. The skeptics suspect that psychical researchers are masking an underlying religious will-to-believe; the proponents, in turn, accuse skeptics of being closed-minded. I surely cannot do justice in this essay to the debate that has been waged for over a century, and the success or lack of success of scientific efforts to confirm the main thesis of the spiritualists, though I submit that the results are negative.

There was a second wave of spirituality, however, that took a new direction. This was stimulated by the founding in 1927 of the first parapsychological lab at Duke University by J. B. Rhine. Rhine deferred the question of survival, and attempted to establish the existence of ESP—clairvoyance, precognition, telepathy—and psychokinesis, using experimental methods. For Rhine, the above- or below-chance calls in a run of Zener cards could not be explained by normal science, but could only be attributed to some underlying paranormal cause.

Did the anomalistic phenomena that Rhine investigated have any relationship to the supernatural? Rhine explicitly stated that one of his primary motives was to reject what he called the "metaphysical doctrine" of the "mechanistic philosophy of man." Rhine made it clear that "it was to refute . . . mechanistic philosophy that parapsychology arose."[3] Among Rhine's tasks was to show the limitations of the "physicalist theory" of the universe and of man. According to Rhine, parapsychology attempts to deal with "nonphysical causation in nature." Psi phenomena, he stated, involved the behavior of living organisms "that fail to show regular relationships with time, space, mass, and other criteria of physicality."[4] Rhine argued that psi was "mental," not physical. "It is now thoroughly clear," said Rhine, "that psi phenomena are identified by the fact that they defy physical explanations and require a psychological one. They . . . involve some associated or at least suspected agency or experience; but at the same time they do not follow conventional physical principles."[5] Rhine thus presupposed a dualistic view of reality in which mind was independent, in some sense, of its material basis. He admitted that this gave some support for religious experience and the religious impulse. He denied, however, that the data of parapsychology were occult or transcendent, for although they could not be understood as natural in the same sense as other phenomena, they were capable of experimental description and interpretation in the laboratory.

According to James A. Hall, Rhine had a deep concern with the relationship of parapsychology to religion. In bringing forth evidence against the physicalist theory of man, he believed that he was indirectly supporting the religious view. Rhine said that, "on the whole, the types of psi that have been quite independently outlined by laboratory research closely resemble the kind of exchange that religious men have assumed in the theologies that arose out of human experience long before the laboratories of parapsychology began their work."[6] Rhine then went on to say that "no matter what one thinks about the theological claims of these religions, he can now at least see that their founders must have built those great cultural systems on a rather good acquaintance with the same powers that have now been independently established as parapsychological."[7] Rhine thus believed that parapsychology was relevant to religion and that it offered a way to reconcile the claims of religion with the principles of science. Among the religious questions it might help to resolve are whether people are free moral agents, whether humankind has a postmortem destiny, and whether the universe is a "personal universe, with a type of intelligent purposive agency within it to which man can, with rational confidence, turn for helpful communication."[8] In this regard, Rhine's interests were similar to the early founders of the Society for Psychical Research, who had hoped to provide a scientific basis for the "spiritual principle in man."

Scientific skepticism about the work of Rhine was widespread. He was criticized by psychologists because of loose protocol, questionable grading techniques, and sensory leakage. A similar tale has been told about G. S. Soal, who attempted experiments to demonstrate precognition and telepathy in London during the Second World War. Fraudulent manipulation of the data by Soal has been clearly demonstrated, so that all of his work is now held suspect.

Since World War II paranormal claims have proliferated, and a new dimension has been added, science fiction, which has opened public imagination to new forms of fantasy and mystery. The mass media continually feed a receptive public with wondrous tales of paranormal miracles. The term *paranormal* has been extended beyond psychical research and parapsychology to include many space-age claims, such as ufology, astrology, and a wide range of pseudoscientific and anomalous claims, including alternative holistic medicines, faith healing, and a return of occult demons and monsters of the deep.

An interesting, and at times heated, controversy has broken out on the borderlands of science between the disciples of the paranormal and the skeptics. The central question raised is: Is there rigorous experimental evidence pointing to the reality of paranormal phenomena, and can the phenomena be replicated in the laboratory? Sheep (believers) maintain that there is sufficient evidence, but goats (skeptics) deny this. In my view, the debate has hidden religious premises, pro and con, between fideists and atheists. The emergence of beliefs in the paranormal, I submit, is primarily a religious phenomenon, and it is intimately related to neospirituality. The new pews are not in the traditional churches, where God is worshiped, but on TV, film screens, and in mass-market books. These mass media offerings are blurring the line between fiction and reality and have become the sacred platforms of our time, satisfying the hunger for existential meaning and filling a void left by the decline of orthodox religious forms. Indeed, the paranormal may be the single largest religious or quasi-religious sect in the world, cutting across cyber, radio, and TV space beyond national boundaries.

There are three areas that I will refer to to illustrate this. The first concerns near-death experience; the second, reincarnation; and the third, extraterrestrial abductions.

THE NEAR-DEATH EXPERIENCE

The widespread fascination today with near-death experience (NDE) is a truly remarkable phenomenon. There have been a great number of books portraying the experience.[9] Raymond A. Moody offers us a collage of various NDE accounts:[10]

A dying person overcome by fear and pain, perhaps lying on an operating table or hospital bed, begins to hear loud buzzing and ringing sounds. He feels himself falling rapidly through a long tunnel. He finds himself outside of his physical body, which he is able to view as an onlooker. He may even hear the doctor pronounce him dead and/or attempt resuscitation efforts. As he enters the tunnel he has a panoramic review of his life. Eventually, he encounters a bright light and meets the spirits of friends and relatives who welcome him, perhaps even Jesus or Krishna. There is a Being of Light that he encounters and he feels peace and joy. He discovers that he must return to his physical body on earth, though he is reluctant to do so. Suddenly he is back in his body, and his consciousness revives. The experience is so powerful that it may have a transforming effect on his life thereafter.[11]

Such accounts of near-death experiences are highly reminiscent of the kinds of experience reported by classical mystics, who claim they have encountered a Being of Light. These reports are introspective and subjective, so that most of the evidence is anecdotal. Nonetheless, the spiritual significance of the experience is unmistakable. Does this provide evidence that there is a spiritual realm? Is there now scientific validity for the claim? Michael Sabom, Melvin Morse, and other researchers maintain that there is.[12] Skeptics, such as Susan Blackmore,[13] point out that there are alternative naturalistic explanations— psychological and physiological—that can be given without postulating the existence of an afterlife. Not everyone who is dying and is resuscitated has the same experience. Moreover, elements of the collage can be experienced in other contexts of life. Out-of-body experiences are fairly common. We find them in hypnogogic and hypnopompic sleep. Alpinists who fall from mountains yet land safely, or people in car accidents who survive unscathed, sometimes experience a panoramic review and an out-of-body experience. Ronald K. Siegel reports that he chemically produced similar NDE-type phenomena by administering drugs.[14] Susan Blackmore has summarized a plurality of possible causes: the experience of a hallucination triggered by the distress of the dying process, the deprivation of oxygen, increased levels of carbon dioxide in the blood, the release of endorphins and other natural opiates, seizures in the temporal lobe and limbic systems, the dissolution of the sense of the self, and so forth. Skeptics point out that the spirits encountered on the "other side" are colored by the cultural experience of the person having an NDE. The proponents of the survival hypothesis deny this. They point out that even atheists, such as A. J. Ayer, have reported NDEs. They maintain that there is a remarkable consistency in all such reports. Skeptics maintain that if there is a consistency in reports, it is because we share a common physical and psychological structure. The person who has had an NDE experience has not died (there is no clear case of brain death), but is undergoing a dying process. The transforming effect that the experience has can be simply explained by the fact that a harrowing brush with death can help us to alter our priorities in life. The dying-brain hypothesis more parsimoniously accounts for the altered states of consciousness.

I cannot in this brief essay do justice to the scientific case pro and con. The point I wish to make is that without benefit of church or clergy, this type of near-death experience illustrates a neospiritualist revival, paralleling traditional religious belief in immortality.

REINCARNATION

Another area of interest that enjoys vogue today is a revival of doctrines of reincarnation. These doctrines do not focus only on the afterlife—though this is implicit in them—but also on the preexistence of the soul. Reincarnation theories are prominent in Hindu and Buddhist literature, in ancient Egyptian sources, and in Greek philosophy. Human beings, it was held, had souls, connected in some way to breath, which was separated from a person's body at death. Likewise, animals and plants were possessed of souls. Upon death, the soul could be transferred from one organism to another. In the Hindu sacred writings, the doctrine of the transmigration of souls was added. This was dependent upon *karma,* the behavior of a person in his past lives. After death, the soul entered a new plane of existence. The person's moral conduct in the past determined his future existence as his soul entered different bodies. In any case, the soul exists eternally, and will be reborn into new bodies, and can be released from the cycle only by earning it.

These classical religious doctrines have taken on a new vogue in this paranormal age by the introduction of allegedly new scientific findings. Reincarnation need not any longer be taken as a mere article of religious faith, say its proponents, for it has been demonstrated empirically by parapsychologists and hypnotherapists.[15]

The first kind of research draws primarily upon the memories of young children who recount to parents and others in their immediate circle incredible tales of previous lives. The best summation of such reincarnation cases, particularly of children in India, is provided by Ian Stevenson, an American physician and parapsychologist.[16] I find the evidence he adduces highly questionable. An alternative naturalistic explanation of such memories is that these have been suggested by those in the immediate circle of relatives, friends, and the cultural milieu. Predisposed to believe in reincarnation, they interpret the experiences of their children in terms of it.

Another area of research today is the experience of "regression," that allegedly enables a person to recall his past lives. Here the evidence comes from adults. Some people claim to have had out-of-body experiences that, when suddenly triggered, return them to their previous existence. Such evidence is highly subjective and anecdotal and is difficult to evaluate. Another type of alleged evidence is hypnotic regressions. When subjects are placed under hypnosis, they are supposedly able to recall details of their earlier lives. For these cases, at least it is possible to evaluate the alleged accuracy of the historical facts recounted. In North America today there are hypnotherapists who maintain that they can treat people for emotional disturbances and anxieties by taking them back to past lives and finding the causes in their previous existences. This regression technique, they say, can have an extremely important transformative therapeutic value. There is a kind of spiritual reawakening (or, as I call it, a placebo effect) that provides the patient with considerable solace by relating their current

experience to previous experience in a prior life. Some hypnotherapists even claim to be able to progress people into future lives,
describing the kind of person he will be at some future date. They
maintain they can go backward or forward on the time scale.

An interesting body of regression data was assembled by the
British hypnotherapist Arnold Bloxham, who had audiotaped more
than four hundred subjects whom he had put under hypnosis. These
are now known as the Bloxham Tapes. The regression of one of those
subjects, Jane Evans, a Welsh housewife, is detailed in the book *More
Lives Than One* by Jeffrey Iverson.[17] Mrs. Evans describes six past
lives. Many find the richness of detail provided by Mrs. Evans to be
uncanny. For example, Evans maintained that she lived as "Livonia"
in the third century near York as a member of the entourage of the
Roman governor of Britain, Constantine, and also as a young Egyptian servant named "Allison" in 1450 in France in the household of
Jacques Coeur, a famous merchant prince.

Melvin Harris, a skeptical paranormal investigator, has examined
these tapes carefully.[18] He maintains that Mrs. Evans's "memories"
can be more parsimoniously explained in terms of source amnesia (or
cryptomnesia), without the need for postulating reincarnation. Harris
demonstrated that Jane Evans's tale of Livonia, a Roman wife, which
began in the year 286 in Britain, was taken directly from a best-sell-
ing novel by Louis B. Woll, *The Living Wood,* published in 1947, in
which Livonia is a fictionalized character. Harris was likewise able to
trace the life of Allison, the teenage servant in Jacques Coeur's household in fifteenth-century France. Coeur was counselor to Charles VII.
Jane Evans knew a great deal about Agnes Sorel, the mistress of
Charles VII, and she was able to describe Coeur's resplendent chateau
and the tomb of Agnes Sorel in a church. But all of those facts were
in H. D. Sedgwick's *A Short History of France,* published in 1930; in
Dame Joan Evan's *Life in Medieval France*; and in other books. Harris maintains that Jane Evans's "past life" was derived from the novel
The Money Man by C. B. Costain, which is based on Coeur's life. Of
particular interest is the fact that Jane Evans's "Allison" never mentions that her master was married and had five children. The reason

for this is that, as the novelist Costain tells us, he had decided not to mention Coeur's family in his novel—and so they do not appear in Jane Evans's regression. Thus the narratives of Jane Evans were a product of her unconscious memories of what she had read plus her creative imagination. These were carefully checked against the historical facts and many were shown to be wrong. Bloxham himself believed in reincarnation, so that suggestibility undoubtedly played a significant factor in eliciting the narratives.

A further consideration to bear in mind is the fact that although hypnotism is undeniably useful in many contexts, it is unreliable in others. Many psychologists are skeptical that hypnosis exists as a "trance state," and it is surely doubtful that it can be used as an accurate tool of historical reconstruction. The hypnotized person may report what he believes to be true and/or what the hypnotist has suggested may be the case, but the rendering should not be taken as veridical. A hypnotic experience is certainly unusual. But does it bring the individual into an alternative, perhaps even "spiritual state of awareness"?

EXTRATERRESTRIAL ABDUCTIONS

Another area in which hypnosis is being used today is in ufology. It is appealed to as providing phenomenological evidence for the reality of abductions by extraterrestrial beings. Such beings are allegedly kidnapping earthlings and performing sexual, reproductive, and genetic experiments on them. A number of authors have reported on their case studies. Perhaps the most puzzling work is that of John Mack, professor of psychiatry at Harvard. In his book *Abductions,* he claims to have investigated seventy-six abductees, though he focuses on thirteen cases.[19] He calls them "experiencers," for they are undergoing anomalous experiences. His narratives of these experiences are based on hypnotic sessions with them. The phenomenological contours of such cases are as follows.

A person is usually asleep in his bed. He or she is awakened by bright red or white lights that infuse the bedroom. At first he or she is paralyzed and unable to move. Visited by small creatures with huge heads and large eyes, he or she is levitated out of bed, through the walls, and brought aboard a spacecraft. Placed on a table, his or her orifices are probed. There usually is some telepathic communication and a feeling, according to Mack, of beneficence and love (others report feelings of terror and the creatures to be malefic). Often there is a message received from the aliens, according to Mack, of peace and good will. Eventually, the abductees are floated back into bed. It is only with some difficulty that the events are recalled under guidance of the hypnotist. As a result of such experiences, the abductees report that their lives are fundamentally transformed.

According to proponents of the UFO abduction thesis, there is a great deal of consistency in the reports of the experiencers. The experience has intense emotional and traumatic effects upon them, and there are small lesions or scars on their bodies that, it is alleged, provide physical evidence for extraterrestrial implants.[20]

What are we to make of these reports? Proponents of the extraterrestrial thesis say that according to national surveys, millions of Americans may have been abducted, since they report some or all of the symptoms of abductions (seeing bright lights, unaccountable missing hours, overlooked scars, etc.).[21] These abduction stories used to be considered fringe phenomena and were even dismissed by most serious ufological investigators themselves only a decade ago.[22] Today they have moved to the very center of the UFO stage.

John Mack claims that his patients are normal, that they believe in the reality of what they have experienced and are troubled greatly by it. The abductees come from all walks of life. Moreover, the abductees often report having been abducted many times during their lives, even as children. Such phenomenological accounts, he says, must be taken as "given." The empirical data received from them profoundly alters our understanding of the world.

Skeptics have disputed the evidence for the extraterrestrial abduction thesis. They maintain that the abduction syndrome is part of a kind of the UFO legend that is sweeping the world. The UFO age began in June 1947 when flying saucers were first reported as skipping above the clouds over the state of Washington. Since that time there have been hundreds of thousands, perhaps even millions, of sightings of strange objects in the sky all over the world. Public interest continues to grow, no doubt fed by a vast media industry.

It is surely possible, given the vast universe that we live in, that under similar conditions, life, even intelligent life, may have evolved elsewhere in the universe. The SETI project conducted by astronomers is attempting to make contact with intelligent life in the universe and thus verify this hypothesis. But this is different from the popular thesis, namely that (a) extraterrestrial craft have visited or are now visiting the planet earth, and (b) the more radical thesis that they are forcibly abducting earthlings, performing sexual experiments on them, and engaging in genetic breeding programs. In regard to (a), there is no single case that provides incontrovertible evidence of visitation. Virtually all the cases, if there is enough evidence, can be given prosaic explanations (meteors, planets, weather or radar balloons misidentified, etc.). Proponents claim that there is a worldwide scientific and governmental cover-up and a conspiracy of silence suppressing the evidence. In regard to (b), naturalistic explanations can be given of the abductee phenomena. Hypnotherapists who believe in the reality of UFO abductions are suggesting ETI responses during the hypnotic session. It has been suggested that many or most abductees are fantasy-prone and are given to confabulation based on creative imagination. Influenced by a cultural milieu in which science fiction abounds, the reality of creatures from the outer world visiting us is accepted by them as true; and abductees believe that they have been specially anointed to receive a message from these extraterrestrials.

Scientific investigators need to keep an open mind about all such claims. They cannot reject beforehand the possibility, or even the probability, however slim, that visitation and abductions are happening. If such extraordinary claims are to be accepted, prudence demands that there be rigorous evidence, not mere conjecture, to support the claims. After sifting through the reports at length, interviewing abductees, and analyzing the UFO literature, I am persuaded that what we are witnessing is, primarily, a spiritual or quasi-religious phenomenon, the emergence of a new space-age religion rather than a carefully documented scientific case. This is part and parcel of the new religion of the paranormal and it has remarkable similarities to psychical research, near-death experience, regression to past lives, and other such claims.

Interestingly, John Mack does not deny, but indeed, he strongly advocates this interpretation. Mack says that many abduction experiences are "unequivocally spiritual, which involves some sort of powerful encounter with or immersion in divine light . . . the alien beings . . . may also be seen as intermediaries, closer than we are to God or the Source of Being!"[23]

The UFO abduction experience, says Mack, "While unique in many respects, bears resemblances to the dramatic transformation experiences undergone by shamans, mystics, and ordinary citizens who have had encounters with the paranormal."[24] Mack maintains that the abduction experience is like the experience of near-death, or out-of-body, or past-life regressions and encounters with strange beings—such as witches, fairies, angels, and werewolves—putting us in touch with another dimension or plane of reality. All of this, he says, challenges the prevailing materialistic, dualistic worldview.

Mack also believes that the extraterrestrials are involved in "breeding a new race of beings." He even speculates that "the alien beings" may have "mastered time travel and come to us from the future."[25] This interpretation may seem amusing, but perhaps no more fanciful than the myths that a special people, as related in the Old Testament, are the Chosen of God and were given a gift of land by Him, or that a carpenter was born of a virgin and that every person who believes in Him will achieve eternal salvation.

A NEW SPIRITUALITY?

It is time to bring together this selective journey through some recent illustrations of the paranormal literature. They have certain features in common.

First, they talk about another reality, or plane of existence that is beyond the space-time physical world and inexplicable in natural causal terms. Second, they believe that it is possible for some individuals to receive glimmers of this reality. Some hold that only gifted mediums, psychics, or abductees can make contact with it. Others believe that all individuals are capable of encountering this plane of existence.

Third, knowledge of this reality is not obtained by the ordinary senses, nor by rational logic; they defy our commonsense standards of understanding. In the above cases, it is only by a near-death encounter, past-life regression, or abductive hypnosis that we can discover it. This knowledge is revelatory. The door to the realm is only by means of *altered* states of consciousness.

Fourth, there may be emissaries who bring this knowledge to us— psychics, mediums, a Being of light, extraterrestrial semidivine beings. The new priests are the scientist-shamans or hypnotherapists who enable us to make contact with this realm.

Fifth, there is a transformation process of "spiritual growth." Once the believer accepts the new faith, his life takes on new meaning and significance and has new moral import.

What are we to make of this new spirituality? It replaces the old mysteries and miracles of the classical religions with new legends and parables appropriate to the new age of science. It substitutes for the ancient myths of a nomadic-agricultural society new scenarios appropriate to a postindustrial information-technological society. This is especially true of the abduction space-age narratives, but it is also true for near-death and past-life regression scenarios, which use psychologists, psychiatrists, doctors, or hypnotherapists, and a number of pseudoscientists to put us in touch with "new realms of reality."

One may ask, Do near-death experiences, hypnotic regressions, or accounts of abduction point to another realm beyond? And has science indeed opened us up to it? There are, after all, an estimated billion trillion stars in our universe. Surely the human species, living on the planet earth, limited by its own evolutionary brain cells, is perhaps only able to comprehend a small part of the vast universe. Perhaps there are other realms, and perhaps individuals under altered states of consciousness are able to grasp some inkling of these realms. Perhaps we are undergoing a new paradigm shift, led by the new physics and permeating all areas of science.

In my view, this may be true, and therefore one cannot dismiss anomalous paranormal reports without careful examination. On the other hand, I have been in the trenches for the past twenty years, deeply involved in examining the new paranormal cults. I am no longer surprised to find that virtually *any* fantasy, however outrageous, may be believed by some group of people somewhere, who become devoted to it, create an organization or a church to support it, develop a sacred literature, and endow certain individuals who cherish the revelation with shamanlike qualities. Recognizing that is the case, an alternative explanation that is more parsimonious is that the key to understanding the new spirituality is to recognize that it is most likely in *the eye of the beholder,* namely, I submit that what this tells us is that there is a profound psychological, perhaps sociocultural, temptation in human behavior; I have called it the "transcendental temptation."[26] There is a hunger for a world beyond, an unwillingness to accept the finitude of human existence, and a demand for a more dramatic beginning and an everlasting end. The transcendental temptation is so profound that in those societies where classical religion declines, new religions sprout up, with new content and new form, to give added meaning and significance and satisfy this hunger. Human beings are prone to magical thinking; they will read in occult or hidden causes to explain the tragic events that they encounter in life. "The corruption of reality" by the transcendental temptation indeed may be, according to John F. Schumaker, a necessary component of life, offering consolation for human finitude and failure and enabling us to persevere in an otherwise meaningless universe.[27]

In my view, the best therapy for fantasy, and the only corrective for the transcendental temptation run amok, is the use of skeptical reason and critical intelligence. I realize it is extremely unpopular for the naysayer or the dissenter to examine the religious, the paranormal, or the occult belief systems of others and, after submitting them to intensive analysis and scrutiny and finding insufficient evidence, to point this out. It is all too common in human history to burn the heretic, to suppress the dissenter, to declare a jihad on the blasphemer. Nonetheless, an impartial observer of the current scene cannot help being dismayed, particularly in the last fifty years, by the growth of a whole new series of paranormal religious belief systems. These are a continuation of the ancient spiritualities and they seem to have a similar function, even though the content may be radically different. No doubt the prevailing orthodox faiths— Christianity, Islam, Judaism, Buddhism, and Hinduism—will be in time supplanted. Waiting in the wings, some still-unknown religious belief system may so enrapture and enthrall humankind on this planet that it will sweep everything before it. Based on credulity and hope, drama and mystery, some new spirituality may overtake us. It is impossible to prophesy the future, but the growth of the paranormal cults of unreason in recent decades may be a harbinger of this new religion.

NOTES

1. Gardner Murphy and R. O. Balbour, *William James on Psychical Research* (New York: Viking, 1969).

2. E. Feilding, W. W. Baggally, and H. Carrington, "Report on a Series of Sittings with Eusapia Palladino," *Proceedings of the SPR* 23 (1909): 306–569.

3. J. B. Rhine, "Comments on the Science of the Supernatural," *Science* 123, no. 3184 (1956): 11–14.

4. J. B. Rhine, "The Science of Nonphysical Nature," *Journal of Philosophy* 51 (1954): 80–110.

5. J. B. Rhine, *New World of the Mind* (New York: William Sloan, 1953), p. 150.

6. James A. Hall, "The Work of J. B. Rhine: Implications for Religion," in K. Ramakrishna Rao, *J. B. Rhine: On the Frontiers of Science* (Jefferson, N.C.: MacFarland, 1982). See also J. B. Rhine, "The Parapsychology of Religion: A New Branch of Inquiry," *Journal of the Texas Society for Psychical Research and the Oklahoma Society for Psychical Research* (1977–78): 6.

7. Ibid., pp. 7–8.

8. Ibid., p. 9.

9. The most popular, longest-running best-seller in America today is Betty J. Eadie's *Embraced by the Light* (Placerville, Calif.: Gold Leaf Press, 1992; New York: Bantam, 1994). In it she reports on an experience that she says she underwent twenty years ago when she nearly died and came back. She claims that she not only went to "the other side," but met Jesus.

10. Raymond A. Moody, *Life After Life* (Atlanta, Ga.: Mockingbird Books, 1975); *Reflections on Life After Life* (Atlanta, Ga.: Mockingbird Books, 1978).

11. According to some estimates, eight million Americans have reported similar experiences.

12. M. B. Sabom, *Recollections of Death* (London: Corgi, 1982); Melvin Morse, *Closer to the Light* (New York: Ballantine Books, 1990); Melvin Morse and Paul Perry, *Parting Visions: Uses and Meanings of Pre-Death Psychic and Spiritual Experiences* (New York: Villard Books, 1994). See also Kenneth K. Ring, *Heading Toward Omega: In Search of the Meaning of the Near-Death Experience* (New York: Quill, 1984).

13. Susan J. Blackmore, *Dying to Live* (Amherst, N.Y.: Prometheus Books, 1993).

14. Ronald K. Siegel, "The Psychology of Life After Death," *American Psychologist* 35 (1980): 911–31; R. K. Siegel and A. E. Hirshman, "Hashish Near-Death Experiences," *Anabiosis: The Journal for Near Death Studies* 4 (1984): 69–85.

15. Today, according to various Gallup polls, an estimated 21 to 34 percent of Americans believe in the reality of reincarnation.

16. Ian Stevenson, *Twenty Cases Suggestive of Reincarnation* (Charlottesville, Va.: University of Virginia Press, 1980).

17. Jeffrey Iverson, *More Lives Than One* (London: Pan Books, 1977).

18. Melvin Harris, "Are 'Past Life' Regressions Evidence of Reincarnation?" *Free Inquiry* 6, no. 4 (Fall 1986). For a good critique of reincarnation, see Paul Edwards, *Reincarnation: A Critical Examination* (Amherst, N.Y.: Prometheus Books, 1996).

19. John E. Mack, *Abductions: Human Encounters with Aliens* (New York: Charles Scribners, 1994).

20. Budd Hopkins, *Missing Time: A Documented Study of UFO Abductions* (New York: Richard Marek Publisher, 1981); Budd Hopkins, *Intruders: The Incredible Visitations at Copley Woods* (New York: Random House,

1987); David Jacobs, *Secret Life: Firsthand Accounts of UFO Abductions* (New York: Simon and Schuster, 1992).

21. Budd Hopkins, David Jacobs, and Ron Westrum, *Unusual Personal Experiences: An Analysis of the Data from Three National Surveys* (Las Vegas: Bigelow Holding Company, 1991).

22. For example, the case of Betty and Barney Hill, who reported an abduction in New Hampshire in the 1960s.

23. John Mack, *Abductions*, p. 397.

24. Ibid., p. 8.

25. Ibid., p. 422.

26. Paul Kurtz, *The Transcendental Temptation: A Critique of Religion and the Paranormal* (Amherst, N.Y.: Prometheus Books, 1986).

27. John F. Schumaker, *The Corruption of Reality: A Unified Theory of Religion, Hypnosis, and Psychopathology* (Amherst, N.Y.: Prometheus Books, 1995).

16

Quantum Metaphysics

Victor J. Stenger

Antony Flew defined spirit as "incorporeal substance." As a physicist, I can relate to that. If such a thing as spirit exists, then I have no problem with it being incorporeal. It does not have to be made of matter as long as it has "substance." I interpret this to mean that although spirit may not be composed of quarks and electrons or other known constituents of matter, it still may be a meaningful concept, amenable to empirical testing or other rational analysis.

One test for whether a concept has "substance" is to use Occam's razor to excise it from all discourse. If the essential content of discourse remains unchanged, then I would say the concept has no substance. Of course, like most scientific tests, this can only be used to falsify the concept, not verify it.

The idea of spirit as a substantial component of the universe is of course an ancient one, fundamental to the traditional dualistic view most humans hold of the universe and themselves as part of that universe. In this view, planets, rock, trees, and the human body are made of matter, but matter is not everything. Beyond matter exists mind, soul, or spirit, an ethereal substance that may even be more "real" than matter—the very quintessence of being.

In the mid-nineteenth century, many scientists thought that the marvelous new discoveries of science and the methods of science could be applied to the world of the spirit as well as to the world of matter. For example, Sir Oliver Lodge, a physicist who had helped demonstrate the reality of electromagnetic waves, argued that if wireless telegraphy was possible, then so was wireless telepathy. Lodge, like most others of the period, believed that electromagnetic waves, including light, were vibrations of a frictionless medium, the *aether*, that pervaded the universe. It seemed plausible that this medium might also be responsible for the transmission of thoughts, that it was the long-sought substance of mind and spirit.

The electromagnetic field, like the gravitational field proposed centuries before by Newton, exhibited a holistic character that fit in well with spiritual ideas. Matter was particulate, occurring in lumps, and analyzed by the distasteful methods of *reductionism* in which objects are reduced to the sum of their parts. Fields, on the other hand, were continuous—*holistic*—occurring everywhere in space, connecting everything to everything else, and analyzable only in the whole. Even today, occultists confuse natural electromagnetic effects with "auras" surrounding living things. A popular con game at psychic fairs is the sale of "aura photographs" that are simply made with infrared-sensitive film. Kirlian photography is another example of a simple electromagnetic phenomenon, corona discharge, that is given imaginary spiritual significance.

Although the atomic theory of matter was well developed by the late nineteenth century, it had not yet been convincingly verified at that time. Many chemists, and a few physicists like Lodge, still held open the possibility that matter might be continuous. The mathematics of fields had been successfully applied to solids and fluids, which appear continuous and wavy on the everyday scale. These scientists suggested that *continuity,* not atomism, constituted the prime unifying principle for describing the universe of both matter, light, and perhaps spirit.

This comforting notion was shattered as the twentieth century got underway. First, the aether was found not to exist. Second, the atomic theory was confirmed. Third, light was found to be a component of matter, composed of particles now called *photons*. And so, *discreteness,* rather than continuity, became the unifying principle of physics, with the universe composed solely of particulate matter. Quantum mechanics was developed to describe material phenomena in all their various, discrete forms.

However, the situation was not quite so tidy as this short and simplified review may imply. The phenomena that originally led people to postulate the wave nature of light did not go away. Those observations were correct. Furthermore, other forms of matter were shown to also exhibit wave properties. Electrons were found to diffract through small openings in exactly the same way as light.

The fact that particles sometimes behaved as waves and waves as particles was called the *wave-particle duality.* Although matter was sufficient to encompass all known physical phenomena, the apparent twofold nature of matter gave die-hard dualists some comfort. Some associated waves with mind. But waves and particles were not two separate elementary substances but characteristics of the same substance.

Whether a physical entity was a wave or a particle seemed to depend on what you measured. Measure its position and you concluded that the entity is a material body. Measure its wavelength, and you concluded that the entity is some type of continuous field. Furthermore, you can imagine deciding which quantity to measure at the last instant, long after the entity had been emitted from its source, which might be a distant galaxy.

Some have inferred from this puzzle that the very nature of the universe is not objective, but depends on the consciousness of the observer. This latest wrinkle on ancient idealism implies that the universe exists only within some cosmic, quantum field of mind, with the human mind part of that field and existing throughout all space and time.

Quantum phenomena seem to be very mysterious, and where mysteries are imagined, the supernatural cannot be far behind. However, despite these misgivings, quantum mechanics developed as a quantitative physical theory that has proven itself capable of making calculations and predictions to a high level of accuracy. After seventy years of exhaustive testing, no observation has been found to be inconsistent with quantum mechanics as a formal, mathematical theory.

Quantum mechanics dealt early with the problem of the wave nature of matter by introducing a mathematical quantity called the *wave function.* Schrödinger's equation was used to calculate how the wave function evolved with time; the absolute square of the wave function gave the probability that a body would be found at a particular position.

In 1927 Einstein initiated a debate on quantum mechanics with Niels Bohr that continues today, long after their deaths, as others have taken up the arguments one side or the other. Initially Einstein objected to the picture, retained today in most textbooks, in which the wave function instantaneously "collapses" upon measurement. He called this a "spooky action at a distance" because it implied that signals must travel at infinite speeds across the wave front to tell the wave function to go to zero in the places where nothing is detected.

To modern dualists, the holistic quantum wave function, with its instantaneous collapse upon the act of observation, has provided a new model for the notion of spirit. They have been wittingly and unwittingly encouraged by various statements made by physicists, some of considerable distinction.

Eugene Wigner is widely quoted in the new literature of quantum mysticism. He once said: "The laws of quantum mechanics itself cannot be formulated . . . without recourse to the concept of consciousness."[1]

A similar statement by John Archibald Wheeler is also often used, to his dismay, in justifying a connection between the quantum and consciousness: "No elementary quantum phenomenon is a phenomenon until it is a registered phenomenon. . . . In some strange sense, this is a participatory universe."[2]

In their book *The Conscious Universe* astrophysicist Menas Kafatos and philosopher Robert Nadeau interpret the wave function as ultimate reality itself. "Being, in its physical analogue at least, [has] been 'revealed' in the wave function. . . . any sense we have of profound unity with the cosmos . . . could be presumed to correlate with the action of the deterministic wave function."[3]

Physicist Amit Goswami sees a "self-aware universe," with quantum mechanics providing support for claims of paranormal phenomena. He says: "psychic phenomena, such as distant viewing and out-of-body experiences, are examples of the nonlocal operation of consciousness. . . . Quantum mechanics undergirds such a theory by providing crucial support for the case of nonlocality of consciousness."[4]

This view was also promoted by the late novelist Arthur Koestler, who said: "the apparent absurdities of quantum physics . . . make the apparent absurdities of parapsychology a little less preposterous and more digestible."

In the United States today, alternative healing is all the rage. Traditional folk healing techniques are touted as holistic, in contrast to the reductionistic methods of modern Western medicine. Again, quantum mechanics provides a source of inspiration. Two recent best-sellers by Dr. Deepak Chopra contain the word "quantum" in their titles: *Quantum Healing: Exploring the Frontiers of Mind/Body Medicine* and *Ageless Body, Timeless Mind: The Quantum Alternative to Growing Old.*[5]

Johns Hopkins psychiatrist Patricia Newton explains the mechanism: "(Traditional healers) are able to tap that other realm of negative entropy—that superquantum velocity and frequency of electromagnetic energy and bring them as conduits down to our level. It's not magic. It's not mumbo jumbo. You will see the dawn of the twenty-first century, the new medical quantum physics really distributing these energies and what they are doing."[6]

Despite the claims made in many books, neither psychic phenomena[7] nor the vast array of alternate healing methods[8] are supported by controlled, replicable laboratory studies. They cannot be used as evidence for mind-over-matter. Nor can quantum mechanics be used to make these claims more credible.

As we will now see, the mysteries and apparent paradoxes of

quantum mechanics arise only when we try to cast the theory in words instead of equations, applying the language of everyday human experience to a physical realm where that experience may not be relevant.

The words used to describe quantum mechanics in conventional physics textbooks were gleaned from the writings of Niels Bohr, Werner Heisenberg, and Max Born, the primary authors of what is called the *Copenhagen* interpretation of quantum mechanics. In Copenhagen the wave function is simply a mathematical object used to calculate probabilities. The results of measurements are not predetermined, but occur randomly according to the calculated probabilities. The measuring apparatus must be treated classically and is separate from the quantum system under study. No mechanism is provided for wave function collapse, and in fact collapse is not predicted by the Schrödinger equation.

Louis de Broglie, who first suggested that particles like electrons have wave properties, proposed in 1927 the first of the class of what is now called *hidden variables* theories of quantum mechanics. He hypothesized that the wave function is a *real* field associated with a particle. However, Bohr and his supporters talked most of the community, including de Broglie (but not Einstein or Schrödinger), out of hidden variables and they lay dormant until being resurrected by David Bohm in the 1950s.

Bohm, who became the major scientific figure in the quantum mysticism movement, had shown that all the results obtained with the Schrödinger equation can be obtained by familiar classical equations of motion, provided that an additional *quantum potential* is added to the equations to account for quantum effects.[9] However, Bohm's theory, as it was proposed, gave no new empirical predictions; neither he nor his followers have yet produced a mechanism for generating a priori the quantum potential.

The hidden variables approach is based on the notion, which Einstein always believed, that quantum mechanics is fine as far as it goes, as a statistical theory, but that some deterministic subquantum theory that lies behind physical events remains to be uncovered. Einstein's famous quotation that "God does not play dice" referred to this notion, although he thought Bohm's version was "too cheap."[10] It should be noted that hidden variables theories are not properly labeled as "interpretations" of quantum mechanics since they imply the existence of a deeper theory not yet discovered.

In the 1960s John Bell proved an important theorem about hidden variables theories. He showed that any deterministic hidden variables theory capable of giving all the statistical results of standard quantum mechanics must allow for superluminal connections, in violation of Einstein's relativity.[11] In the jargon of the trade, deterministic hidden variables theories are *nonlocal*. In popularized language, they are *holistic,* allowing for simultaneous connections between all points in space. Bell proposed a definitive experimental test that has now been repeated many times with ever-increasing precision.[12] In all cases, the results are fully consistent with quantum mechanics, requiring deterministic hidden variables, if they exist, to be nonlocal.

Instead of giving up on hidden variables because of their apparent conflict with relativity, proponents have taken Bell's theorem to imply hidden variables are even more profound, providing for the holistic universe of the mystic's fondest desires. The problem of nonlocality is dismissed by claiming that no communication of signals faster than light takes place. This conclusion can be proven to be a general property of quantum theory,[13] and will be true for Bohm's theory as long as Bohm's theory is consistent with quantum mechanics. But, as we have seen, Bohm's theory by itself has no unique, testable consequences. We can use Occam's razor to excise it from our discourse, and nothing substantial is changed. The notion of hidden variables has no use *unless* superluminal connections are observed. This has not yet happened, and so hidden variables remain a nonparsimonious alternative to conventional quantum mechanics.

Another interpretation of quantum mechanics that has caught mystics' inner and outer eyes is the *many worlds* interpretation of Hugh Everett.[14] Everett was able to develop a formalism that solved some of the problems associated with the conventional Copenhagen view. In particular, he included the measuring apparatus in the system being analyzed, unlike Copenhagen where it must be treated as a separate, classical system. In many worlds, the wave function of the universe does not collapse upon a measurement. Instead, the universe splits into parallel universes in which all possible events occur. In Everett's view, these parallel universes are deemed to be "equally real."

The idea that the universe is continually splitting into parallel universes whenever a measurement or observation is made strikes many people as a rather extreme solution to the interpretation problems of quantum mechanics. Nevertheless, as long as the parallel universes cannot interact with one another, we can never disprove the concept. If we reject it, we must do so on aesthetic or parsimonious grounds.

More recently, a number of theorists have found ways to recast Everett's ideas in a more economical, commonsensical way. This new interpretation, which some say represents only a small extension of Bohr's thinking, is called *consistent histories*.[15]

In the consistent histories view, as in Copenhagen and many worlds, the wave function allows you to calculate the probabilities that the universe will take various paths. Unlike many worlds, these paths are not deemed to be "equally real." Instead, the path taken in our universe is chosen randomly, as the toss of coin. The indeterminism of Copenhagen is retained but, unlike Copenhagen, the wave function "decoheres" rather than collapses upon the act of measurement.

Theoretical work has provided for a logically consistent histories theory that agrees with all known data without the introduction of holistic, nonlocal, or mystical elements. In this theory, the only consistent paths (or histories) are those for which probabilities add as they do classically. The quantum-to-classical transition occurs by the mechanism of *decoherence* induced by measuring instruments or the environment.

The idea of decoherence is quite simple. Quantum effects are characterized by phenomena, such as interference and diffraction, that are understood to be coherent properties of the wave function. These occur because the universe is *granular*, with matter existing in lumps separated by empty space. Only where lumps of matter exist, either in the form of a measuring instrument or environmental body, can particle paths be logically defined. At these points, the particles scatter and decohere and classical paths are produced.

Classical mechanics follows as the limit of quantum mechanics in a fine-grained universe. In our experience, ordinary light is coherent in air because the probability of a visible photon colliding with an air molecule over the distances involved is small. Gamma ray photons, on the other hand, appear to travel classical paths because they have high probability to scatter, and decohere, over the same distances.

By being nondeterministic, consistent histories avoid the problem of nonlocality associated with hidden variables. Some still argue that the wave function is nonlocal, but if it is not a "real" field but a mathematical convenience, who cares? In any case, no signals move faster than the speed of light.

Still some commentators argue that any nondeterministic quantum mechanics, be it Copenhagen or consistent histories, is still incomplete. What "causes" the universe to take the path it does, they ask? Deterministic, nonlocal hidden variables are one answer. But, we have seen that they are necessarily nonlocal and we have no empirical evidence for any superluminal or subquantum processes.

Another even more poorly justified answer is that the path selection is made by consciousness itself. In the *quantum mind* interpretation of quantum mechanics, the path taken by the universe, whether you care to describe it in terms of wave function collapse or universe-splitting, is *actualized* by the action of mind.[16]

Now here the theories become impossibly vague and untestable, so I can only indicate some of the language. In some sense, the wave function of the universe is an etheric cosmic mind spread throughout the universe that acts to collapse itself in some unknown way. The human mind (spirit, soul) is, of course, holistically linked to the cosmic mind and so exists in all space and time. Once again we have an example of what Paul Kurtz calls the "transcendental temptation."

And so, quantum mind rescues the dualists from the damage caused by the destruction of the electromagnetic aether. But like so many similar proposals, the theory of quantum mind will get nowhere until it makes some prediction that can be tested empirically. In the meantime, it must be rejected as nonparsimonious, especially since we have in our hands a perfectly economical and logically consistent

theory that agrees with all the data and requires no additional component in the universe beyond matter.

NOTES

1. E. P. Wigner, "The Probability of the Existence of a Self-Reproduc-
ing Unit," in M. Polanyi, *The Logic of Personal Knowledge* (Glencoe, Ill.:
Free Press, 1961), p. 232.

2. John Archibald Wheeler in *Mind in Nature,* ed. Richard Q. Elvee
(San Francisco: Harper and Row, 1982), p. 17.

3. Menas Kafatos and Robert Nadeau, *The Conscious Universe: Part
and Whole in Modern Physical Theory* (New York, Springer-Verlag, 1990),
p. 124.

4. Amit Goswami, *The Self-Aware Universe: How Consciousness
Creates the Material World* (New York: G. P. Putnam's Sons, 1993), p. 136.

5. Deepak Chopra, *Quantum Healing: Exploring the Frontiers of
Mind/Body Medicine* (New York: Bantam, 1989); Deepak Chopra, *Ageless
Body, Timeless Mind: The Quantum Alternative to Growing Old* (New York:
Random House, 1993).

6. Patricia Newton, talk before the Ninety-eighth Annual Meeting of
the National Medical Association, San Antonio, Texas, 1993. Quotation provided by Bernard Ortiz de Montellano (private communication).

7. Victor J. Stenger, *Physics and Psychics: The Search for a World
Beyond the Senses* (Amherst, N.Y.: Prometheus Books, 1990).

8. Kurt Butler, *A Consumer's Guide to Alternative Medicine: A Close
Look at Homeopathy, Acupuncture, Faith-Healing, and Other Unconven-
tional Treatments* (Amherst, N.Y.: Prometheus Books, 1992).

9. David Bohm, "A Suggested Interpretation of Quantum Theory in
Terms of 'Hidden Variables,' I and II," *Physical Review* 85 (1952): 166.

10. M. Born, ed., *The Born-Einstein Letters* (London: Macmillan, 1971).

11. J. S. Bell, *Physics* 1 (1964): 195.

12. Alain Aspect, Phillipe Grangier, and Roger Gerard, "Experimental
Realization of the Einstein-Podolsky-Rosen *Gedankenexperiment*: A New
Violation of Bell's Inequalities," *Physical Review Letters* 49 (1982): 91.

13. Phillippe H. Eberhard and Ronald R. Ross, *Foundations of Physics
Letters* 2 (1989): 127.

14. Hugh Everett III, *Reviews of Modern Physics* 29 (1957): 454.

15. Roland J. Omnès, *The Interpretation of Quantum Mechanics* (Princeton, N.J.: Princeton University Press, 1994).

16. Henry P. Stapp, *Mind, Matter, and Quantum Mechanics* (New York: Springer-Verlag, 1993); Henry P. Stapp, *Physical Review* 50 (1994): 18; Euan Squires, *Conscious Mind in the Physical World* (New York: Adam Hilger, 1990).

Contributors

J. E. BARNHART is professor of philosophy at the University of North Texas.

CLINTON BENNETT lectures in the study of religion (Islamic Studies) at Westminster College, Oxford, and is editor of the interfaith journal *Discernment*.

STEPHEN BIGGER is principal lecturer in religious education at Westminster College, Oxford.

H. JAMES BIRX is professor of anthropology, Canisius College, Buffalo, New York, and contributing editor of *Free Inquiry*.

MARGARET CHATTERJEE was formerly professor of philosophy at the University of Delhi, India, and Spalding Fellow at Wolfson College, Oxford.

BERNARD C. FARR is head of the School of Theology, Westminster College, Oxford, and a trustee of the International Interfaith Centre.

ROBERT N. FISHER is lecturer in philosophy and theology at West-minister College, Oxford.

ANTONY FLEW, professor emeritus of philosophy at Reading University, has written extensively on the philosophy of belief.

R. JOSEPH HOFFMANN is director of the Oxford Centre for Critical Studies and editor of the *Journal for the Critical Study of Religion, Ethics, and Society.*

PAUL KURTZ is professor emeritus of philosophy, State University of New York at Buffalo, and chair of the Council for Critical Studies.

JUSTIN MEGGITT (Ph.D., Cambridge) is Junior Research Fellow (New Testament Studies) at Cambridge University. His research centers on the social world of the early Christian movement.

PEGGY MORGAN is lecturer in the study of religion at Westminster and Mansfield Colleges and lecturer in the faculty of theology, Oxford University.

ISABEL MUKONYORA lectures in the study of religion at the University of Zimbabwe, Harare.

JAMES PENNEY is lecturer in theology and contemporary studies, Westminster College, Oxford.

VICTOR J. STENGER is distinguished professor of physics at the University of Hawaii and an authority on the new metaphysics.

M. M. THOMAS is a distinguished theologian and former president of the World Council of Churches.